LIVING IN

God's Grace

MARCIA KLINE-LIBERTZ

Printed in the United States of America

ISBN 979-8-89114-137-7 (hc)
ISBN 979-8-89114-136-0 (sc)
ISBN 979-8-89114-138-4 (e)

Library of Congress Control Number: 2024922344

2025.02.19

MainSpring Books
5901 W. Century Blvd
Suite 750
Los Angeles, CA, US, 90045

www.mainspringbooks.com

LIVING IN
God's Grace

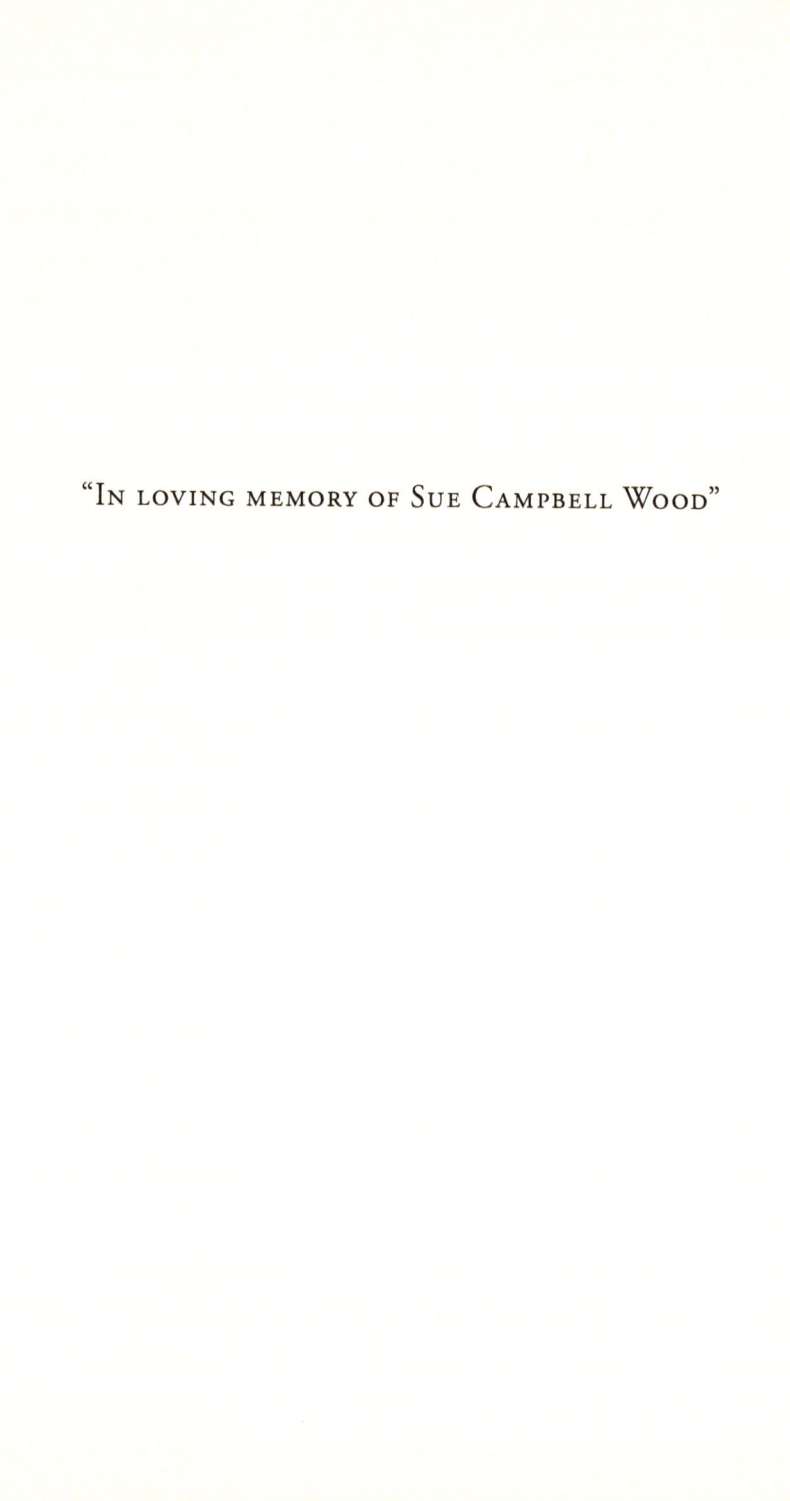

"IN LOVING MEMORY OF SUE CAMPBELL WOOD"

JANUARY 1

MATTHEW 3:13-18

Then Jesus came from Galilee to John at the Jordan, to be baptized by him. John would have prevented him, saying, "I need to be baptized by you, and do you come to me?" But Jesus answered him, saying, "Let it be so now; for it is proper for us in this way to fulfill all the righteousness." Then he consented. And when Jesus had been baptized, just as he came up from the water, suddenly the heavens were opened to him and he saw the Spirit of God descending like a dove and alighting on him night. And a voice from heaven said, "This is my Son, the Beloved, with whom I am well pleased."

Heavenly Spirit, I pray that all who know you and love you are in dialog with you. It can be difficult sometimes to pray to someone with whom you have never seen. May they just start praying and asking to be filled with the Holy Spirit, your spirit loving God. Help each one to depend upon you and to begin a dialog with you. Fill our hearts with your love and help us to find comfort and love you, too. Encourage each one to live a life that is pleasing in your sight. Be with those who do not yet know you and your love. Lord, I pray for all of those who are suffering, hungry or lost. Keep your people warm this winter day, be with the lonely, the sick and those whose days are limited. Lord, comfort those who have lost a loved one by bringing them comfort and the assurance promised. Help them to know your loving grace awaits. Be with us, Lord God as a new year begins. We pray for our world which seems to struggle to find peace, I pray for our country, which has spent a year seeing a government in turmoil, be with those who govern, may they begin to think about what is best for each nation and her peoples. Be with the sick, the lonely and the lost. May their struggles lead them to you and to a peace they can only dream about. Lord, be with us in the facing of each day, forgive us our sins and know that we seek your love and guidance in all we do and say. In your blessed name, Amen.

JANUARY 2

PSALM 18:1-3, 49-51

I love you, O Lord, my strength
The Lord is my rock, my fortress, and my deliverer,
  my God, my rock in whom I take refuge,
  my shield, and the horn of my
  salvation, my stronghold.
I call upon the Lord, who is worthy to be praised,
  so I shall be saved from my enemies.

For this I will extol you, O Lord, among the nations. and sing
  praises to you name.
Great triumphs he gives to his king, and shows steadfast love
  to his anointed,
  to David and his descendants forever.

———————————————

Holy Lord, your servant David praises you with words of devotion and love. We join in this Psalm and others throughout the Bible. The teaching of your love and divine power give us the same hope David speaks about in the Psalm. May we sing praises to you and give thanks for your saving grace and love for us. Be with us this day as we go about our lives. Help us to hold your love in our hearts and minds as we strive to do your will in a world that seems more than challenging to us. We know, through you, all things are possible. Be with us and help us have "God moments" to bolster our fears and doubts. Be with those who are most needy, help us be generous with our more than ample food supplies and resources, and please keep those who are fearful safe and warm. We pray all for all who are anxious or frightened. Help them find peace and comfort in your love. Be with us, each one and save us, I pray in your glorious name. Amen.

JANUARY 3

PSALM 90:12-18

*So teach us to count our days that we may gain a wise
    heart.*
Turn, O Lord! How long? Have compassion on your servants!

*Satisfy us in the morning with your steadfast love, so
that we may rejoice and be glad all our days. Make
us glad as many days as you have afflicted us, and
as many years as we have seen evil. Let your work be
manifest to your servants, and your glorious power
to their children. Let the favor of the Lord our God be
upon us, and prosper for us the work of our hands—
O prosper the work of our hands!*

———————————

Teacher, we place our love and trust in you! Thank you for all that your hands have provided. Today I pray for a compassionate heart for all of your people. Help us live our days in service to you. We often forget to share our abundance, Lord and sometimes we waste what we have without regard to others who are in need. Out of our abundance may we clothe the naked and cold and feed the hungry. May we be compassionate to the sick and dying that their suffering may be soothed. May we be as generous with our love and praise as we are with our abundance. Help those in need to find warm places to sleep and tables laden with healthy and delicious food. Lord, comfort those who must do without this day. Help us all to remember the children of the world, for we are all children. Keep your children safe from the evils in this world. We pray for those who do evil, may their hearts and minds be turned to do only good. Be with us this day, O Lord and save us from our sinful, wasteful ways, in Your name we pray. Amen.

PSALM 98:1-3

O sing to the Lord a new song, for he has done marvelous things.

His right hand and his holy arm have gotten him victory. The Lord has made known his victory; he has revealed his vindication in the sight of the nations. He has remembered his steadfast love and faithfulness to the house of Israel.

All the ends of the earth have seen the victory of our God.

———————————————

Savior God, you have indeed done marvelous things and created so many talented people. Today I give thanks to the parents of Sandy Hook Elementary School and the students of Parkland High School. Adults and youth had formed coalitions to work to end the scourge of gun violence in our country. Lord God, help us find a way to rein in the violence in ways that save innocent people from heinous acts that forever scar them and their communities. The motivation has come from many, however, these two groups in particular have steadfastly worked to help our country escape the all-too-frequent blast from gun violence. The violence stems from hate. Hate from anti-Semitic, hate from White Nationalists and the Ku Klux Klan, hate from differing religions and cultures, hate resulting in mental illness, etc. Lord be with innocent boys and girls who have had their lives taken from them by Human Traffickers. They shall be forever scared by their "handlers" who are evil and seeking only ways to enrich themselves without regard to the innocent children whose lives will never be the same. Lord, you have done marvelous things, help us to find ways to live harmoniously with one another in a world where guns of war are not on our streets. May we learn to celebrate our differences and diversity. Be with those who continue to mourn their unspeakable losses, comfort them. Help those who are committing such atrocities by softening their hearts and minds. May we seek to do your will and help all peoples learn to live grace-filled lives. Be with those who struggle with the ravages of hate, and the perpetrators of hate. Turn this unsettled world into one of peace and love. Be with us, Holy Lord, and save us, I pray. Amen.

PSALM 101:1-4

I will sing of loyalty and of justice to you, O Lord, I will sing.
I will study the way that is blameless.
When shall I attain it?

I will walk with integrity of heart within my house;
I will not set before my eyes anything that is base.

I hate the work of those who fall away; it shall not cling
  to me.
Perverseness of heart shall be far from me;
I will know nothing of evil.

Holy God, How do I process what is happening? Merciful God, I am worried about my homeland. I fear for all the peoples of the world. I fear for those who are charged with upholding the Constitution of the USA. Will they remain silent too long? Will the president become a dictator? What will happen to people who rely on their Social Security, Medicare and other government sponsored earnings? What will happen, when we cannot afford food for ourselves, much less "the least of these"? Please help our elected leaders to do their jobs and to right the things which the president is doing to harm citizens of this United States. I pray today for the turmoil in Asia due to the military actions taken. Please be with us as we struggle with the issues that our President set into action without having a dialog with other elected leaders. I pray that You will restore our government and our people, and I pray military actions will not escalate further. Be with us and save us Lord as we are a sinful people living in a world in turmoil. Amen.

JANUARY 6

PSALM 104:1-4

Bless the Lord, O my soul. O Lord my God, you are very great. You are clothed with honor and majesty, wrapped in light as with a garment.
You stretch out the heavens like a tent, you set the beams of your chambers on the waters, you make the clouds your chariot, you ride on the wings of the wind, you make the winds your messengers, fire and flame your ministers.

Gracious and loving God, thank you for the psalmists! They wrote such beautiful poetry filled with love. Those who have gone before us teach us as you taught them! Thank you Lord! I am drawn even closer to you, especially when I see beauty in nature. Your world, the world you gave us, and your son, whom you also gave us has completed our lives in rich and blessed ways. Help us to contain the spirit of your majesty and love for us each day. Be with those who have yet to learn of your abiding love and care. Help us to represent you and be inspiring to those with whom we interact. We praise your Holy name, Lord and I pray for forgiveness of our sins and for those who do not know you, yet. Help them realize You are the answer for each person. Be with us and help us to be good stewards of your plan for the world. In the name of Jesus. Amen.

JANUARY 7
PROVERBS 27:1-6

Do not boast about tomorrow, for you do not know what a day may bring.
Let another praise you, and not your own mouth—a stranger, and not your own lips. A stone is heavy, and the sand is weighty, but a fool's provocation is heavier than both. Wrath is cruel, anger is overwhelming, but who is able to stand before jealousy?

―――――――――――――――

Wise and wonderful Lord God, thank you for the psalmists! You know how to calm our anxieties and fears. We have become a "me first" ... "how awesome am I?" boastful people. Help us Lord to be more humble as we walk this walk, with you in our hearts. We want our youth to have a sense of pride, but I fear the self-satisfaction they exhibit frequently is not worthy of such boastfulness. Help us all to recognize and praise when one is deserving. May we withhold undeserved praise. We must listen to the words of the psalmists and their warning about wrath, anger and jealousy. Help us be mindful of their warnings and give us grace to know when to praise another. The world seems to be spinning out of control by leaders who are so full of themselves, they are not keeping their attention on what is most important. Help the leaders learn to be generous to those who are needy and to be cautious of wolves in sheep skins. Guide the leaders of the world, helping them to help those in need, to be good neighbors for countries who are the most needy of assistance. Where there is abundance, may they share their bounty and help improve those who are needy. Be with us this day and each of our days. Forgive our sinfulness and help us grow as we grow closer to you. Amen.

PROVERBS 28:1-6

The wicked flee when no one pursues, but the righteous are as bold as a lion.
When a land rebels it has many rulers; but with an intelligent ruler there is lasting order. A ruler who oppresses the poor is a beating rain that leaves no food. Those who forsake the law praise the wicked, but those who keep the law struggle against them. The evil do not understand justice, but those who seek the Lord understand it completely. Better to be poor and walk in integrity than to be crooked in one's ways even though rich.

Loving God, please help me understand what is happening in the world I love. Daily our nation and many others throughout the world seem to be spinning out of control. We find neighbors butting heads against neighbors and countries in chaos and unimaginable struggles complicate each day. If it is true, "a ruler who oppresses the poor is a beating rain that leaves no food," where is the hope against such oppressors? Those who follow oppressors instead of standing for what is right do not understand justice. How can that be, Lord? People are suffering, dying. I praise your name, Lord and await a time when sound minds can restore order out of chaos and love out of hate. Soften the hardened hearts in the world and help us restore integrity throughout our lives. Lord, I pray for the people and all living creatures who are suffering terrible fires throughout the land. Bring the gentle rains to wash away the fear and terror of fire. Help us Lord to remember those who are less fortunate and who need assistance. May we be bold to remember what your expectations are of us and help us to use our leadership for good. Be with us this day and save us from our sins. I pray in the name of Jesus. Amen.

ECCLESIASTES 5:1-3

Guard your steps when you go to the house of God; to draw near to listen is better than the sacrifice of fools; for they do not know how to keep from doing evil. Never be rash with your mouth, do not let your heart be quick to utter a word before God, for God is in heaven, and you upon earth; therefore let your words be few. For dreams come with many cares, and a fool's voice with many words.

———————————

Lord, your teachings comfort me. Thank you for helping show the way to listen and learn about Jesus and your expectations of humankind. You encourage us to hold silent our tongues in order that we might listen for your words, your will. It is easy to judge others when one is spouting words that are contrary to your understanding of what is good, what is just, what is fair. Help me find a way to express fewer words in opposition, rather to be more positive regarding my thoughts words and deeds. May I continue to seek your will and listen for your guidance. When I see the dawn of each new day and especially when your majesty is on display, it reminds me Your mighty power and love. I especially love waking to the beautiful sight of snow painting barren branches white, colorful birds dotting the landscape and most of all, I love the peaceful quiet. Thank you God, for the blessings of each moment and for being the force that informs each day. Be with us as we search for answers and help us to be ever ready to listen and to hear. Forgive our sins, Lord and know that although imperfect, we are trying to do your will. Your saving grace gives us hope for tomorrow and a pathway to you. In Jesus' name, I pray. Amen.

ECCLESIASTES 5:4-7

When you make a vow to God, do not delay in fulfilling it; for he has no pleasure in fools. Fulfill what you vow. It is better that you should not vow than that you should vow and not fulfill it. Do not let your mouth lead you into sin, and do not say before the messenger that it was a mistake; why should God be angry at your words, and destroy the work of your hands.

Good morning, Lord! You have given us a new day and this day prayers for all who have struggled through the night. In slumber, you enter our thoughts and calm our fears. The light of each new day is also a reminder to do your will. It is not always easy, Lord, but of course you know that, and are providing the light of each new day to guide our ways. Help me Lord to find ways to bring your expectations out of darkness and into a world awaiting your word and improving the lives of those who are struggling. You have told us it is not "my will" but yours. May we ever enlighten those whose lives are searching. They may not even know just what it is they are seeking. You, all knowing Lord know. May each person take a few moments each day to read and to learn of your power and your love. Help each of us Lord, to seek and to speak the truth as you have instructed. Help us to follow the path set before us through Christ Jesus as your will for us has been laid out. Lord, I pray for all of your children and especially the young who depend upon others for each day. May the "caretakers" of children do their jobs with integrity, strength and most of all faith. Help these caretakers teach goodness, love and Your will to each one in their charge. Keep them and the young ones safe and may grow up to be models of your expectations for goodness. Be with each of us, Lord and forgive our sinful moments. In Your blessed name, I pray. Amen.

JANUARY 11

ECCLESIASTES 5:10-12

The lover of money will not be satisfied with money; nor the lover of wealth, with gain. This also is vanity. When goods increase, those who eat them increase; and what gain has their owner but to see them with his eyes? Sweet is the sleep of laborers, whether they eat little or much; but the surfeit of the rich will not let them sleep.

———————————

Loving God as a new day dawns, let us be ever-mindful of your admonition to not be filled with avarice The poet, Geoffrey Chaucer wrote, "avarice is the root of all evil." He understood the love of money leads one to evil. As I contemplate today's world, I realize in that regard not much has changed through the centuries and that reality is heartbreaking. The love of money has found greedy people who do not seem to know or care they have more than they need, and yet they are unwilling to share with others. May we give to food pantries, to shelters and to those in need. Help us to use what we have to Your glory and good. I pray for the children who are abused in any way, especially for those ensnared by Human Traffickers. Be with them, Lord, and show them love and kindness. Give them hope that one day they shall be free once again. Be with us Lord, help us to use our excesses for good, save us from our sinful ways and know that You, Lord are our way, our truth and our light. In your holy name, I pray. Amen.

PSALM 66:4

All the earth worships you, they sing praises to your name. Come and see what God has done: he is awesome in his deeds among mortals.

Holy and loving God, I am awakening to another day of challenges. And yet, personal challenges of any of us do not even hold a candle to yours. We praise you and give up,those things which we cannot change. Help us to reconcile with them as we give the burdens of our hearts and minds to you. Strengthen our faith in you and show us the way you would have us go. Lord, help me step up and face those things that I can influence: I want to help females and especially young girls find a way to be safe and free from sexual exploitation and human trafficking. I have a plan and I pray that plan will enable you innocent children a way to escape the bondage they have become ensnared in. And Lord, I pray for those who are hungry and homeless. Help us stop throwing away good food and make it available in safe ways for those whose stomachs are growling from hunger. Help our nation be a leader in the search for affordable healthcare and medicine and help us honestly face the issues of climate change to save the planet for generations. Be with us Lord as we struggle to love the heaven and earth created by you and to keep it at the same time. Save us Lord from our sinful and wasteful ways. Please, Lord, watch over all of us, especially vulnerable and abused children. In your name I pray. Amen.

JANUARY 13
PSALM 108:1, 3-4

My heart is steadfast, O God, my heart is steadfast. I will sing and make melody. Awake my soul! I will give thanks to you, O Lord, among the peoples, and I will sing praises to you among the nations. For your steadfast love is higher than the heavens, and your faithfulness reaches to the clouds.

T hank you God for the first snowfall of winter. I am amazed at the stillness of a blanket of snow, it calms our lives and opens our hearts and minds to you. The blanket of snow, enfolds us with awe and wonder and at the same time provides nourishment for the glory you will bring. Just like the first flower of Spring, you provide quiet brilliance of your mighty power. May our faith nourish others just as your love and care nourishes me. Just like the first flower of Spring, you provide quiet brilliance of your mighty power. Lord, be with those who do not have a warm home in winter who perhaps lack adequate food and clothing. May those in their quiet brilliance, those with abundance who are your humble servants, step up and help take care of those who need food, clothing, medical attention or a place to live. I pray for all who are needy in body or spirit. Help them Lord and may we each take a moment to pray for the unnamed sufferers. Help them to find peace and the light of your love through our actions and deeds. Be with us on this journey. Lord God and I pray you will watch over us and save us, in your holy name I pray. Amen.

JANUARY 14

PSALM 145:21

My mouth will proclaim the Lord's name, and every living thing will bless God's holy name, forever and always.

———————

Holy God, the psalmist has given us a succinct and clear direction of what is expected . Lord, the proclamation is clear and in our hearts and often via unspoken words, we do proclaim your blessed name. Unspoken words are not enough, Lord, we know we need to be bold, as you were bold, sending your son to take away the sins of the world. Help us to boldly live our faith and love for you in what we say, what we do, and how we think. It is not enough to be silent with our unfailing love for you. We must live our faith in such a way, there is no doubt of our love for you. We know at times we are not faithful. We do not always praise your name and works. Be with us and remind us that You are the reason and how joyful we are for that. May we give thanks and praise to you, loving God for all that you have provided. May we find ways to be good shepherds in your flock of Christians. Let us teach our children to grow up praying and loving you. May we set examples inside our homes, and outward in our lives, helping others to see the light of the world provided by your amazing grace. Help us, I pray to be a beacon of light that others might see and hear what a loving and omniscient God you are, now and into eternity. Lord, today I pray for the lonely, the bereaved, and the sick. They need your loving touch to help them through lonely and painful nights. Be with them and with me as we prayerfully come to you in a quiet moment of each day. Forgive the sins committed and help us to control our ways to your glory and honor. Lord, we love you and humbly ask for your saving grace, in your name we pray. Amen.

JANUARY 15

ECCLESIASTES 7:1-4

A good name is better than precious ointment, and the day of death, than the day of birth. It is better to go to the house of mourning than to go to the house of feasting; for this is the end of everyone, and the living will lay it to heart. Sorrow is better than laughter, for by sadness of countenance the heart is made glad. The heart of the wise is in the house of mourning; but the heart of fools in the house of mirth.

———————————

Lord of Hosts, you tell us how important your name is. Sometimes, we lose sight of that, and dishonor ourselves and you in the process. You mean the name is important as it is associated with us. Our good name means honor, giving glory to You and being a good shepherd of your words and deeds. We must guard our good name from all evil and temptation. Lord, I have learned the comfort of sadness. It is a validation of what one once had or loved that is gone.

Sadness is made glad by the mere validation of what was. Comfort those who mourn a loss by helping the bereaved realize the one lost, will be reunited in Heaven one day. Help us Holy One, in order that all that we do and all that we say will glorify you and your wonderful, powerful, loving name. Be with those who mourn, reassure them that you have gone to prepare a place for them, and where you are, there we shall also be one day. May we be comforted by your words, your promise and live lives to your glory. Be with us each day and forgive us our sins, save us Lord, I pray in your name. Amen.

JANUARY 16

PROVERBS 2:6

For the Lord gives wisdom; from his mouth comes knowledge and understanding. Wisdom makes decisions today that will stand the test of time.

Wise and omniscient God, help us to move through these days as gracefully as possible. I pray for leaders in cities and towns, in counties, states and in each country in the world. The times are frightening to the people subjected to despots and dictators. Lord comfort them, and help those who would act on behalf of others to be mindful of the burdens they carry. May they seek to do what is right for the world and not what is financially, economically or advantageous to a few. Help us to live by the "Golden Rule" and may those who represent others always consider the full measure of their actions before making decisions. Holy God, may the municipalities and leaders strive to take care of the physical and mental well-being of others. Help lawmakers to be mindful especially of the needs of those suffering from mental illness. May they find ways to keep these individuals safe, from themselves and from harming others. May our lawmakers find sensible ways to reign in the use of deadly weapons, such as weapons of war, biochemicals and the like. Help our leaders boldly work to make our planet clean for the future as well as today. May the choices made now stand the test of time and make our world a better place, pleasing to you. Be with each one and save us I pray. Amen.

JANUARY 17
PSALM 145:15-16

All eyes look to you, hoping and you give them their food right on time, opening your hand and satisfying the desire of every living thing.

Dear Lord, as Shakespeare once wrote, "a rose by any other name is still the same", so too are the loving names you have for your disciples. We depend on your Devine care to meet our needs and call out to you in times of plenty and in times of desperation. You generously care for each one, even though we are unworthy. Thank you for giving your unconditional love to the flock that is often lost, neglectful and yes cruel. Today I lift up the people who need your love and grace as they are suffering health issues and for their loved ones and caretakers who unselfishly devote countless hours to help loved ones in uncertain times and days. It is painful to see friends and loved ones struggle to "make it better" when there will be no "better." Comfort them and give them peace throughout the process. Please be with and heal those who are suffering. You know their names and their circumstances. It is stressful watching a loved one die, and yet, there is great rejoicing knowing that when earth loses one, heaven gains one. Be with those who are left behind and comfort each one. Be with them and us as we strive to follow your example and love one another as we love ourselves. Lord your constant and abiding love is with us. I pray to be saved from my sinful ways. Soften my heart when I say or do unkind acts. In the name of the Risen Son. Amen.

JEREMIAH 5:20-24

Declare this in the house of Jacob, proclaim it in Judah: Here this, O foolish and senseless people, who have eyes, but do not see, who have ears, but do not hear.

Do you not fear me? says the Lord, Do you not tremble before me? I placed the sand as a boundary for the sea, a perpetual barrier that it cannot pass; though the waves toss, they cannot prevail, though they roar, they cannot pass over it.

But this people has a stubborn and rebellious heart; they have turned aside and gone away. They do not say in their hearts, "Let us fear the Lord our God, who gives the autumn rain and the spring rain, and keeps for us the weeks appointed for the harvest."

God of our lives, why are we so reluctant to honor, to believe or to love you? In a world of goals, objectives and "To Do" lists, how is it You, loving, and patient God are not on any of them? What we need, Lord is to find ways to be intentional with You as our guide and way. The start of each day will be our way to learn from your teachings. As the morning dawns, may we commit to prayer and a genuine conversation with you guiding our thoughts and informing our prayers. We know there will be obstacles as we walk in faith and love with you. Give us eyes to see and ears to hear your truths, our truths. Calm our fears and keep us ever on the path to being faithful and resolute in our learning and living as sensible Christians. Keep us from turning away from you and your son, and leaning into your love and teachings. Be with us on this journey of intentional prayer and devotion to you, and save us as we acknowledge our sins, we pray. Amen.

JANUARY 19
JOHN 14:1-7

"Do not let your hearts be troubled. Believe in God, believe also in me. In my father's house there are many dwelling places. If it were not so, would I have told you that I go to prepare a place for you? And if I go and prepare a place for you, I will come again and will take you to myself, so that where I am, here you may be also. And you know the way to the place where I am going." Thomas said to him, "Lord, we do not know where you are going. How can we know the way?" Jesus said to him, "I am the way, and the truth, and the life. No one comes to the Father except through me. If you know me, you will know my father also. From now on you do know him and have seen him."

Wise and loving Lord of All, how proud you must have been as your son, sent to be the Savior of the World, undertook a loving and profound ministry in your name. Reading the words he spoke and feeling the love he had for his mission is powerful and humbling. I feel his love and reassurance, even when he answers Peter's question in the Upper Room, he knew Peter would betray him. Even the disciples failed to recognize and accept the true identity of Jesus, even after saying "I am the father and the father is in me...". Powerful words as were those spoken just moments before. Lord, history has recorded the greatest gift, the gift of the Savior, Jesus, who came to take away the sins of the world. We praise you and Jesus' life. We know that through your love of us, you gave us your only son. Thank you Lord, for giving us all a chance to know you through your son and to love and worship in a faith-filled community of Christians. It was the greatest, everlasting gift! May our lives continue to be enriched because of our faith and because your son came to take away our sins. Be with us and save us this day and each of our days. Amen.

JANUARY 20

CORINTHIANS 1:2

Grace to you and peace from God our Father and the Lord Jesus Christ.

———————————

Dear Lord, you have set the world in motion. We know there is much we do not always understand, or for that matter, even what is happening in our world. By your grace and with our faith in you we know that all things are possible. When I stray from your will, I pray your guidance will help me return to your plan. Yes, sometimes I grow impatient and push for answers that need time to become part of my reality. Help me to be patient and open to the possibility of each answer. I pray to glorify your name and please you in thought, word and deed. Be with enemies who would have believers stray from your will and guide us in the way you would have us go, in peace and with your grace. Lord, Jesus came to bring a very real answer to a world that was in chaos. I think the world continues on chaotic exercises, denying your rule and your expectations. Help us, Lord God, to right the ship, set the true path to our futures by dedicating our lives to you and to helping people. I am thankful for all who teach us about you and who help to provide the solutions to complex issues, like world peace, climate change, and devotion to you. Lord, may we learn to live our lives in grace-filled love and devotion to you and following the example of The Risen Son all of our days. Be with us and save us, Lord. Amen.

ROMANS 1:8-12

First, I thank my God through Jesus Christ for all of you, because your faith is proclaimed throughout the world. For God, whom I serve with my spirit by announcing the gospel of his Son, is my witness that without ceasing I remember you always in my prayers, asking that by God's will I may somehow at last succeed in coming to you. For I am longing to see you so that I may share with you some spiritual gift to strengthen you—or rather so that we may be mutually encouraged by each other's faith, both yours and mind.

———————————

Holy Lord, we give your thanks and praise for your servant, Jesus' disciple, Paul. He was faithful to his charge, and thus Paul went to Rome to spread the world about your power, power for salvation to everyone who has faith. He wrote to the Romans and he proclaimed "For in it the righteousness of God is revealed through faith for faith; as it is written, "The one who is righteous will live by faith." May it be so Lord. May you continue to be with us and may our salvation from sin be secure because of our faith in you. Amen.

JANUARY 22

MATTHEW 7:24-28

"Everyone who hears these words of mine and acts on them will be like a wise man who built his house on rock. The rain fell, the floods came, and the winds blew and beat on that house, but it did not fall because it had been founded on rock. And every one; who hears these words of mine and does not act on them will be like a foolish man who built his house on sand. The rain fell and the floods came, and the winds blew and beat against that house, and it fell—and great was its fall."

Loving and merciful Lord, the world is filled with abundance and abject poverty. Each season that passes we learn of calamity caused by humans. The world has acknowledged the phenomena of "Climate Change" and yet, some greedy decisions by those who would deny it. Laws were made based on the recommendations of scientists that would help save our lands and the very air we breathe and the water we drink. However, many in positions of power broke the laws apart in order to save and/or make more money. The resulting changes have harmed the planet and all life on it. Please help brilliant minds repair the damage climate change has on the planet and make it a safer place environmentally for all. Too often Lord, the greedy, are looking out for no one but themselves. We have to be cognizant of the repercussions of our actions. May we be good stewards of the environment and leave a healthier one for those who are yet to come. Lord, help us to avoid having a great planetary fall. Help the world leaders act on your words of warning and the science that struggles to bring about change for all who inhabit the earth. Be with us Lord and save us from our sins, especially the environmental sins, I pray in Jesus' name. Amen.

JANUARY 23

PROVERBS 4:1-5

Listen, children, to a father's instruction, and be attentive, that you may gain insight; for I give you good precepts: do not forsake my teaching. When I was a son with my father, tender, and my mother's favorite, he taught me and said to me, "Let your heart hold fast my words; keep my commandments, and live."

Dear God, this morning I pray that your words will be with me as I continue to walk through life. I have much to learn from you, teacher. Help me to be a leader, by leading others following your commandments. I pray for those who do not know of your love and teachings. Keep me on your path and let my words reflect your words. Heavenly teacher, help us this day and every day to continue the path you set for us. May we live our lives by gently following your instructions, for you are the way, the truth and the light. May we go forth this day and all of our days following your teachings and saved by your grace. Amen.

JANUARY 24

JOHN 3:11-16

"Very truly, I tell you, we speak of what we know and testify to what we have seen; yet you do not receive our testimony. If I have told you about earthly things and you do not believe, how can you believe if I tell you about heavenly things? No one has ascended into heaven except the one who descended from heaven, the Son of Man. And just as Moses lifted up the serpent in the wilderness, so must the Son of Man be lifted up, that whoever believes in him may have eternal life. For God so loved the world that he gave his only Son, so that everyone who believes in him may not perish but may have eternal life."

———————————

The song title, Because He Lives is poignant. God your teaching comes in many ways. You have touched my life in ways spoken and unspoken. We all have them Lord. I pray today that as we listen to this beautiful song, we will sing along and feel the power of your Holy promise. Lord, your disciple John was eloquent when he wrote the familiar words. The words are quite revealing, John has written about your very nature and connected us with your beloved son, Our Savior, Jesus. The scriptures help us to understand the prophecy of the Old Testament. The link is undeniable and. I see a loving God, a parent who loves a son deeply and who is tender and compassionate. I know a God who is ready to forgive. Holy God, your love for earthly beings you sacrificed the love of your only Son for believers. I feel the relationship and your love for me. Help me to continue the journey with you, knowing that through you, all things are possible. Be with us and save us, I pray in your name. Amen.

MATTHEW 12:18-21

"Here is my servant, whom I have chosen, my beloved, with whom my soul is well pleased. I will put my spirit upon him, and he will proclaim justice to the Gentiles.
He will not wrangle or cry aloud, nor will anyone hear his voices in the streets. He will not break a bruised reed or quench a smoldering wick until he brings justice to victory. And in his name, the Gentiles will hope."

———————————

Holy one, you know what is in our hearts and minds. I pray that you will calm us enough to see the signs that you are with us always. I pray you will help us open up to whatever it is that we can do to "please" you. Your teachings have shown many "the way," following in the pathways you have instructed us to follow is not always easy. Things of value, goals to attain, are never easy, however, the journey is the only way to find you, to find forgiveness for sins and mostly to have my spirit lifted to heaven on my final earthly day. In your name, I have hope. Listening or reading your words of long ago set a high bar for humankind. May all we do please you as we walk through life always remembering that what we do and say must be according to your teaching. I know Lord, sometimes the bar seems too high, but I also know that if what we do, we do softly and gently, hopefully you will be pleased. May the end of each day bring us to feel our work was well done. Be with us each day and save us, I pray in your name. Amen.

PSALM 98:4

Make a joyful noise unto the Lord, all the earth; break out in loud songs, and sing praises.

———————————

This is the day that the Lord has made. Let us rejoice and be glad in it. Lord, sometimes picking the hymns which have become "oldies but goodies" takes your people back to a time before. And sometimes Holy One, it makes me long for a new way to worship you. Be with your servants this day and every day, making us open to the "old" and the "new." Let us praise your Holy name in tangible ways to glorify you and keep a song in our heart as we pass a sabbath holding you in word, deed and especially in our hearts. Be with those who are suffering and need to know of your love. Thank you for all whose life's work is to help others: ministers, doctors, teachers, firefighters, and all who strive to help people in need. Let us rejoice for those who give unselfishly of their time and talents. Help those who are searching for you and an understanding of your powerful love and devotion to us. Lord, you know what is in our hearts and minds. Be with us as we walk with you and save us, I pray in your name. Amen.

JANUARY 27

JOHN 3:1-3

Now there was a Pharisee named Nicodemus, a leader of the Jews. He came to Jesus by night and said to him, "Rabbi, we know that you are a teacher who came from God; for no one can do these signs that you do apart from the presence of God." Jesus answered him, "Very truly, I tell you, no one can see the kingdom of God without being born from above."

Have you ever awakened, feeling like although alone, you are not? Do you sometimes say to yourself, "Thank you God for showing me the way"?

Lord, thank you for the testimony of Nicodemus. It helps me carry our Savior, in my heart and mind. Lord, I pray for those who might not think they have heard. May they keep listening and praying, it will come. Lord God, thank you for all who bring your messages to the people. Be with the ministers, pastors, teachers and leaders, who are doing good work without much pay, but with love in their hearts for you and for those with whom they spend their devoted time. Help us to keep listening and praying as we seek to learn your will for each of us and just how precious your love for us is. Be with those who are struggling with their faith, and help them to become true believers. Loving God, please help all people today and every day face obstacles that may bring doubt. Help us see you and love you each day. I also pray for all who venture out this day into freezing cold and blizzard-like conditions. Be with the workers who clear the roads and sidewalks, deliver the mail and packages, and those whose jobs require a lot more on inclement weather days. Keep each one safe as they venture out into the storms of nature this day. Keep them and us warmed by your love. Be with us this day and each of our days and Lord, we ask for the forgiveness of our sins, in your Son's name. Amen.

JANUARY 28

JOHN 14:1-2
JESUS THE WAY TO THE FATHER

Do not let your hearts be troubled. Believe in God, believe also in me.
In my father's house, there are many dwelling places.
If it were not so, would I have told you that I go to prepare a place for you?

Loving God, we are often troubled by things which we can neither embrace within our senses nor control. We seem to be in an age of accountability. From the moment our children are born they are tested to prove their viability: first medical tests, and at a tender age test after test, benchmark after benchmark to prove the student or rather the teacher is successful. Lord God, thank you for only placing one test for success. There is sure and just knowledge that those who place their trust in you will be saved. The "trust thing" is sometimes difficult for a doubting mind, not for me! When I lose my way and things don't go just as hoped, often I get so busy trying to "fix" the issue that I neglect to start the "fixing" with you! Help me to turn to you, and to bring you with me as I face life's challenges. Today Lord, I'm praying for all of your children who will be in harm's way today. May each one find warmth and safety as temperatures drop or other issues challenge their physical being. Warm the hearts of those who provide help for the homeless: a warm meal and a shelter from the cold. Lord, be with those who feel lost or lonely, those who turn to others for their daily safety. Lord, I pray for the lost ones who are suffering and abused. May your love be enough to get them through a day that will be lost to them, until your love strengthens them in spirit and in body. Thank you Lord for being my savior throughout each second of each day. Be with each one and save us from harm and our own sins, in your name I pray. Amen.

ACTS 28:26-29

Go to these people and say, You will indeed listen, but never understand, and you will indeed look, but never perceive. For this people's heart has grown dull, and their ears are hard of hearing, and they have shut their eyes; so that they might not look with their eyes, and listen with their ears, and understand with their heart and turn—and I would heal them. Let it be known to you then that this salvation of God has been sent to the Gentiles: they will listen."

———————————

L ord God, your servant, Paul dedicated his life at great cost, to bring the message of salvation to all who would hear. Paul tried several times and ultimately spoke of your gift of salvation given to those who would listen, at that time, it was the Gentiles. It is so in our lives today. Lord, help us to bring your message of salvation into our hearts and to spread the "good news" of your gift of Jesus Christ. I pray that as we walk through life, our lives might be an example of how to live out our lives in thought, word and deed. Be with us all of our days Lord, help those who are suffering, homeless, abandoned, or abused to feel your love. I pray for safety throughout your world, especially for those who suffer under the auspices of cruel and illegal enslavement. Comfort them until the day they shall be free and whole again. Be with us all, and help us to demonstrate how to live a faith-filled life that others might know of your love and receive the gift of salvation. Through your son, Jesus Christ, I pray. Amen.

JANUARY 30

PSALM 92:1-4

It is good to give thanks to the Lord, to sing praises to your name, O Most High; to declare your steadfast love in the morning, and your faithfulness by night, to the music of the lute and the harp, to the melody of the lyre. For you, O Lord, have made me glad by your work; at the works of your hands I sing for joy.

Heavenly Teacher, to you all glory and power. Thank you Lord God, for the time you have given us to nourish our faith in you. You remind each of us about an important task we have, to praise you night and day, waking and sleeping, and to be filled with joy. We know that joy when we live our lives as you wish and when we bring our faith together with our sisters and brothers, in Christ. Your teachings sustain us and lead us. Sometimes God, we are so "busy" we may not take time to praise you, however, we are trying to demonstrate that love through our actions, our faith and our love for one another. While there are seven days in a week and we are to love you each day, Sunday is your day and it is then when our souls and spirits are replenished as we worship with brothers and sisters in Christ. Lord, I pray for those who do not know your love and that your "flock" will find the way to bring others into joyful love and your amazing grace. Teach us how to bring those who do not know you; to learn of your great works and abiding love. Lord, help those too busy to reclaim "church time" for themselves, their children and their families. Be with us this day, heal the sick, keep us warm during the cold weather, especially help all who have no source for warmth, and all who are hurting. Forgive our sins, and save us, I pray in your blessed name. Amen.

JANUARY 31
ROMANS 10:1-4

Brothers and sisters, my heart's desire and prayer to God for them is that they may be saved. I can testify that they have a zeal for God, but it is not enlightened. For, being ignorant of the righteousness that comes from God, and seeking to establish their own, they have not submitted to God's righteousness. For Christ is the end of the law so that there may be righteousness for everyone who believes.

———————————

Our Father in heaven, help us to know you through the life, works and teachings of your beloved son, Jesus Christ. You sent him to walk among mortals and to take away the sins of the world. We know to receive forgiveness, we have but to ask. Thank you Lord, for holding each one in your head and heart. May each parent teach their children from conception throughout their lives, keeping foremost in their child rearing responsibilities the requirement to teach each child of your love and about the forgiveness of sins which can be theirs for the asking. Remind each one of us the importance of demonstrating and teaching Your word and helping shape each child with whom we encounter. Forgive our sins, Lord, especially this day the sin of neglecting our duty to testify in Your name. I pray for each parent who might have let the busy world interrupt the important parental duties for children. May they find time to take their children to Sunday School and Church, and to pray with them each day and use teachable moments with each child with whom they interact. May we each day model your love and the way to enter into the gates of heaven with you. I pray for each parent today, in the name of your precious son. Help us lead lives in service to you and the world you have created for us. Be with us each day and help us to be better Christians. In Jesus' name we pray. Amen.

FEBRUARY 1

LUKE:3:21-22

Now when all the people were baptized, and when Jesus also had been baptized and was praying, the heaven was opened, and the Holy Spirit descended upon him in bodily form like a dove. And a voice came from heaven. "You are my Son, the Beloved: with you I am well pleased."

Heavenly Spirit, I pray all who know you and love you are in dialog with you. It can be difficult sometimes to pray to someone with whom you have never seen. May we all just start praying and asking to be filled with the Holy Spirit. Help each one to depend upon you and to begin a dialog with you. Fill our hearts with your love and help us to find comfort and love you, too. Encourage each one to live a life that is pleasing in your sight. Be with those who do not know you and your love. Lord, I pray for all of those who are suffering, hungry or lost. Keep your people safe and free from harm this day. Please be with the lonely, the sick and those whose days are limited. Help them to know your loving grace and also that salvation awaits. Remind us daily, Lord of your presence and love for us and forgive our sins, I pray. Amen.

FEBRUARY 2

MARK 16: THE SHORTER ENDING OF MARK*

And all that had been commanded them they told briefly to those around Peter. And afterward Jesus himself sent out through them, from east to west, the sacred and imperishable proclamation of eternal salvation.

Heavenly Father of Jesus, on this day, sometimes a "short version" works for those who need to heed your proclamation, like right now. For others, I pray the knowledge of eternal salvation dwells within their hearts and minds. Knowing a simple request for forgiveness of our sins, and elaborating on the specifics is what we often unnecessarily feel compelled to pray for. The fact of the matter, Lord God is that you already know our petitions for forgiveness before the first word is spoken. As we sin, and it is often difficult not to, especially via the spoken word, may we feel a power greater than ourselves, your power and love. Hopefully, we will begin to exercise self control over our negative thoughts, words and deeds. I pray Gracious Lord, you will help those that sin, may we receive the "sacred and imperishable proclamation of eternal salvation." In praise and gratitude I ask you to be with us this day and all the days of our lives. Save us and forgive our sins, in Jesus' name. Amen.

---

* Some ancient authorities believe that Mark concluded with verse 8. One authority concludes the book with shorter ending, others extend Mark, however, it is reported the longer version is marked as being doubtful.

FEBRUARY 3
LUKE 18:1

Jesus instructs his disciples to pray always and to not give up hope.

Healing God, your son, instructed his disciples to have faith and to continue to pray. We are assured that God will be us as we pray. I pray for all who do not "know how to pray." Help each of us, Lord, to just start praying. I also pray for patience when answers to prayers may not be forthcoming, in the way I want. Lord most high, we know our prayers have been heard, and our petitions considered. Help us Lord to not lose hope and to pray trusting that you will be with us. We know sometimes, the prayers we pray, the miracles we hope for, may not be the miracle we receive. However, it may indeed be the best miracle for our situation. Be with us Lord, help us to pray and be saved through your grace and Jesus' gift of salvation for all. Amen.

FEBRUARY 4

MALACHI 3:16-17
THE REWARD OF THE FAITHFUL

Then those who revered the Lord spoke with one another. The Lord took note and listened, and a book of remembrance was written before him of those who revered the Lord and thought on his name. They shall be mine, says the Lord of hosts, my special possession on the day when I act, and I will spare them as parents spare their children who serve them.

Fearless and loving Lord, we have learned of your plan for every believer. This morning I pray that your spirit and grace will live in my heart this day and every day. I know how the glory of this gift warms my soul. May your spirit dwell in each one, that we might serve our lives as faithful people, proclaiming your glory. Only then, my Lord will we be prepared to face judgement day. May what we do and what we say be pleasing in your sight. I pray for those who do not know your name and for all who are struggling. Comfort the sick and broken hearted. Be with us and save us, I pray in your name. Amen.

MATTHEW 15:1-2, 8-9

When the Pharisees and scribes, came to Jesus from Jerusalem and said, "Why do your disciples break the tradition of the elders? For they do not wash their hands before they eat." He answered them, "And why do you break the commandment of God for the sake of your tradition? These people honor me with their lips, but their hearts are far from me, teaching human precepts as doctrines."

Dear Lord God, you and your son, alone, were able to instruct the Pharisees and scribes. It is clear to us through your leadership and teachings to the Pharisees, a deeper understanding of your teachings is required. Help me to be open to the true meaning of how it is we are charged to live. What is expected of us in today's world, loving God is to honor our God from our very soul. We are blessed by the words and deeds of your son, Jesus the Christ. Help us Lord to honor you by speaking, teaching traditions and most importantly help us live our lives in ways that are pleasing to you. We shall be intentional and faithfully praise your holy name and teach your children how to live a more Christ-like life. Each day, we pray for our salvation from sins and your grace to grant our humble petitions. Amen.

FEBRUARY 6

JOHN 3:11, 16

"Very truly, I tell you, we speak of what we know and testify to what we have not seen" "For God so loved the world that he gave his only Son, so that everyone who believes in him may not perish but have eternal life."

———————————

Fairest Lord, sometimes we need to read your words and the words of your son to be reminded of just what You did for my sake. When I was taking instruction to be baptized, I learned an important lesson. The words of the baptism and feeling the pastor's hand, that was dipped into the holy water, changed me. Although symbolic to many, when one accepts Jesus Christ as Lord and Savior, it changes everything in a person. I pray that those who do not know of your teachings, begin in earnest to learn of your earthly mission and heavenly promise. Be with those who have lost loved ones, give them comfort and peace, knowing that their loved one has earned eternal life. Help those who are walking in your footsteps and comfort them as they face the end of their earthly lives. Lord, thank you for the gift of eternal life and for the forgiveness of sins. Be with each one on their journey to be a Christian, I pray in the name of Jesus. Amen.

FEBRUARY 7

PSALM 46:1-3, 11

God is our refuge and strength, a very present help in trouble. Therefore we will not fear, though the earth should change, though the mountains shake in the heart of the sea, though its waters roar and foam, though the mountains tremble with its tumult.

The Lord of hosts is with us, the God of Jacob is our refuge.

L ord of hosts be with us as we walk through life. It is hard when people suffer "natural disasters' ' and man-made ones, too. There are troubled waters in our private lives and in our universe. Sometimes, it is difficult to be fearless with all the upsetting events that shake us to our very core. God, be with those in "leadership" who have become lost on our local, state and private lives and on the national/global level. We read your words and try to follow your teachings, but when our leaders sin, we have difficulty standing up and becoming fearless. God it is not acceptable to turn away from difficulty. Help us to lead by example by making a difference. Help us to maintain integrity when considering our actions in the face of different genders, different races, different generations, different faiths, different beliefs in how we treat one another. May our attitude towards others be less judgemental and more welcoming. It is the way to change the framing of who we are. God, please help me find a way through the potholes in life when tumultuous incidents muddy the waters in my daily life. Be with us this day and save us, I pray. Amen.

FEBRUARY 8

PSALM 23
THE DIVINE SHEPHERD,
A PSALM OF DAVID

The Lord is my shepherd, I shall not want.
He makes me lie down in green pastures;
He leads me beside still waters; he restores my soul.
He leads me in right paths for his name's sake.

Even though I walk through the darkest valley,
I fear no evil, for you are with me, your rod and your staff—
they comfort me.
You prepare a table before me in the presence of my
enemies; you anoint my head with oil; my cup overflows.
Surely goodness and mercy shall follow me all the days of my
life, and I shall dwell in the house of the Lord my whole life
long.

Shepherd God, we truly are a blessed people. We are generally hard-working people with lives that are filled with seemingly endless "To Do" lists. Our calendars are filled with our plans for each day. Help us to make time, Lord to begin our day with You and end our day with prayers of gratitude on our lips. Help me Lord to plan so that what is between the "bookends" of prayer is a life completing obligations and may I be richer because You are in it. May a generous and loving spirit help those who need a kind word, a simple deed of friendship and caring gestures for those less fortunate. Lord, I pray you will be with me and save me from my sins. In Jesus' name, I pray. Amen.

FEBRUARY 9

1 CORINTHIANS 12:4-6

There are different spiritual gifts but the same Spirit, and there are different ministries and the same Lord; and there are different activities but the same God who produces all of them in everyone.

Everlasting God, sometimes it is hard to believe in something one cannot see or touch. From time to time, all of us have struggled to find words for the prayer that is in our heart and head. What changed, for me, was all the people living their faith that encouraged and showed me that what is in my heart and head is real. God, you comforted me when everything seemed to cave in around me. You are the one who saved me when I struggled. Thank you for comforting me in my darkest hours and for showing me a way to move forward. My prayer is for those who do not know you, trust in you or believe in you to find you in the random acts of kindness they receive. I pray for a way for each to become one with you. It is written "Whatever you do, whether in speech or action, do it all in the name of the Lord Jesus and give thanks to God the Father through him. (Colossians 3:17). May it be so, and may my words and actions demonstrate a way to show my love and faithfulness to you. Be with us Lord, and grant forgiveness for our sins. In the name of Jesus, I pray. Amen.

FEBRUARY 10
MATTHEW 14:24-26, 30

"The kingdom of heaven may be compared to someone who sowed good seed in his field; but while everybody was asleep, an enemy came and sowed weeds among the wheat, and then went away. So when the plants came up and bore again, the weeds appeared as well.

Let both of them (the weeds and the wheat) grow together until the harvest; and at harvest time I will tell the reapers, "Collect the weeds first and bind them in bundles to be burned, but gather the wheat into my barn."

L ord of all, I pray this morning that today we can pause and give thanks to you. Thank you for all you have provided to us. Be with those who know you and who spread the "Good News" of Jesus' birth, life and resurrection. Lord, thank you for the songs and hymns of praise shared this day. Help us nourish our souls, our goals and learn to rid our hearts of the "weeds" that choke our loving and caring ways. May we become more generous with our abundance and helpful to those in need. Today Lord, I ask you to be with us and help us to be people who will in some way demonstrate our abiding faith where we live, work and play. Be with us each day and save us, I pray in your name. Amen.

FEBRUARY 11

ECCLESIASTES 3:1,2,4,8.
EVERYTHING HAS IT'S TIME

For everything there is a season, and a time for every matter under heaven:
  a time to be born, and a time to die,
  a time to weep and a time to laugh;
  a time to love; and a time to hate;
  A time for war; and a time for peace.

D ear Holy Savior, your words provide insight into my walk with you. There are some "times" I don't like what is happening in the world very much. I am encouraged when many moments give me hope. Passages of loved ones from a life on earth to heavenly life, is comforting, but God, it is so very painful. I am comforted, Lord, that loved ones shall "dwell in the house of the Lord, forever." I pray that you will walk with me, all the way from this world to the next. Be with us Lord, and warm us with the saving grace of Jesus Christ. Amen.

FEBRUARY 12

Today is Abraham Lincoln's Birthday. He was the sixteenth President of the United States. He is celebrated for his leadership and how one should treat all people equally. Via (Emancipation) Proclamation 95 came change in the United States. The proclamation changed the legal status of more than 3.5 million enslaved African Americans in the designated areas of the South from slave to free. Lincoln's life was cut short by John W. Booth in 1864.

Quotes from Lincoln:

> *Those who deny freedom to others, deserve it not for themselves.*
> *I walk slowly, but I never walk backward.*
> *Tact is the ability to describe others as they see themselves.*

HEBREWS 11:1-3
THE MEANING OF FAITH

Now faith is the assurance of things hoped for, the conviction of things not seen. Indeed by faith our ancestors received approval as righteous. By faith we understand that the worlds were prepared by the word of God, so that what is seen was made from things that are not visible.

Lord of hosts, I read your words and embrace your teachings. My faith gives me hope for all of the world. God, thank you for the conviction of our forefathers (and foremothers). I am especially thankful that President Lincoln was bold enough to instruct Americans that all people are to be treated equally. Although just saying those words then, had dire consequences, it was a first step toward freedom for those enslaved. I do not understand how in our country and world, there continues to be unjust treatment of numerous people. I pray for those people, that you might melt their cold hearts and turn their prejudices into love for all. Be with those who have lived and taught racism, sexism, anti semitism to generations. Warm their cold hearts. Lord God, I pray your words and deeds will instruct and create within our world one that is open, caring, inclusive, accepting, and loving. Be with those who do not yet know of your love for all people. God, help those who need to have minds and hearts softened. Be with them and us, forgive our sins and help make all people free from the enslavement they feel. I pray all in your Holy name. Amen.

PSALM 9:1-2

I will give thanks to the Lord with my whole heart. I will tell of all your wonderful deeds. I will be glad and exalt in you; I will sing praise to your name, O Most High.

Lord God, I pray that your truth and light will be a steady guide. You are a comfort when other issues in life seem to be unsettling and even frightening. My trust is in you and I am learning to be patient and also how to pray. You provided ways for me to have "thought prayers" that helped me find my way to speaking and writing them. We do not always know the way, and stray off the path, but your forgiveness Lord is assured. Guided by your actions and words I pray for all who seek a way to move closer to you. I pray for those who are suffering from physical or emotional issues. Be with each one who receives these prayers and save us all, I pray in your Holy name. Amen.

FEBRUARY 14

EPHESIANS 4:1-6

I therefore, the prisoner in the Lord, beg you to lead a life worthy of the calling to which you have been called, with all humility and gentleness with patience, bearing with each other with love, making every effort to maintain the unity of the Spirit in the bond of peace. There is one body and one spirit, just as you were called to the one hope of your calling, one Lord, one faith, one baptism, one God and Father of all, who is above all, in all and through all and in all.

On this day Father, I pray for all of your people both near and far. May we take to heart your words and encourage us to "love thy neighbor as thyself". I pray for each of us to try to recall our baptism, or a baptism witnessed. Help each one to remember how it felt at that sacred event and that the love for all of humankind will warm each heart. Holy God, I pray the "calling" be acknowledged by each, for as unique as the "calling" itself, is the heartfelt love of one another. Knowing what God's plan is for me sometimes took time for me to find. Thank you Lord for leading your people in hope and love. This Valentine's Day, I pray for all who are alone and praying for companionship. Let a random act of kindness renew their faith. Healing God, be in the hearts and minds of all. Help our special friends heal and be warmed with the knowledge of your love. Be with all who are suffering physically or mentally. Lord God, help those who feel unloved and the need to anesthetize the pain life is making them feel. Be with us all and save us. I pray in the name of Jesus. Amen.

FEBRUARY 15

PSALM 10:2

In arrogance the wicked persecute the poor—
Let them be caught in the schemes they have devised.

F orgiving Lord, sometimes we get caught up in a big old pity party. We rage on and on about things over which we really cannot change all that easily. Help us to be patient and to learn to use our voices calmly and deliberately. Be with us as we ponder what is in our hearts and let us choose our words carefully, prayerfully. Be with those whom we might think of as "enemies" that their hearts might hear our petitions. Lord I pray for all who seek your grace and for those who do not may they become instruments of your love. I pray for forgiveness this day and for all of those who are hurting, ill, perplexed, lost and lonely. Be with us Lord this day and all the days of our lives, and forgive us our trespasses. I pray for traveling mercies and for those who need to feel your healing power. Amen.

FEBRUARY 16

MATTHEW 13:31

"The kingdom of heaven is like a mustard seed that someone took and sowed in his field; it is the smallest of all the seeds, but when it has grown it is the greatest of shrubs and becomes a tree, so that the birds of the air come and make nests in its branches."

Lord, help me to grow in the sure knowledge of your love. Be with me, as I strive to do your will and to be a good parent, spouse, sister, friend, and a kind and gentle teacher. I pray to exude my faith and joy on my life's walk with You. May I cease from following the advice of those who do not know you. May the prayers I write, bring you into the hearts and minds of those searching for you and a reason to pray. My happiness comes from you, loving God and from learning Your amazing power and love. I pray that my heart, mind and soul will grow like the mustard seed. May my faith grow into one which welcomes all, helps them to learn of you and your mighty works. Be with me on this walk, O Lord, and save me in the name of your son, Jesus. Amen.

FEBRUARY 17

PSALM 8:1-9
DIVINE MAJESTY AND
HUMAN DIGNITY

O Lord, our Sovereign, how majestic is your name in all the earth!

You have set your glory above the heavens. Out of the mouths of babes and infants you have founded a bulwark because of your foes, to silence the enemy and the avenger. When I look at your heavens, the work of your fingers, the moon and the stars that you have established; what are human beings that you are mindful of them, mortals that you care for them? Yet you have made them a little lower than God, and crowned them with glory and honor. You have given them domination over the works of your hands; you have put all things under their feet, all sheep and oxen, and also the beasts of the field, the birds of the air and the fish of the sea, whatever passes along the paths of the seas. O Lord, our Sovereign, how majestic is your name in all the earth!

All praise and glory to you, our Lord! Thank you for giving us the Sabbath for it is a sacred time when we can join brothers and sisters in Christ to worship you and enjoy time with brothers and sisters in Christ. It is time set aside to worship and praise your holy name. Lord God, you have entrusted us with taking care of the precious gift that you have given us. Help us to be faithful stewards of this earth and all that dwells upon it. There is much to do, and at times it seems as if many do not value preserving this earthly gift. I pray that you will help those who are working to protect our environment to be successful in restoring your gifts and preserving them for all generations. Be with those who seek to preserve this planet earth and with those who have dedicated much of their lives for the sake of future inhabitants. Be with those who are suffering physical or mental issues, help them, through your power to enable them to be whole again. Be with the sick, the lonely, and those who are grieving. Be with each of us this day and every day and save us, I pray. Amen.

FEBRUARY 18

PHILIPPIANS 4:4-7

Rejoice in the Lord always, again I will say rejoice. Let your gentleness be known to everyone. The Lord is near. Do not worry about anything, but in everything by prayer and supplication with thanksgiving let your requests be known to God. And the peace of God, which surpasses all understanding will guard your hearts and your minds in Christ Jesus.

God of heaven and earth, be with us this day and every day. At times, I know that my words are not as gentle as they should be. I am a work in progress, knowing God. I pray for many things in my heart and mind. I hand my worries and petitions over to you, it is hard, but I am working on it. Help me to use my time of prayer to be more inclusive of what is on my heart. Help calm my anxious fears and soften my anxious fears Loving God, you are always 'there' for me. I shall be forever thankful to your ears that hear and calm my worries. I know through your love and care, all worries will be handled and often my fear is for naught. Be with each one as we all strive to turn to you first. May I rest knowing you have a handle on the issues which are on my heart. I pray today for all who need your blessing, may each one feel your love and seek your guidance. Be with me and forgive my sins this day and all the days of my life that my prayers may be gentle. Amen.

FEBRUARY 19

PHILIPPIANS 4:8-9

Finally, beloved, whatever is true, whatever is honorable, whatever is just, whatever is pure, whatever is pleasing, whatever is commendable, if there is any excellence and if there is anything worthy of praise think about these things. Keep on doing the things that you have learned and received and heard and seen in me and the God of peace will be with you.

Excellent Lord, I praise your name and your teachings. It is often difficult for me to remain grounded in the positive. I hear about building walls, struggles for health care, people who have emotional or mental issues that need to be addressed, homelessness, human Trafficking and I worry about dwindling attendance in the houses of worship in the USA. I worry about people who building walls off what has been called "the least of these; like the children are forced into cages with tin foil blankets and without their parents, like the young people who are scooped up by human traffickers who pretend they want to love and help vulnerable young girls and boys when they only seek the financial gains of their enterprises. The words written in letters by Paul to the Philippians are a reflection of how we can be faithful to you. May it be so before our country is unrecognizable. Sometimes, the reflections of how one can be faithful to you and yet keep silent when we see our people and values obliterated is repugnant to me. Help me to always speak the truth and praise God often. I struggle with how to remain on track and faithful to you, Lord of Hosts. I pray that you will continue to help me find my way when the world around seems to be upside down. You have taught me to use my voice and I pray that when I do, it will be pleasing in your sight. Please be with us this day and every day. May we help those who are hungry or ill, be with all as we face extreme weather conditions, and save us this day, loving God of peace. Amen.

FEBRUARY 20

PHILIPPIANS 4:10-13

I rejoice in the Lord greatly that now at last you have received your concern for me; indeed you were concerned for me, but had no opportunity to show it. Not that I am referring to being in need; for I have learned to be content with whatever I have. I know what it is to have little, and I know what it is to have plenty. In any and all circumstances, I have learned the secret of being well-fed and of going hungry, of having plenty and of being in need. I can do all things through him who strengthens me.

Generous Provider, your words proclaimed by Paul have been eloquently re-stated. And so, the take away I have learned is to (1) Pause to pray, (2) Give love, and (3) Receive Peace.* For a busy person sometimes less is more. The clear and sure message to the people of Philippi, The Lord is to acknowledge you. So Lord God, I feel empowered to praise you. Be with all who search for a way out: out of poverty, out of loneliness, out of ... all things that give joy. I pray to do all things through you, the one who strengthens me. Help me let others know the joy and love that comes when they feel your hand, Lord God. Lord, thank you for the beauty of the white snow, covering the ugliness of resting trees and plants. Through your plan, there is a time to rest and a time to grow. May it be so in my personal life as well. Be with those who are out in the cold and who are hungry. Keep watch over our words and deeds, may they all be to honor and glorify you. Save us from temptation and evil and remain in our hearts forever. Amen.

FEBRUARY 21

Only together, hand in hand, as God's family and not as another's enemy can we ever hope to end the vicious cycle of revenge and retribution

– Desmond Tutu
God Has a Dream:
A Vision of Hope for Our Time (2003)

LUKE 6:31

Do to others as you would have them do to you.

———————————

Hear my prayers, O Lord. Time throughout the ages reveals humans often ignore Jesus' teachings. Help your teachers reach those who do not know you. Through the ages, great people have been steadfast in treating others the way you would want them to be treated. The question is, why is doing unto others, so hard? Lord help us to follow the "Golden Rule." We hear you God, it does take daily practice. It takes time and really sincere practice to love and treat all as one thinks and wishes to be treated. Sometimes, Lord, I struggle with this principle. Jesus, you remind me when my words or deeds stray. Remind me to ask the question: how do I wish to be treated? Help us begin to change the way we live in this town, state, nation and world. May our words be used to praise your name and our lives show our love for neighbors, modeling your teachings. Be with us when we stray and help us to find our way back to what is pleasing to you and helpful in our world. Be with us as we learn better ways to resolve differences, help our friends and family and all who are suffering hunger, cold, or pain from deeds committed or received, this day. May their strife be softened and a productive conversation begun. Lord, be with us this day and save us, I pray in your name. Amen.

FEBRUARY 22

On this day in 1732 George Washington was born. He was wise and led the United States in the efforts of a new nation's colonization process. He was the first President of our country. Washington's career began as a surveyor. I read recently, many of his reports on boundaries in and around Virginia, continue to be valid. And no, he did not chop down a single Cherry Tree!

Later in life General Washington's reputation as a great leader was acclaimed by the colonists during the early days of our country. General Washington led colonial USA in defeating the British in the Revolutionary War. He is known as "the father" of our country. Washington's leadership was further established as he became the first President of the United States (voted unanimously by the electoral college). A famous quote from President Washington is, "The foundation of our national policy will be laid in the pure and immutable principles of private morality, and the preeminence of free government be exemplified by all the attributes which can win the affections of its citizens and command the respect of the world."

PSALM 1

Happy are those who do not follow the advice of the wicked, or take the path that sinners tread, or in the seat of scoffers; but their delight is in the law of the Lord, and on his law meditate day and night. They are like trees planted by streams of water, which yield their fruit in season, and their leaves do not wither. In all that they do, they prosper. The wicked are not so, but are like chaff that the wind drives away. Therefore the wicked will not stand the judgement, nor sinners in the congregation of the righteous; for the Lord watches over the way of the righteous, but the way of the wicked will perish.

L oving God, I pray that others might also walk in faith and love with You. We know, Lord, when we are filled with a clean heart we are walking in the light of your love. We want to follow a right path, however, sometimes, Lord we stray. Thank you for watching over us and helping us along the way. Lord, if I think my doing something may not be right, I know I need to stop, re-think that action and if it is not something I think will be pleasing to you, I don't do it. Some might think that is an unconscious action, but I believe my core ablity to know right from wrong will aid me when perhaps I might 'think' about doing something that is wrong. It may not be illegal, but my conscious simply causes me to pause and re-evaluate the efficacy of my actions. I pray for those who's filter does not slow them down before performing a sinful or unkind action. Continue to watch over me in my waking and in my sleeping. Help me to be one of your earthly representatives. Please continue to guide my ways sharing your love and blessings with others. Be with me this day, Lord God and save me.In your holy name I pray. Amen.

THESSALONIANS 1:2-6
THE SALUTATION OF PAUL
TO THE THESSALONIANS

We always give thanks to God for all of you and mention you in our prayers, constantly remembering before our God and Father your work of faith and labor of love and steadfastness of hope in our Lord Jesus Christ. For we know, brothers and sisters beloved by God, that he has chosen you, because our message of the gospel came to you not in word only, but also in power and in the Holy Spirit and with full conviction...

...so that you became imitators of us and the Lord, for in spite of persecution you received the word with joy inspired by the Holy Spirit.

Holy God, I pray that the words from my faith journey will always be pleasing to you. Hope is in the power of the Holy Spirit. Sometimes it is a struggle to understand your will and what it is you want your people to do. It is with full conviction that I pray to you. The hope is that those who pray this prayer will use, maintain or rekindle the spirit of your love and expectations for us and to spread the message of the gospel. Lord God, sometimes we get distracted and hesitate to be intentional in our faith practices. I do know, however, that we carry your spirit wherever we go and whatever we do. You saved me when all around my world was falling apart. It is because of my steadfast faith in you that sustained me when I was alone. I have felt your love and passion to be "my rock" and to guide me in the best of times, and in times when I was totally lost. I would be lost without you, Lord God. Thank you for being ever-present and for loving me on my worst days. Be with us each day as we go about our daily activities. Help those who do not yet know of your wondrous power, May we become imitators of you, Lord God, and receive the word with joy and inspiration by the Holy Spirit. Amen.

FEBRUARY 24

Only together, hand in hand, as God's family and not as one another's enemy, can we ever hope to end the vicious cycle of revenge and retribution.

Desmond Tutu in God Has a Dream:
A vision of Hope for Our Time (2003)

PSALM 52:1-9

Why do you boast, O mighty one, of mischief done against the godly? All day long you are plotting destruction. Your tongue is like a sharp razor, you worker of treachery. You love evil more than good, and lying more than speaking truth. You love all the words that devour, O deceitful tongue. But God will break you down forever; he will snatch and tear you from your tent; he will uproot you from the land of the living. The righteous will see, and fear and will laugh at the evildoer, saying "See the one who would not take refuge in God, but trusted in abundant riches, and sought refuge in wealth!" But I am like the green olive tree in the house of God. I trust in the steadfast love of God forever and ever. I will thank you forever, because of what you have done. In the presence of the faithful I will proclaim your name, for it is good.

Hear my prayer Lord, in our changing lives we are struggling with accommodating those who are 'different'. For some it is the difference of skin color, for others beliefs. I pray for those who have an ideology of evil, may they will turn to you. I pray others will work as diligently as possible to change the framing of evil by modeling and being a welcoming change of ideals. Throughout the world there are factions of negativity as well as harmful acts being committed by some whose vision is of hate and destruction. I pray this day that the words "do unto others as you would have others do unto you" might become a way for our world to work its way back. Help us to see the goodness in our neighbors, doing good so that we might one day embrace a lasting peace. Lord, please be with those who disseminate hate and do harmful acts, help our country to reset and become a country of helping "thy neighbor". May we find ways to move from a nation that allows people to build bombs, collect an arsenal of weapons of war and replace the ideology of "me" at all costs. Teach our children to love one another. Be with us this day and wrap your arms around those who are suffering and facing troubled times. Save us and keep watch over those struggling with health issues and those who are mourning. In your holy name I pray. Amen.

FEBRUARY 25

Churches across the country are joining World Vision to participate in the Matthew 25 Challenge. You are invited to join in and experience God's Word in community through a week-long daily text challenge. To participate: TEXT: M25 TO 44888 sign up today! Daily texts will challenge and encourage you with powerful stories of children around the world. SHARE on social media #M25Challenge. If texts are not your thing, Get daily emails at world vision.org/25.

World Vision is a Christian humanitarian organization dedicated to working with Children and their communities worldwide to reach their full potential by tackling the causes of poverty and injustice.

MATTHEW 25:35-40

Jesus said:
"For I was hungry and you gave me something to eat.
I was thirsty and you gave me something to drink. I was a stranger and you invited me in. I needed clothes and you clothed me. I was sick and you looked after me.
I was in prison and you came to visit me.

Truly I tell you whatever you did for one of the least of these brothers and sisters of mine, you did for me."

Generous Provider Savior, thank you for showing the way in today's world. Help us all learn how to participate in humanitarian efforts to help your children as we begin to understand the plight of some of "the least of these". As we participate we stand in solidarity with them. Holy God, we take the challenge to understand "the least of these" throughout the world. I pray we will begin to look outward from our own situations and begin to find ways to help someone in need. Lord God, be with those who are hurting, sick, frightened or fearful. Calm their anxious hearts and make them safe again. Be with all who are giving back to help raise the well being of others. Save us from our greed and sinful ways, I pray in Jesus' name. Amen.

ON THE PULSE OF MORNING

Excerpts from the poem by Maya Angelou

You, created only a little lower than
The angels, have crouched too long
The bruising darkness
Face down in ignorance

Lord God the almighty, I pray for those who are ignorant in their apathy and lack of curiosity of your abiding love for us.

The Rock cries out to us today, you may stand
But do not hide your face.

Leader of our souls, may we stand proudly in our affirmations of you and your abiding love for us. Melt the hearts of the ignorant and arrogant, that they might find the one who proclaims, "I am the way, the truth and the light..."

Your armed struggles for profit
Have left collars of waste upon
My shore, currents of debris upon my breast.

Yet, today I call you to my riverside.
If you will study war no more. Come.

Loving and all-knowing God, there are rivers of strife in our private lives, in our workplaces and our country. Be with us as we muddle along, in an effort to find a way for peace, in our lives, our nation and in the world. May we leave our complacency to find a way to set aside indifferent and uncomfortable relationships in all areas of our lives and universe. Help us to follow your teachings and learn how to live in peace.

The horizon leans forward,
Offering your space to place new steps of change.

Here on the pulse for this new day
May you have the grace to look up and out
And into your sister's eyes,
And into your brother's face, your country
And say simply
With hope
Good Morning.

Almighty God, may it be so. Amen.

JOHN 9:15-17

Then the Pharisees also began to ask him how he had received his sight. He said to them, "He put mud on my eyes. Then I washed, and now, and now I see." Some of the Pharisees said, "This man is not from God, for he does not observe the. Sabbath." But others said, "How can a man who is a sinner perform such signs?" … He said, "He is a prophet."

Healing Lord, I give thanks to you for the most perfect way to speak to those who doubt you and your healing powers. Those who walk with you, do not doubt you. When one of your servants was driving home from work one day, a car ran a light and t-boned her car causing her vehicle to cross two lanes of traffic before coming to a stop. She sat in the car and you came and comforted her. Emily told me she knew she was ok, because "God told me." When the police and rescue squad came to assist, they found she had already been assisted. Thank you for your saving graces and for her proclamation of how you comforted her and saved her, again. I pray Lord, that others may have such abiding faith in you and tell of your healing powers. Be with those today who are hurting in body or spirit, with the sick, those facing surgery, and the families of those who mourn, keep each one named or only known to you safe and secure in the knowledge that they are loved. Be with them and enfold your loving grace to them and to us. Be with us. As we go about our day and save us I pray. In your holy name I pray. Amen.

FEBRUARY 28

JOHN 10:7-10

So again Jesus said to them, "Very truly, I tell you, I am the gate for the sheep. All who came before me are thieves and bandits; but the sheep did not listen to them. I am the gate for the sheep. Whoever enters by me will be saved, and will come in and go out and find pasture. The thief comes only to steal and kill and destroy. I came that they may have life, and have it abundantly.

Dear Lord and gatekeeper of our minds, bodies and souls, I give all thanks and glory to you and your beloved son, Jesus Christ. I believe in your truth, life, and freedoms. May your blessings and love for us be an avenue to help others learn of your awesome power and amazing grace. I pray that you lead "the flock" to discern truth, wisdom and to learn of your forgiveness of sin. Bless all those who are searching, may they find you. Help the doubters, Lord. May they feel your love through those who interact with them. Help those who are struggling with their life and relationships. I pray they will find in you, help to overcome adversity. Be with us each day, lead us to your loving grace, and save us all, in Jesus Christ. Amen.

FEBRUARY 29
Leap year, when February's days are 29!

LUKE 6:23

Rejoice in that day and leap for joy, for surely your reward is great in heaven; for that is what their ancestors did to the prophets.

———————————

Fairest Lord Jesus, help me to be filled with your spirit and to rejoice when my thoughts, words and deeds inspire others to ponder your greatness. I know the words of the prophets were not received with neither joy nor excitement. I pray one day every ear shall hear and know of your mighty power and love for all peoples. Help me Lord, to keep my vision of helping others learn about your mighty works and deep love for each one in the kingdom. Help me pray for your loving guidance as I pray, that others might become a chorus of love and prayers to you most holy and loving God. Although, I sometimes feel sad when someone dies, my feelings are selfish, for I know each one has truly gone home, to be with you. Let us learn to rejoice in that blessed homecoming! Thank you God for the promises made and the love freely given. Lord, until the day when I shall be with you, may my words and prayerful thoughts help Christians learn to use their words and their devotion to you spread throughout their communities. Be with us, Lord God, and save us. I pray in the name of your blessed son, Jesus. Amen.

MARCH 1
JOHN 10:11
JESUS THE GOOD SHEPHERD

"I am the good shepherd. The good shepherd lays down his life for the sheep.

Faithful and loving God, you sent your beloved son, Jesus to walk with others for all the days of his life. Jesus shows us "the way, the truth and the light." I pray that others will come to know you, and by faith, believe also in your son, Jesus Christ. Help them to learn of your deeds and stories of your son who faced many of the same issues we do. Learning of his untimely death speaks to all who live with the knowledge that someone they know has also left this life, too soon. Help each one who struggles with doubt or perhaps wonder, welcome you into their hearts and minds. I pray for them and those who may feel their faith is bruised or challenged. May each be comforted and feel your blessing and love. Be with those who mourn, the sick, those facing serious health issues, and those who have addictive personalities. Today, our world is dealing with many people who think there is no hope for them. Show them the way, Lord God. Help the depressed and those contemplating self harm to find an abiding faith that can lead them out of their inner struggles. Be with our neighbors across the world as they face challenging health issues or do not have adequate food, water and basic necessities that I take for granted. Lord, I pray you will help all who are sick and broken hearted. Be with them and us this day and save us, I pray in your holy name. Amen.

MARCH 2

MARTIN LUTHER KING, JR.

Faith is taking the first step even when you don't see the whole staircase.

Heavenly God, I give thanks for the words and life of Dr. Martin Luther King, Jr. Although he has left this life, his words and deeds are left as a beacon of light that is sometimes hiding under a basket just waiting to be discovered, I learned from him that my faith is present in my daily life. Dr. King's understanding of faith in oneself is not based on seeing and touching. He said, "This is the same as when you have faith in your life's journey, you might not see the complete picture, but as long as you keep going and trying, you know where you will be when your journey is complete...". Dr. King was a brilliant man and yet, like each of us, a sinner. You loved him and accepted him into glory, just as you will accept me and all who come to you asking for the forgiveness of sin. May we keep going Lord, living in a manner that is pleasing to you. Lord God, I know of your amazing grace and thank you for walking with me even when I did not know how to walk with you. You have saved me from a life that did not glorify your name. I know you are patient and that sometimes when things are difficult in life, your love and guidance saves me. Thank you for your patience Lord, for you know your flock well and sometimes just cannot turn toward you on our time, but yours. Loving Shepherd, thank you for your patience with your wayward flock. I pray that each one will see you and live a life that is pleasing to you; for it is then that all shall know what it means to be saved. Help doubting souls take the first step knowing that in the last step one shall be together in Your house, forever. Amen.

MARCH 3

SAINT TERESA OF CALCUTTA

I used to pray that God would feed the hungry, or do this or that, but now I pray that he will guide me to do whatever I'm supposed to do, what I can do. I used to pray for answers, but now I'm praying for strength.

———————————

All knowing Creator, you have taught me to pray and to lean into my faith and insecurities. It is a daunting task at times. I am finding my voice and learning how to pray as I lean into the roadblocks life presents. You comfort me and lead the way when I want a different outcome. You must be so frustrated with my stubbornness. As I pray and wonder if my prayers are heard, help me slow down, and to be open to find the strength to stay on the path you have set for me. Lead me in the ways that you would have me go. Bless those who need your healing touch, and those who are searching for answers. Strengthen efforts to help those whose day to day needs are a constant struggle. Thank you Lord God for the message you gave us through your son, Jesus. His coming made real your unconditional love. Be with me each day and help me live out my life in the sure and sacred knowledge of your unconditional love. Be with those who are hurting, or in need. You are the way, the truth and the light, lead me on the path of wisdom and truth. Be with all your children, forgive our sins and strengthen my resolve to carry your message. Thank you for Saint Teresa of Calcutta. She worked for poor children who learned of your love through her untiring efforts. Thank you for finding a place for me to share your truth to others. Be with us, save and strengthen us Lord. Amen.

MARCH 4

JOHN 10:17-18
JESUS THE GOOD SHEPHERD

For this reason the Father loves me, because I lay down my life in order to take it up again. "No one takes it from me, but I lay it down of my own accord. I have the power to take it up again. I have received this command from my Father."

COLOSSIANS 1:19-20

For in him all the fullness of God was pleased to dwell, and through him God was pleased to reconcile to himself all things, whether on earth or in heaven, by making peace through the blood of his cross)

CORINTHIANS 2:5:18

All of this is from God, who reconciled us to himself through Christ, and has given us the ministry of reconciliation.

Dear Lord, what an horrendous march to the cross your son took. When I think of the horrifying indignity of it, I am repulsed. Repulsed because of the cross and the blood and because Jesus' death was so violent. Those who spat on him and stole his clothes and although this was no accident, it was no less brutal nor unintentional. For Jesus was born to die. How you knew, Lord God what it would take for the faithful to believe was to send your son, to save us. I pray as we move through the season of lent, you will be with us, reminding us of just how powerful your love for us is. Can it be Lord God that Jesus suffered and died on the cross simply because he loved us? I know the answer is "yes." Did this humiliating death of your son bring us into a right relationship with You? Oh Lord, make it so. Through you, our Giving Lord, we discern Jesus

Christ died for us in order to allow us to live with you [...] forever. I give thanks for the scriptures, for providing no room for doubt nor hate. Loving God, please help me find ways to show love and acceptance of my brothers and sisters here on earth. Be with all who suffer and mistreat others and help each one find ways to turn that hate into love and acceptance. Teacher, I pray for the sick, may they become healthy; for the lost, may they might find their way to you; for the homeless, may they find a place to be safe and their needs met; finally Lord I pray all shall know of your love and of the sacrifice of your son, Jesus, you made for us. Be with us this and every day and save us, I pray. Amen.

MARCH 5
JOHN 1:1-4

In the beginning was the Word, and the word was with God, and the Word was God. He was in the beginning with God. All things came into being through him, and without him not one thing came into being. What has come into being in him was life and the life was the light of all people.

Lord God, I give thanks to you for the prophecies that predicted the Passion of the Christ, made hundreds of years before Jesus' crucifixion. The four Gospel writers recorded Jesus' formal and majestic arrival in Jerusalem. We read of his arrival on a donkey, the palms. The prophet Zechariah foretold Judas Iscariot's betraying of your Son. The contempt, scorn and punishment of Jesus was horrifying; and yet it was to be his destiny, to give his life for us. Help us Lord to embrace the prophecy that brought Christianity into our lives. You know how we anguish over loved ones who are suffering and have perhaps died. Your steadfast love is comforting when we are feeling the pain of loss when a loved one has died. Be with us this season of Lent and help us draw closer to you. God I pray for comfort for those who have lost loved ones and for those who are ill. Be with us as life "happens" and please help us find a way to cope with "unthinkable" issues and messes that complicate our lives. Be with us this day and every day, and save us in the name of your son, Jesus Christ. Amen.

MARCH 6

PSALM 111:1-10

Praise the Lord! I will give thanks to the Lord wit my whole heart, in the company of the upright, in the congregation. Great are the works of the Lord, studied by all who delight in them.

Full of honor and majesty is his work, and his righteoushness endures forever. He has gained renown by his wonderful deeds; the Lord is gracious and merciful, he provides food for those who fear him; he is ever mindful of his covenant. He has shown his people the power of his works in giving them the heritage of the nations. The works of his hands are faithful and just; all his precepts are trustworthy. They are established forever and ever. Holy and awesome is his name. The fear of the Lord is the beginning of wisdom; and all those who practice it have a good understanding. His praise endures forever.

Lord God, you are my rock and my salvation. The psalmist's prayer fills me with renewed hope. My hope is in your blessed promises sent to all believes through the life, death and resurrection of none other than your beloved son, Jesus. Help me Lord to not put off praying for the forgiveness of my sins. Let me be open and honest and most of all, help me to show humility and sincerity when I ask for your forgiveness of my sins. I sometimes move too quickly from one day into the next, Lord, calm my "too busy" attitude and help me set aside just a few minutes each day, at the start of the day to give praise and thanks and to ponder the portion of my yesterday which brings me shame. May I humbly pray for your forgiveness. And Lord God, help me to say "I'm sorry" with sincerity of heart and head to those whom I may have offended. You have taught us of your capacity to perform many wonderful works, and while mortals works pale by comparison, we have the capacity, I have the capacity to be generous in thought, word, and deed. May those deeds seek to help those who need the assistance I am able to provide. I am grateful, Lord, for the capacity to teach your children, although even then, not always with a gentle and kind tone. Forgive my impatient ways and instill in me a kinder heart. Lord, help all of your people to emulate your capacity for love and forgiveness with others. Be with us and help us with each day and all of the myriad of activities in which we engage. Be with those who suffer and feel the loss of a loved one, may you comfort them and all who suffer. Lord, how awesome is your name! May I never doubt nor forget all that I have and all that I know is because of you and your gift of Jesus. Be with me this day and save me, I pray in your awesome name. Amen.

MARCH 7
HEBREWS 4:1-3

Therefore, while the promise of entering his rest is still open, let us take care that none of you should seem to have failed to reach it. For indeed the good news came to us just as to them; but the message they heard did not benefit them, because they were not united by faith with those who listened. For we who have believed enter that rest, just as God has said.

Oh God of promises, be with each one in your earthly flock this day. Help us God, to pray and to believe in those promises. You have taught us it is never to late to reach out to you and to ask for the forgiveness of our sins. I know how easy it is to say, "Lord, I have sinned and I am truly sorry. Lord, please forgive me and help me walk the path toward life everlasting. Help me Lord, to be a better person and to live a life that pleases you." That's all one can do, live a life that is pleasing to you, Lord God. May we rest in the peace of your promise to Christians if we ask for the forgiveness of our sins, there is a place in heaven for us. Lord, your teachings are clear, "let us take care" in order to reach out to you in this life in order to "enter that rest" with you in the next. Amen.

MARCH 8
HEBREWS 4:14-16

Since then, we have a great high priest who has passed through the havens, Jesus the Son of God, let us hold fast to our confession. For we do not have a high priest who is unable to sympathize with our weaknesses, but we have one who in every respect has been tested as we are, yet without sin. Let us therefore approach the throne of grace with boldness, so that we may receive mercy and grace to help in time of need.

Dear Lord God of all, thank you for showing all believers the way to you! Lord, I know there are times of doubt and despair which have entered my life. It was and is in those times Lord, when I feel the most comforted because of your promise. I know that no matter how alone I may feel, one thing I know for sure is you are always with me. What a comfort that knowledge is, knowing I am never alone for your are in my heart and in my head. I pray others will also find that inner peace and never feel alone. You have made me want to be a better person here on earth and to spread the news of Jesus Christ and your love for him and for each believer. Help me improve the message and tell the stories of your abounding love for each one. You sent your son to save all who believe and repent their sins. May it be so, God. Lord be with us this day and every day, and save us as we petition forgiveness for our sins. Amen.

MARCH 9

EPHESIANS 2:4-10

But God, who is rich in mercy out of the great love with which he loved us even when we were dead through our trespasses, made us alive together with Christ—by grace you have been saved—and raised up with him and seated us with him in the heavenly places in Christ Jesus, so that in the ages to come he might show the immeasurable riches of his grace in kindness toward us in Christ Jesus. For by grace you have been saved through faith, and this is not your own doing; it is the gift of God—not the result of works, so that no one may boast. For we are what he has made us, created in Christ Jesus for good works, which God prepared beforehand to be our way of life.

Loving God, there it is, simple as it can be stated: "for by grace you have been saved through faith." Thank you for the saving grace you have for those who profess their faith in you and who ask for divine forgiveness for their sins. I am filled with joy, knowing you knew some of us would require an "aha" moment to believe salvation is that simple. Sometimes, Lord God, I think of people who do evil things and wonder where do these people come from? How can they possibly treat their fellow neighbors with wicked or cruel deeds? I imagine you shaking your finger at us, and reminding us that You are the one who will save us, and I am the one who wants to face you one day with an abiding faith in you and Jesus Christ. I give thanks to you each day for saving me. Lord, please be with us, guiding our ways and when it is time, opening the door so that we may walk side by side with the host of angels and you. Amen.

MARCH 10
JOHN 1:14-18

And the word became flesh and lived among us, and we have seen his glory, the glory as of the father's only son, full of grace and truth.

From his fullness we have all received, grace upon grace. John testified to him and cried out, This was he of whom I said, 'He who comes after me ranks ahead of me, because he was before me." From his fulness we have all received, grace upon grace. The law indeed was given through Moses; grace and truth came through Jesus Christ. No one has ever seen God. It is God the only Son, who is close to the Father's heart, who has made him known.

———————————

Loving God, I am thankful for your disciple, John. He spelled out the the divinity of Jesus, fully human and fully divine. I have read John's gospel countles times and yet this day I am reading it with "fresh" eyes. The words link us back to Genesis and the Old Testament. Once again I am in awe of the plan you made for all of humanity, for me! What you set in motion was for the destiny of humankind. The beauty and intracacies of your plan was clearly motivated by your love for generations to come. You loved us even before we were born! Lord, a more perfect way to show your love for humanity and the new religion could not be made. Thank you for giving Jesus to the world and for his faith-filled teachings. And Lord, thank you for showing me your deep plan and loving ways. I will remember your plan and think of Jesus in a different way from this day forward. Fresh eyes and a joyful heart motivate the time spent reading and rereading the Bible. I have always taken time to pray, mostly "thought prayers," and now Lord, I am one who feels your call to share my prayers with others. I pray it will motivate others to begin or reconnect with you through prayer. You shall forever be close to my heart and in my head. Be with me this day, and save me from my sin in your blessed name, I pray. Amen.

MARCH 11

MATTHEW 5:4-7

Blessed are those who mourn, for they will be comforted
Blessed are the meek, for they will inherit the earth
Blessed are those who hunger and thirst for righteousneess
for they will be filled
Blessed are the merciful, for they will receive mercy"

Dear Lord, I pray for those who do not know you nor your son, Jesus. I pray for those who have turned away, or perhaps interrupted a conscious walk with you be their side. You sent Jesus to us that all humanity might learn of how we are to live. Truly, you are the way, the truth and the life. Today, I pray for those in need: food, clothing, medical care, and for those who carry deep concerns for themselves, and their futures. Be with each one who struggles, those who are ill or who have family members who are ill. Be with both and help them find a way to be joyful in their love for you, reassured their prayers are heard. Knowing the "miracle" we pray may not be the miracle we receive, is for your divine wisdom to discern. I pray for your guidance as each of us march forward into each new day, sometimes a day fraught with uncertainty, fear or trepadation. Lord, knowing You are with us and You know our petitions even before they are voiced, is a great comfort. The undeserved blessings you give provides tangible evidence of your forgiving and loving heart. Merciful God, help us to live a life pleasing to you and one which is an example for our children and families as they grow in faith and devotion to you. Be with us in our waking and in our sleeping, and save us, I pray. Amen.

MATTHEW 5:9-11

Blessed are the peacemakers, for they will be called the children of God.
Blessed are those who are persecuted for righteousness' sake, for theirs is the kingdom of heaven
Blessed are you when people revile you and persecute you and utter all kinds of evil against you falsely on my account.
Rejoice and be glad, for your reward is great in heaven, for in the same way they persecuted the prophets who were before you.

I hope those who are pure in heart see You and may they have their faith renewed. What a blessing it is when faith is tested in such a way that not only is my faith in you renewed, but faith is multiplied when I encounter you. Jesus was telling his disciples they are when they are at their end of their rope. He is saying "with less of you there is more time in their lives for God and his wisdom and rule. When I feel most like throwing in the towel, I pray and it is then, I feel your love the most. pray for the peacemakers of the world hoping they will use their hearts and voices to soften the loud voices of hatred and turn the conversation toward peaceful solutions. I pray for all peacemakers knowing that peace will be pleasing to you while they seek solutions to end all wars and internal conflicts. May ohapsur leaders be creative as they work with one another to discover ways to peacefully stand up for the people of our country and others throughout the world. I pray especially for Tunisia, where my World Vision "daughter" lives in poverty. I pray that we respect our environment and care for the sick and elderly. We want to leave a world healthier by doing our part to reduce pollution of our streams, creeks and rivers. Be with those who need help doing the simplest of chores, and for those who are lonely. Help me to do a better job of recycling and to be less wasteful knowing many could benefit from things I carelessly throw away. Holy God, I ask for courage to stand firm on the right to worship you without our houses of worship and communities being the target of hate crimes. I am seeking to find a way to use my prayers as an outreach to those who do not know you. Be with us all this day and every day, help us to advocate for you and the teachings we learn about in the Bible. Amen.

MARCH 13

LUKE 1:46-55
MARY'S SONG OF PRAISE

And Mary said,

"My soul magnifies the Lord, and my spirit rejoices in God my savior, for he has looked with favor on the loveliness of his servant. Surely, from now on all generations will call me blessed; for the Mighty One has done great things for me, and holy is his name. His mercy is for those who fear him from generation to generation. He has shown strength with his arm; he has scattered the proud in the thoughts of their hearts. He has brought down the powerful from their thrones, and lifted up the lowly; he has filled the hungry with good things, and sent the rich away empty. He has helped his servant Israel, in remembrance of his mercy, according to the promise he made to our ancestors, to Abraham and to his descendants forever."

Merciful God, you made way for your son in Mary's womb. Jesus was born to take away the sins of the world. The boldness of your plan to select an engaged woman and a carpenter named Joseph, was to awaken and instruct. Mary was honored to be carrying the Christ child and clearly, although initially perplexed, moved forward and was fearless regarding her 'condition.' Joseph took Mary in, to care for her and love her during the most amazing pregnancy of all time. Thank you Lord, for helping Joseph understand and love Mary. What a blessing for this couple to have unconditional love for the special mission You had for them. Lord, your powers do not know boundaries. I am in awe, you brought your son, the most magnificent Jesus, into being. Your wisdom Holy One shed a light throughout the land, offering the people a new way to live and think. I pray the story of the birth, life, and death of Jesus will continue to be a catalyst for change. The world needs to learn of your mighty power and love, and hopefully it will become sensitive and responsive to the needs of and for the good of those who are deprived of basic life requirements. Find a way to bring food, clean water and medicine to those who are denied. Help all people understand why humanitarian efforts should be paramount, especially for a greedy world that has largely turned its back on "the least of these". Teacher, I pray that from our homes, pulpits and Sunday schools, a renewed devotion to your teachings will be rekindled. Help all to feel empowered to help those in need, and to pay attention to the changing topography of the lands and waters. Lord God, I pray for the leaders of the world may they treat one another with wisdom and compassion. Be with those who are ill and those who care for them. Soften the stubborn or ignorant leaders' minds and hearts to "see the big picture," to do what is right for the world. Be with educators across the world, teaching subjects and at the same time teaching peace, wisdom, love and mercy. Be with and save us today and always. Amen.

MARCH 14

PSALM 27:1-4

The Lord is my light and my salvation whom shall I fear? The Lord is the stronghold of my life; of whom shall I be afraid? When evildoers assail me to devour my flesh—my adversaries and foes—they shall stumble and fall. Though an army encamp against me, my heart shall not fear; though war rise up against me yet I will be confident. One thing I asked of the Lord, that I will seek after: to live in the house of the Lord all the days of my life, to behold the beauty of the Lord.

Teacher, Savior, Lord of all, your blessing and timing is what I call "spot on." When I listen and hope for a word, a sign, an answer I am never let down, although at times my patience is tested. The problem is, I am impatient and think I know what is best, until You interrupt my petitions with a different plan. When a beloved local teacher and coach suffered an illness and passed, it was then, Holy God, I realized You know best for me, for everyone. I found myself writing to a friend, trying to be comforting, and yet honest, "the miracle" we prayed for, was not the miracle the friend received. However, it was a beautiful miracle. And so, you took a friend to live in your house forever which was as it should be. I am thankful for your wisdom and awed by your power. I pray for strength and confidence in the words I write or say. May they glorify you and make a difference to all, friends I know and those I've yet to meet. When I behold your beauty and glory, I shall be joyful and awed. In the meantime, God please forgive my missteps and shortcomings. Trying to be faithful is sometimes hard and often conflicting. I pray for patience and your guidance to step into each new day. Be with me Lord God, save us all as we seek to walk confidently into all of our tomorrows. Blessed assurance, Jesus is mine. Amen.

MARCH 15

ROMANS 8:26-28

Likewise the Spirit helps us in our weakness; for we do not know how to pray as we ought, but that very spirit intercedes with the sighs too deep for words. And God who searches the heart, knows what is the mind of the Spirit because the Spirit intercedes for the saints according to the will of God. We know that all things work together for good for those who love God, who are called according to his purpose.

Lord, thank you for the "Spirit" assisting me during times of fear and weakness, and for helping me through each day. I am learning Lord God, how to use my words in prayers to you, and I feel your loving grace and power a little more each day. Thank you God for being patient as I learn from amazing people, some who perhaps do not know just how inspiring and instructing they are. I pray for all who are searching for an "unknown". May they find the "unknown" is a loving God who wants each person to live a life filled with grace and a loving spirit. May each one's soul be in a trajectory towards you. Thank you for the gift of your son, Jesus who came to show the way to salvation. Help us to rejoice in this knowledge and to be "freed" from worry about our own mortality. May each one feel "the call" and help others by thoughts, words and deeds intended for your glory, Lord. Be with us this day and save us, I pray in the name of Jesus Christ. Amen.

MARCH 16

LUKE:1:57-66
THE BIRTH OF JOHN THE BAPTIST

Now the time came for Elizabeth to give birth, and she bore a son. Her neighbors and relatives heard that the Lord had shown his great mercy to her, and they rejoiced with her. On the eighth day they came to circumcise the child, and they were going to name him Zechariah after his father. But his mother said, "No, he is to be called John." They said to her, "None of your relatives has this name." Then they began motioning for his father to find out what name they wanted to give him. He asked for a writing tablet and wrote, "His name is John." And all of them were amazed. Immediately his mouth was opened and his tongue freed, and he began to speak, praising God. Fear came over all their neighbors, and all these things were talked about throughout the entire hill country of Jude's. All who heard them and pondered them and said, "What then will this child become?" For indeed, the hand of the Lord was with him.

Lord, thank you for John the Baptist. You provided numerous miracles: you gave Elizabeth (a cousin to Mary, Jesus' mother) at age 88 a child. What a blessing for Elizabeth and Zechariah and when the child was not named after his father, you provided yet another miracle. You gave Zechariah his voice! I wonder, how would people feel if these events occurred now? Lord, would they even notice a miracle? What force would work against us to deny one?

Please, God, stop the killing in the world. I awaken to more senseless killings: Once, it was Columbine High School, then Sandy Hook Elementary School, the an African American Church, and any one morning an Amish School. The mass shootings and senseless deaths of innocent people is ripping our country and world apart. Each time the attack has killed innocent men, women, or children. Lord, even our elected leaders have not been spared. Please Lord, help this world find ways to put an end to sensless killings and terriorism. Help us to find ways to be complicit in stopping the carnage in our world by refusing to be sucked into the hateful rhetoric spewed by zealots and despots. Be with leaders who choose peace and please make random acts of organized massacres cease. Save us Holy God and be with us this day. I pray in the names of Mary and Elizabeth and all mothers and fathers. Amen.

MARCH 17

PSALM 27:1-2; 4, 6

The Lord is my light and my salvation; whom shall I fear? The Lord is the stronghold of my life; of whom shall I be afraid? When evildoers assail me to devour my flesh—my adversaries and foes—they shall stumble and fall. One thing I asked of the Lord, that I will seek after: to live in the house of the Lord all the days of our lives, to behold the beauty of the Lord, and to inquire in his temple. Now my head is lifted up above my enemies all around me, and I will offer his tent sacrifices with shouts of joy; I will sing and make melody unto the Lord.

Loving Lord, I pray for those who do not yet know you. You are the stronghold of my life, even when things are not going well, I feel your gentle guidance and love, assisting me on the way to face each new day. Although the world around me is somewhat of a mess, the calming and steady reassurance from you, comfort me. You have helped me realize many of the temptations in our world and have gently and lovingly watched over me. I give praise, honor and glory for all that I have needed your hands have provided. Help me, Savior Lord to use my talents for your glory. I pray what I do and say glorifies your name. Please guide me in the ways you would have me go. I pray especially today for those who are being persecuted for their race or faith. The world is in turmoil and I pray for all families, may they be safe and protected from antisemitism, intolerance of race, gender, or religious persecution. Prayers also for resolution of all the oppressed or threatened people, those with mental or physical illness and those fearful for each new day. Continued prayers for those who are hurting and in need of your presence in their lives. Be with those who have been abducted for human trafficking by evil people. Help them survive until they shall once again be free. Be with each one of us, save us and help us to be part of the solution to our national and international challenges. I pray all in your holy name. Amen.

PSALM 27:11-14

Teach me your way, O Lord, and lead me on a level path because of my enemies. Do not give me up to the will of my adversaries, for false witness have risen against me, and they are breathing out violence. I believe that I shall see the goodness of the Lord in the land of the living. Wait for the Lord, be strong, and let your heart take courage; wait for the Lord!

———————————

Holy God, you are the warrior who fights against evil in the world. How wonderful it would be if all of our enemies were once and for all dispersed and silenced. But we know Lord God there will always be another enemy of your people and today I pray for the warriors who carry your flag, who work hard to dispel evil in our world. Help us all to rally around your teachings and to do good in the world. Where there are the evils of White Supremacy, or Nationalism, or Anti Semitism or Jihad or Racism or Exclusion, may we sew the fabric of an inclusive and peaceful society. Help us turn the hearts of those whose evil practices and welcome them into peaceful dialog with a goal of reforming their evil ways. May we show them the way you would have us all live. I pray for those who are confused or hurting, may they learn of your love and begin to have their hardened hearts turned towards you. Be with each one of your children this day and every day and help those who mourn or who worry about a friend or loved one. Help those who do your work here on earth that their mission of peace, inclusion, and love will resonate throughout the land. Give us the courage and strength to carry your message of peace. Be with us each day and save us from evil all the days of our lives. Amen.

MARCH 19

PSALM 121:1-4, 7-8

I lift up my eyes to the hills—from where will my help come?
My help comes from the Lord, who made heaven and earth.
He will not let your foot be moved; he who keeps you will not
slumber. He who keeps Israel will neither hunger or sleep.
The Lord will keep you from all evil; he will keep your life.
The Lord will keep your going out and your coming in from
this time on and forevermore.

Loving God, I give praise and thanks to you for always being there. I know that at times the miracle I am praying for is not the one I receive, but you know what is best. It is painful to go on a journey when one feels lost or alone, but loving God, you are always there with me, with us. Sometimes in our hurried lives, it takes slowing down to ponder what exactly your will is for us. It should be easy knowing that you are always "on duty" watching over us. Perhaps we are just in too big of a hurry to thoughtfully, prayerfully listen to you. We want easy fixes, when easy fixes are rarely representative of the "big picture". What you have taught is peace. It is a struggle when our world continues to have enormous and profound issues. I pray for peace and I sincerely hope we find it hiding in the weeds of larger divisions of hate; the events happening all around us are most disturbing. In New Zealand, mosques are persecuted and many were senselessly killed, primarily because of religious intolerance. Holy God, how is it that the world's leaders are not able to respect one another's differing opinions, religious and political beliefs? I pray that where there is anger may there be joy, where there are differences let there be understanding and peace, where there is poverty, may there be sharing the abundant resources we have. A world that leans into ``love one another as yourself" and away from evil and selfishness would bring not only peace, but salvation. May it be so. Be with each of us as we seek to do your will and to be saved. Amen.

HEBREWS:11:1-3

Now faith is the assurance of things hoped for, the conviction of things not seen. Indeed, by faith our ancestors received approval. By faith we understand that the worlds were prepared by the word of God, so that what is seen was made from things that are not visible.

Holy God, you have provided our world with so many examples of your glorious power! I give thanks and praise to all of the people teaching and sharing by example how to understand and how to live a life that is pleasing to you. As young children we were instilled with a way of following the edict (as in the Gospel Luke 6: 31) "do unto others as you would have them do unto you." It seems so simple and yet, so many struggle with accepting what they can neither see nor hear. Jesus taught his disciples and those who came to believe in his miraculous powers. The restoration of life to Lazarus of Bethany is but one example of your power. Lazarus died, four days later Jesus was asked to restore his life, and he did! For those who witnessed this miracle, faith was real, perhaps even validated. Today, Holy God, we learn of your powers through your teachings, and although we were not with Jesus when he performed miracles, we believe. We are assured by faith witnesses, things that are seen and unseen. We know your spirit has found a home in our minds and hearts. This I believe. Thank you for the words of the prophets and the host of witnesses who tell us of the miracles of life and yes, death. I felt you with me in the wee hours. You heard my prayers and relieved my husband from pain and suffering. It was a beautiful moment, I covet the memories of your love with me always. Be with those who suffer and their caregivers. Give each one hope and strength in the promise of those who repent. In your Holy name, I pray. Amen.

MARCH 21
MATTHEW 28:1-20

Now the eleven disciples went to Galilee, to the mountain to which Jesus had directed them. When they saw him, they worshiped him; but some doubted. And Jesus came and said to them, "All authority in heaven and on earth has been given unto me. Go therefore and make disciples of all nations, baptizing them in the name of the Father and of the Son and of the Holy Spirit, and teaching them to obey everything I have commanded you. And remember, I am with you always, to the end of the age."

L oving God, the prophets extolled your glory and told of your love and the powerful impression your words and deeds made to all who witnessed your son's work. I am thankful for those who have journeyed through life reflecting your love and their faith and love in you. I give thanks to those who are on this walk, for they have taught me of your Glory and how to believe in the teachings and examples that Jesus taught the disciples. Also, I give thanks to the many who helped me to learn of your love, power and promise of salvation. It saved me from a tumultuous life. They were and are faithful people

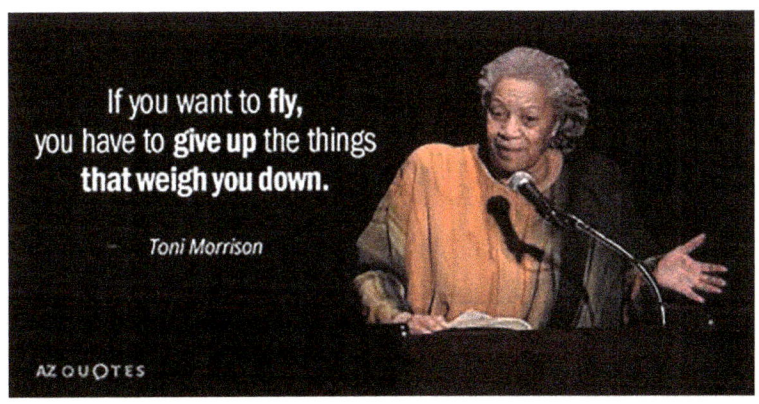

If you want to **fly,** you have to **give up** the things **that weigh you down.**

— Toni Morrison

AZ QUOTES

who have led congregations and embraced your example. Pastors and church leaders were and are crucial to our understanding of how you want your "flock" to live. Even in times where I felt alone, I was comforted just listening to the pastors messages and singing hymns of praise. It has been my own salvation. I give thanks for the lessons learned and especially how they impacted my life. Lord, every time a child is baptized, we hear the solemn words spoken long ago. We agree to support and teach the infant in the right ways and know you and to love you. Thank you God for showing us the way. Be with those who are suffering, facing serious health or personal concerns or those who seek your blessing. I pray for your continued love and guidance. Be with all of your children and save us, I pray. Amen.

MARCH 22

PROVERBS 2:1-8

My child, if you accept my words and treasure up my commandments within you, making your ear attentive to wisdom and lining your heart to understanding; if you indeed cry out for insight, and raise your voice for understanding, if you seek it like silver, and search for it as for hidden treasures—then you will understand the fear of the Lord and find the knowledge of God. For the Lord gives wisdom; from his mouth comes knowledge; He stores up sound wisdom for the upright, he is a shield to those who walk blamelessly guarding their paths of justice and preserving the way of his faithful ones.

Precious Savior, I am in awe of your majesty, your insight, planning and energy in preparing the faithful to embrace life with wisdom and love. I struggle, Lord God, with how many leaders rule in ways that seem harsh, even cruel to the very ones they represent. Where is the understanding? Where is the sound wisdom? Where is the justice? Holy God, I am praying today for those whose leadership is toxic and for those who perhaps have forgotten to "love thy neighbor as yourself". May we peacefully and prayerfully help the "downtrodden" and simultaneously continue to "line our hearts' ' with courage to speak your truths and wisdom to reset our "paths' '. Be with us Lord as we seek to help the downtrodden, the oppressed and those whose lives on earth are coming to an end. Give courage to those who reject anti Semitism, homophobia, narcissism, and your teachings of inclusion and love. Help those who lead from strength, love and inclusion. Be with us and save us as we continue our walk with you. Amen.

PROVERBS 3 :1-8

My child,do not forget my teaching, but let your heart keep my commandments: for length of days and years of life and abundant welfare they will give you. Do not let loyalty and faithfulness forsake you, bind them around your neck, write them on the tablet of your heart. Trust in the Lord with all your heart, and do not rely on your own insight. In all your ways acknowledge him, and he will make straight your paths. Do not be wise in your own eyes; fear the Lord, and turn away from evil.

Teacher, your words of wisdom are instructive for the mind and the heart and a lifetime of generosity of spirit. Sometimes I get lazy and forget the path you have set for me. I am well intentioned, however, the path I take is not always "politically" correct, nor kind. Help me to slow down, pray about and to be generous with my comments. I do trust in you, Lord, for when I have needed you desperately, you were there for me. The least I can do is honor your instructions and the wisdom of your words. You are my North Star and the light that guides my days and nights. I will work hard to stay the course and make my words and deeds more pleasing to you. Knowing I have much to learn, Lord, teacher, please do not give up on me. May the words of my mouth and the thoughts on my heart reflect the love I have for you. Be with me and forgive my transgressions and short comings. In you name I pray. Amen.

MARCH 24
JOHN 10:7-10

So again Jesus said to them, "Very truly, I tell you, I am the gate for the sheep. All who come before me are thieves and bandits; but the sheep did not listen to them. I am the gate. Whoever enters by me will be saved, and will come in and go out and find pasture. The thief comes only to steal and kill and destroy. I came to realize that they may have life, and have it abundantly.

———————————

Savior God, why is it that sometimes in the "crazy busy" of my day, I neglect morning prayers. When my day seems to be taking over, I am reminded that you are always with me. You, Sovereign God, I do know that it is not "my time" but yours and I give you thanks for walking with me each day and night. I so appreciate your guardianship. You are my Lord and Savior all the time. Sometimes, I struggle to answer the tough questions. I struggle when it seems as if I am on an unfathomable journey. It is then Lord God, I remember the circumstances of how your son, Jesus, lived and died. He died for me, for all of your children, that we might have abundant life. You never said life would be easy, but no matter what the situation may be, You are always with me. Thank you, for your abiding faith and love. Be with us always and save us, I pray in your holy name. Amen.

JOHN 10:17-18

"For this reason the Father loves me, because I lay down my life in order to take it up again. No one takes it from me, but I lay it down of my own accord. I have the power to lay it down and I have the power to take it up again. I have received this command from my Father."

———————————

All knowing God, I thank you for the life, death and resurrection of your son, Jesus Christ. Jesus' life fulfilled the prophecy, and Jesus knew the path to life eternal was to act on your command. I pray our faith and our life's journey will be an example not only to our children, but also to those who do not know of your wondrous powers.

Loving God, I give thanks for the writings of Toni Morrison. She was much more than a gifted author, her writings enlighten our world. Ms. Morrison understood that "things" weigh us down and keep us from being what we are meant to be. So, what is it that is weighing us down? I suspect the answer is not readily discerned. Does our answer represent one's true self, or does it represent a possible dream? How likely is it that it will come true? In large part the dream will come true when we seek to know You and when we follow your teachings and those of Jesus. Our journey shall continue and God willing, we shall be with you when our life's journey ends. Amen.

HEBREWS 12:1-4
GOD HAS SPOKEN BY HIS SON

Long ago God spoke to our ancestors in many and various ways by the prophets, but in these last days he has spoken to us by a Son, whom he appointed heir of all things, through whom he also created the worlds. He is the reflection of God's glory and the exact imprint of God's very being, and he sustains all things by his powerful word. When he had made purification for sins, he sat down at the right hand of the Majesty on high, having become as much superior to angels as the name he has inherited is more excellent than theirs.

Most excellent Lord, thanks be to you for your wisdom, and your patience with us, members of your flock. I know how hard it is at times to go boldly and fearlessly into some of our tomorrows, and yet, our journey cannot hold a candle to the pain you must have felt seeing your son on the cross. Help us remain focused on your teachings and especially your love of an unworthy flock. Your powerful words Lord God, and your love gives hope and strength as we struggle to calm our 'crazy busy' lives. May we never be too busy to be present in the assurances you have given. Your love for us is powerful and unfailing. Sometimes I may not feel "worthy" but you love me regardless of my insecurities. Your love comforts me and rekindles my resolve to walk with you each and every day. Be with the sick, the downtrodden and those who feel loneliness or depression. I ask that you save us all, in the name of your blessed Son, Jesus Christ. Amen.

MARCH 27

PSALM 46:1-3, 10-11

God is our refuge and strength, a very present help in trouble. Therefore we will not fear, though the earth should change, though the mountains shake in the heart of the sea; though its waters roar and foam, though the mountains tremble with its tumult.

"Be still, and know that I am God! … The Lord of hosts is with us; the God of Jacob is our refuge."

Lord God, your words are mighty and powerful, and yet there are times when things happen, and our faith is shaken. When life seems to give one punch after another it is a struggle to hear you, and to feel your love. Give us peace, Lord, until with the passage of time we are able to feel your loving comfort. Help our country to be comforted in times of unrest. May our leaders find ways to lead through compromise and sound decisions for the people.

I pray, Healing Lord, that you will be with us. Your teaching is for us to "be still" and you will provide for us. That is the hard part, waiting. Help us remain strong when times are challenging or when we are neither prepared nor ready to be reassured. This day I pray for all who are 'lost' or lonely. Hear the petitions given and comfort them. Be with the sick and those who have mental disorders. This world is ever changing, murders and suicides are increasing. I pray Lord that you will be with us all in times of trouble, give us courage and strength. Be with fathers and mothers who are bringing a new life into this world. Help those who may need you, but are unable to pray for themselves. Give them peace, Lord, until with the passage of time they are able to feel your comfort. Be with each one, and save us, I pray in your name, Amen.

MARCH 28

MARK 3:31-34
THE TRUE KINDRED OF JESUS

Then his mother and his brothers and sisters came; standing outside, they sent to him and called him. A crowd was sitting around him; and they said to him, "Your mother and your brothers and sisters are outside asking for you" And he replied, "Who are my mother and my brothers?" And looking at those who sat around him, he said, "Here are my mother and my brothers! Whoever does the will of God is my brother and sister and mother."

Sovereign Lord, your words inform the multitude of followers and the curious who quickly learned from the very mouth of Jesus, that every person who follows Him and Your will, shall be included, part of the family. Once again we learn of the holy affirmation of your beloved son. Lord God, the phenomenon of Jesus' words and deeds have been preserved for the people throughout the universe. The faithful who believe that Jesus Christ is your son, believe it by their faith. By our faith in you, we seek to serve you and to share the word throughout. Help us God, to carry our faith from our first breath to our last. Today Lord, I also pray for those who do not know you, to your people who are suffering serious illnesses and to those who are privately suffering in any way. Help all of them and also help us to peacefully be with our leaders who strive to respond to those who move through the cover of darkness to defile our homes with anti Semitic acts, or those with phobias against people of differing religions, or those with differing sexual preferences. Be with all of us as we seek to be faithful servants in spreading the word. Heavenly Teacher, instruct us in the ways you would have us go. Believers seek Your forgiveness, it is in your Holy name that I pray today. Amen.

MARCH 29

Here and Now
Living in the Spirit

– Henri Nouwen

"To live in the present, we must believe deeply that what is most important is the here and now. We are constantly distracted by things that have happened in the past or that might happen in the future. It is not easy to remain focused on the present. Our mind is hard to master and keeps pulling away from the moment. Prayer is the discipline of the moment. When we pray, we enter into the presence of God whose name is God-with-us. To pray is to listen to that voice of love. That is what obedience is all about. The word "obedience" means to listen with great attentiveness. When we no longer pray, no longer listen to the voice of love that speaks to us in a moment, our lives become absurd lives in which we are thrown back and forth between the past and the future."

Heavenly Lord, we know 'our world' is mostly occupied with the present. Distractions come from many sources; events of the past and perhaps those events yet to come. When we become distracted, we must stand firm. Thank you for teaching us how to pray and how to be in Your presence, God with-us. Lord, may those who may not feel the glory you freely share be quiet and "unplugged" from any and all distractions. May they hone their senses to the possibilities you offer. Perhaps when they see a double rainbow or take a walk in a quiet place, they will learn of your mighty power and existence. I pray adults will instruct their children from an early age to pray to you. When someone knows they have had a "God moment", may they give witness and share it. For it is the sharing that we learn to seek You. Be with us this day, and each day, Holy God and save us from our sinful ways and many transgressions. In Your name we pray. Amen.

MARCH 30

THE COST OF DISCIPLESHIP

"Judging others makes us blind, whereas love is illuminating. By judging others we blind ourselves to our own evil and to the grace which others are just as entitled to as we are."

– Dietrich Bonhoeffer

I give praise and thanks to you Lord for the wisdom of Dietrich Bonhoeffer, who reminds us that "spiritual life is not a life of then and there, but a life of here and now. It is a life in which the spirit of God is revealed in the ordinary encounters of everyday." Sometimes it is so hard not to judge others. I wonder, is it avarice that causes one to judge others? I also pray this day that through your benevolence those who are in search of meaning in their lives, those who know something is missing in their hearts, will realize that the answer is You! Lord, be with the "lost" help them find their way to spiritual renewal through your words and the teachings of your Son. Help those who seem to overlook "the least of these" and I pray for them that a spirit of generosity and love will move them to help others. I pray especially today for the work that strives to to stop human trafficking. Lord, there are many young girls and boys enslaved into a practice of prostitution. Help us find a way to free these young people. May our society accept them and help them recover from the abuses they have suffered. Be with them and any who are in situations beyond their control. Prayers for your love and wisdom as we find ways to help the oppressed, restore their faith in humankind and You. May your saving grace and love abide in us today and all of our days. Amen.

MARCH 31

Here and Now
Living in the Spirit

– Henri Nouwen

"One of the discoveries we make in prayer is that the closer we come to God, the closer we come to all our brothers and sisters in the human family. God is not a private God. The God who dwells in our inner sanctuary is also the God who dwells in the inner sanctuary of each human being."

Heavenly God we recognize you are present in our hearts and minds. And God, we realize and are thankful for our community of friends, believers. When we see and hear examples of others in community, we are walking in the glory of our Risen Lord.

Believers seek out other believers, however, they also resist friendships that are not conducive with how you expect believers to be. All of those who follow evil sayers and doers are not part of the community. Here's the thing, there is a pathway for all. You, Lord God have provided for the non-believers to be in a community of believers. The evil ones have but to ask for forgiveness. The sincerity of the "ask" is followed by the sincerity of the thoughts, words and deeds, although that is for you to decide. God, you teach us we are not the 'judges' of others, You are. We are to accept and love them. For it is when we see God within ourselves, that we will also see God in others. Thanks be to you, loving God for your abundant grace and love this day and every day. Amen.

APRIL 1

And the cup he brings, though it burns your lips, has been fashioned of the clay which the Potter has moistened with His own sacred tears."

– Khalil Gibran, The Prophet

Holy Potter, you know our hearts and minds even when what is inside of us is sometimes not something we want to come to the surface. Are we afraid to take a deep look? Why do we hesitate to acknowledge that You, Holy God are with each one of us?On this day, at this moment let your "sacred tears" remind us of your deep and abiding faith in us. Help us walk in the light, knowing that You are with us on this crazy journey. Forgive our transgressions and help us to lead a life pleasing to you. Strengthen the faint of heart, be with those who are sad or lonely. Give each one an extra measure of your love. Be with those who are carrying heavy burdens of health or worry. It is you loving God who can lesson the pain and worries we have. Be with us on our walks, saving us all, by your grace. In the name of your son, Jesus Christ I pray, Amen.

APRIL 2

Nature holds the key to our aesthetic, intellectual, cognitive and even spiritual satisfaction.

– E. O. Wilson

Lord, the morning beauty provides a magnificent picture of the glory you have provided. Washington, D.C. has provided a pop of pink, delicate flowers of the Japanese cherry trees. The blooms are a welcome to the beginning of Spring. They are like us, Holy God, plentiful and yet at times so delicate. We look to the beauty of new birth to march boldly into a time where we take care of ourselves and a time that propels us to take care of our environment by weeding, feeding and planting. We also look to spring as a time when we come out of our homes and begin to plan what we did not start after writing those pesky resolutions for a new year. Lord, we meant to follow them, but somehow we let the days go by without the enthusiasm of the resolutions. Today, we are diving into our surroundings as we make plans to take care of ourselves, inner and outer. I pray for help and direction you want each one of us to take. I pray also for leaders to help our environment so that future generations will rejoice in the glory of planet earth. As we prepare flower beds and plantings, we know it is only through our love and care the fruit of our work may be successful. I pray for all who are struggling with their faith. May this season be a time for us to care for our bodies inside and out. I pray that we will add a pop of color to our love for you and your son, Jesus Christ. Be with those who struggle and help them find their way in this complex world. Bring to the seekers of your truths a spiritual satisfaction, new growth as the journey continues. Be with each one and save us, I pray in the name of your son, Jesus. Amen.

APRIL 3

Autumn is a second spring when every leaf is a flower.

– Albert Camus

God, you have provided the beauty we see during most of the year. The spring flowers, following a cold winter which turned everything grey, brightens my soul. Just in time, you have made your presence known via the beauty of the last week when the dogwood trees, jonquils, and tulips begin to explode in joyful colors. Thank you for creating our earth and especially locales where seasons of the year can be appreciated. I pray for the beauty of this earth, may it be reflected by the people who enjoy it. Prayers for consistent efforts to insure that our seasons will always be discernible, that our streams, rivers, lakes, seas and oceans will be clean and safe for your children to enjoy for many years. Many throughout the world have lost homes and all of their worldly possessions to forest fires, tornadoes and other causes. Our national disasters continue to destroy much of what has been built. Help us to encourage conservation of the air we breathe and the water we drink. Help the poor in Africa, for many who have a six mile walk just to get to water, and then the return trip with jugs full of clean water. Help the effects of our climate by pollution which causes many to have breathing issues. Many throughout the world have lost homes and all of their possessions. Our national disasters continue to destroy many of the things we have built. Make this the year when we get serious about climate change as new babies are born and new foliage is coming. Protect our forests and our people. God, I pray for all of the concerns about our environment and for those who have been harmed by unclean air and water. Be with us this day and always. Save us and forgive us for our sins. In the name of your son, Jesus Christ. Amen.

APRIL 4

For the beauty of the earth, For the glory of the skies
For the love which from our birth Over and around us lies
Lord of all to thee we raise This our hymn of grateful praise.

O Lord, thank you for the beautiful words in the hymn For the Beauty of the Earth. This hymn of praise tells of the author's was in awe of the beauty of your creation. He was amazed and fixated on the beauty of the countryside with rolling fields in front of a harvest. We pray today for the wonders of your world. Walking this wonderful planet, we see your power and what a loving God you are. Thank you God for the beauty of the earth and for loving us. Be with us this day, rejoicing in your majesty and the forgiveness of our sins, we pray. Amen.

APRIL 5

"Here is your country. Cherish these natural wonders, cherish the natural resources, cherish the history and romance as a sacred heritage, for your children and your children's children. Do not let selfish men or greedy interests skin your country of its beauty, its riches or its romance."

– Theodore Roosevelt

Creator God, help us find ways to preserve our natural wonders, that have not fallen prey to the avarice of developers and selfish people. Bit by bit, the natural wonders of the world are being obliterated. Lord God, we have to preserve our "treasures" so that your world will see your mighty creations. I remain concerned about endangered species like the monarch butterfly and bees who help pollinate and grow numerous trees and plants. Clean air and delicious food products from the land suffer from the ever-present bulldozers. Why Lord God, has humanity and greed taken over common sense and preservation? Help us to be sensible about what the world needs in order to protect our natural wonders, sustain and maintain life. Be with each of us as well as local, state and national electorates. May each one be more sensible when permitting changes to our environment. Lord, our polar ice caps are melting and our beach fronts are shrinking, helping us maintain an ecosystem that is kinder and mindful of your creations. I pray for clean air to breathe and clean water to drink; safety for all, that "inventions" do not put your people, creatures in the wild and lands in danger of extinction. In the sure knowledge of Your powers, I pray. Amen.

APRIL 6

MR. ROGERS

"I'm fairly convinced that the Kingdom of God is for the broken-hearted. You write of 'powerlessness.' Join the club, we are not in control. God is."

(Fred Rogers, Letter to Tim Madigan)

I am thankful Savior Lord, for the gift of your servant, the Reverend Fred Rogers. His ministry was gentle and thoughtful and loving. He gave hope to many young children for whom he directed his ministry. He had a soothing voice, which drew in everyone. I know that he is still singing and I am sure those around him are pleased with his song and his words of hope, "It's a beautiful day in the neighborhood, won't you be mine?" Lord, when Mr. Rogers learned of the unreasonable fears some white people had and refused to swim in waters with African American people, he made an example in a wading pool with a brother in Christ. He showed all, there is no need to fear your brothers and sisters, in Christ. Thank you for your servant Fred Rogers. May we learn the lessons he taught us. Be with all who share and live lives serving You. Be with us as we learn and change and save us. Amen.

I CORINTHIANS 13:1-3 THE GIFT OF LOVE

If I speak in the tongues of mortals I am a noisy gong or a clanging cymbal. And if I have prophetic powers and understand all mysteries and all knowledge, and if I have faith, so as to remove mountains, but do not have love, I am nothing. If I give away all my possessions, and if I hand over my body so that I may boast, but do not have love, I gain nothing.

Holy God, I understand that living one's life without love may be cold and lonely. Lord of all, be with those who feel cold and lonely, those who have lost a loved one. We know you will help heal their broken hearts. May they turn towards you for comfort and courage to move forward. It will take time for their hurt to heal. Lord, please be with them as they mourn and help them find a way to love and joy.

Without love, there is nothing and that is when bad things happen. Today I also pray for those who do not have or have never had love in their hearts. When mortals are bereft of emotion (love), often their mental state becomes flawed. I suppose, Lord, in some ways those people have a post traumatic stress disorder, and they need help finding their way back to feelings and emotions. I pray for your intercession on their behalf.

Savior, the mysteries why people carry out the hatred in their hearts and harm other human beings are the "noisy gong or clanging cymbals." They do not know you and make decisions based on the beliefs they have obtained from others just like them, or in their entrance into evil groups and ideologies. Those people have become sociopaths acting out with weapons of war (knives, bullets, fire, fists) and without regard for those they hurt. I pray for these people, Lord God, may the hate in their minds and hearts be softened. Often there is no hope change will occur. Help us to be advocates for You and to change those for whom change may seem impossible. It is hard to find adequate mental facilities and to identify those needing help. Help society to help the lost and those needing interventions. May they be healed.

Lord, be with us this day and every day, you have saved so many, please find a way to help those who do not have loving hearts. Be with us this day and save us all, I pray in the name of your Son, Jesus. Amen.

CORIENTHIANS 13:4-7
THE GIFT OF LOVE

Love is patient; love is kind; love is not envious or boastful or arrogant or rude. It does not insist on its own way; it is not irritable or resentful; it does not rejoice in wrongdoing, but rejoices in the truth. It bears all things, hopes all things, endures all things.

———————————

Loving God, your words of inspiration and warning make all who read them know what love is and what love is not. You tell us to be patient with our loved ones and also to be be kind. Sometimes our patience wears thin when a child refuses to be rushed into leaving the house and heading to school or to a caregiver so the adult in the room can get to work on time. In circumstances like these, it is hard to refrain from being irritable or filled with angst. And patient God, when I am set in my own ways and someone else thinks of a 'better way' to do something, I have to check my attitude. After the passage of time, I have learned to rejoice in truth and joy instead of being overwhelmed by grief. I know, just thinking how you must have felt when your beloved son's life was brutally ended, it seems to make my sorrow seem less. Holy and loving God, I pray You will help us to control negative emotions and to present a loving, patient attitude in all we say and do. Enduring the loss of a child or a spouse or anyone beloved to us is hard. You have taught us to endure all things. That one is so very hard, I pray for your love to enfold all who are suffering the loss of a loved one, or perhaps living with a sad heart of loneliness or longing. May your love help those whose lives have forever been changed by debilitating events. Becoming a caregiver is exhausting and expensive. Help those caregivers to know the hard work it takes to be patient and kind with a person who is slipping into an unknown life of mental and/or physical decline. Theirs is a loving, unselfish gift of love. I pray for your spirit and love be with each caregiver. Be with them, healing God and save us all, in the sure knowledge of your love and patience. Amen.

APRIL 9

PSALM 118:1, 14

O give thanks to the Lord, for he is good; his steadfast love endures forever!
The Lord is my strength and my might; he has become my salvation.

———————————

Lord God, as morning dawns and the moon retreats, you are with me, in my waking and my sleeping. To you I give all the glory for your grace, saved me. Be with your flock this day and night; show them the way. I am praying for everyone these last two weeks before the glory of your son's resurrection is celebrated. Learning exactly what happened to Jesus at the hands of evil people was the ultimate sacrifice. I used to think that I could not stand the pain, my faith had yet to be developed and my life was full of bullying, turmoil and without love. You saved me Lord God! You brought me out of a household without love and without you. My refuge and strength came from the mouths of loving and wise servants of you, loving God. I am praying for those lost souls who suffer now, that they might find solace and a new beginning which will give them strength to escape whatever it is that inflicts mental or physical pain. May each one find a way into sanctuaries where they too, shall learn of your power, strength and loving ways. I pray for the oppressed and forgotten victims, may they be comforted and stronger, loving advocates for the next generation of victims. Be with those who are seeking a way out of oppression. Heavenly Teacher, teach the bullies/oppressors to learn of a better way to treat your children. Let the suffering end and the light shine in loving hearts of those frightened or bullied. May all who believe in you and salvation join in saying. Amen and amen.

PSALM 106:1-2, 48

Praise the Lord! O give thanks to the Lord, for he is good; for his steadfast love endures forever. Happy are those who observe justice, who do righteousness all times. Blessed be the Lord, the God of Israel, from everlasting to everlasting. And let all the people say, "Amen." Praise the Lord!

Lord, thank you for your patience. Sometimes it is hard for me to be patient, especially when I want something…now! I know when I ask something of you, I must learn to listen patiently. I have tried to do that on many occasions. I have discovered, when I take my time, when I am paitient and listening, you answer. Thank you God for giving me time to ponder what I want versus what I need. You usually take care of the second part. Coming to you in prayer reallly is the way. Lord, thank you for all of the blessings you have sent my way. You have taken me as I am, as imperfect as I am and made me whole again. You gave me gifts to love the "least of these" in my classroom and enabled me to help others learn life's lessons in addition to the curricula I was there to teach. Your love and blessings renew a spirit and love for those who are hurting and that love enables me to help those in need in many ways. Be with me this day, holy God and forgive my sins, I pray in your blessed name. Amen.

APRIL 11

ROMANS 10:17

*So faith comes from what is heard,
and what is heard comes through the word of Christ.*

"I believed that there was a God because I was told it by my grandmother and by other adults. But when I found that I knew not only that there was a God, but that I was a child of God, when I understood that, when I comprehended that, more than that, when I internalized that, ingested that, I became courageous."

*Maya Angelou's Faith
Made Her A Courageous 'Child of God.'*

———————————

All-knowing God, thank you for the life and vision of Dr. Maya Angelou. She walked her life with you, and it is because of that walk, we have a greater understanding of just how powerful and how wonderful you are. You, loving God are the answer to so many confounding events in our lives. For Dr. Angelou and for many like her, like me, you were there when we needed you. You are now the caretaker of my soul. You have provided all I need. Many times, you were all I had. And yes, it was enough. Thank you for the comfort you provided when I was lost and in despair. Be with each one Holy Savior and lighten the burdens of those who have yet to feel loved or your loving grace. Be with us as and forgive us our sins and save us I pray, in your glorious name. Amen.

APRIL 12

ROMANS 12:9-13
MARKS OF THE TRUE CHRISTIAN

Let love be genuine, hate what is evil, hold fast to what is good; love one another with mutual affection; outdo one another in showing honor. Do not lag in zeal, be ardent in spirit, serve the Lord. Rejoice in hope, be patient in suffering, persevere in prayer. Contribute to the needs of the saints; extend hospitality to strangers.

Lord God, I give thanks to Paul and his extensive Biblical writings. He was a true and faithful servant, called by Jesus Christ to be an apostle. Paul has written numerous letters spreading the "good news." I pray your people will demonstrate the "marks of the true Christian." I join those who find being "patient in suffering" a real challenge. As Paul wrote, "persevere in prayer," the petitions are heard, as we have also learned, a return to a healthy body is not going to happen necessarily on "our time" but yours, Holy God. Be with the sick, if it is your will may they return to improved health and strengthen those who are weary. May we be quick to praise and slow to admonish. Paul's words give us hope and inspiration as they map the ways and expectations for how we should lead our lives. Be with us this day and save us. In the name of your son, Jesus, I pray. Amen.

APRIL 13

Every morning is an opportunity. Choose joy this morning!

LUKE. 19:37-40
JESUS' TRIUMPHANT ENTRY INTO JERUSALEM'

As he was now approaching the path down from the Mount of Olives, the whole multitude of the disciples began to praise God joyfully with a loud voice for all the deeds of power that they had seen, saying, "Blessed is the king who comes in the name of the Lord! Peace in heaven, and glory in the highest heaven!" Some of the Pharisees in the crowd said to him, "Teacher, order your disciples to stop." He answered, 'I tell you if these were silent, the stones would shout out.'

Heavenly Father, what a proud and profoundly sorrowful moment Jesus' entry into Jerusalem must have been for you. However, all knowing, Lord, you knew what Christians everywhere have learned; your beloved son would die, fulfilling the prophecy. Jesus would die and rise again. The Bible tells us of Jesus' triumphant entry into Jerusalem. The news to all Christians is Jesus' entry was filled with joy. I know Lord God, the intentional journey into the city of his birth, was a conundrum, however, it was filled with many lessons. The disciples, following Jesus' instruction became leaders and spread the 'good news' about him. Jesus was confident and joyful while at the same time 'all knowing.' Lord God, when we face trials, help us hear you. As believers, we know those praying will not be silenced. By faith, we help those who mourn, which is God's gift. When a loved one passes, the loved ones, family and friends unite to bring love and comfort. When our life's journey becomes difficult, I pray God for wisdom and discernment to bring comfort to those who mourn. Help all who move forward into the unknown of "tomorrow" to be comforted and to find joy, and a peace, which "passes all understanding." The truth, Holy one, is failure to praise and glorify your holy name, will raise up other voices. I live secure in your love, and for all of those who honor you and your beloved son. I cannot fathom a chorus of rocks praising your holy name. Lord, I give thanks to you and to your son. I pray one day, to be welcomed into your 'house' and to live there forevermore. Be with the sinful and may each one receive forgiveness and your abundant love. Amen.

APRIL 14

PSALM 121

I will lift up my eyes to the hills—from where will my help come?
My help comes from the Lord, who made heaven and earth.

He will not let your foot be moved; he who keeps you will not slumber.
He who keeps Israel will neither slumber nor sleep.

The Lord is your keeper; the Lord is your shade at your right hand.
The sun shall not strike you by day, nor the moon by night.

The Lord will keep you from all evil; he will keep your life.
The Lord will keep your going out and your coming in from this time on and forevermore.

Lord, you are my strength and hope. Often we stumble in our faithful practice of giving thanks to you for the loving care you give to us. I am humbled when I think about what you have done for the human race and the painful personal cost of your deeds. Thank you for sending Jesus into the world. We are told in Biblical writings Jesus ws fully divine, all-knowing, fully present and powerful. The Bible makes it abundantly clear Jesus was fully divine. Lord, in times of great suffering throughout the world, I feel your healing and comfort for those who are sick and dying. I pray you will help calm our fears. May my faith grow, Lord. Thankyou for your glorious and unselfish gift of Jesus Christ, who came into the world that we might have life and have it abundantly. By taking away our sins, our tomorrows are in front of us. Lord, be with us as we continue our earthly journey. Help calm our fears and worries during times of unrest, illness, and world events. When we are frightened or worried for ourselves, for family members an loved ones; those receiving treatment or ill, those facing surgeries and Lord, those infants about to be born. Those Mary's who perhaps may be frightened or feel alone, without perhaps even one person known to them during their labor and delivery, help them know you are with them. Lord thank you for the caretakers, medics, paramedics, physician's assistants, nurses and doctors, and all who help heal the sick. Give them courage, strength and confidence in you, may they know brighter days will come. I pray all will know we are in your house where ever we are! Be with us and save us, I pray. Amen.

APRIL 15

PSALM 122

I was glad when they said to me, "Let us go to the house of the Lord!" Our feet are standing within your gates, O Jerusalem. Jerusalem –built as a city that is bound firmly together. To it the tries go up, the tribes of the Lord, as was decreed for Israel, to give thanks to the name of the Lord. For there the thrones for judgment were set up, the thrones of the house of David. Pray for the peace of Jerusalem: "May they prosper who love you. Peace be within your walls, and security within your towers." For the sake of my relatives and friends I will say, "Peace be within you." For the sake of the house of the Lord our God. I will seek your good.

Precious Savior, your words written by the psalmists humble me. In a quiet pastoral setting or in a bustling city and everywhere in between, You are there for all of humanity. And so, Lord God, I shall remember this Psalm when I throw up my hands in despair, when I am frightened, when pandemics, flu or other calamities threaten my life or the lives of loved ones, and yes, even strangers. Sometimes Lord, I cry for the unknown person in a nursing home or hospital emergency room who is facing an unexpected or hideous demise. I cry for the young people who, because of a virus have strokes. While they might live, their lives and the lives of loved ones shall forevver be altered in ways that change their life's plan. God, show them and me your purpose and grace as we adjust to what befalls your people. Help me remember this beautiful Psalm and the beauty of your grace, your wisdom and your love for everyone. Lord, I will keep you in my heart and in my mind, knowing you will and have saved me. Be with all who are struggling this day, Lord. Show them your beautiful grace, comfort those who are left to mourn, in the sure knowledge they now have eternal life in your heavenly world. Until the time when we too shall meet them again, help us to be good people, doing your will on earth. Be with us and sae us, keeping us safe to do your will. Amen.

APRIL 16

COLOSSIANS 1:19-20

For in him all the fullness of God is pleased to dwell, and through him God was pleased to reconcile to himself all things, whether on earth or in heaven, by making peace through the blood of his cross.

Our God, your God and my God, how majestic is your holiness and wisdom throughout the world. The cross that Jesus suffered was "not for nothing;" it was for EVERYTHING! Jesus had to be a true sacrifice in order that we would be in harmony with You. It was You, Lord who sacrificed Jesus, those who sentenced him were the vehicles used to attain his death. Thank you Lord God, for sending your son to put us in a 'right relationship' with you, thus allowing believers to be saved. Thank you, Loving God, for the Savior who paid for our sins throughout eternity. All that Jesus did while he was on earth was for each one of US! He paid the ultimate price to save us. Knowing you loved us so much that your own son, Jesus had to die on a cross for our salvation was the greatest gift one could ever receive. Through the Resurrection of your beloved son, we were given the right or privilege to be with you, through faith and by your powerful grace. I pray to you, Loving Lord, and give thanks for keeping me on the right path which allows me to move through my days knowing you will continue to guide my ways. Be with all your people and save us. I pray in your holy name. Amen.

APRIL 17

MATTHEW 3:13-17
THE BAPTISM OF JESUS

Then Jesus came from Galilee to John at the Jordan, to be baptized by him. John would have prevented him, saying, "I need to be baptized by you, and do you come to me? But Jesus answered him, "Let it be so now; for it is proper for us in this way to fulfill all righteousness." Then he consented. And when Jesus had been baptized, just as he came up from the waters, suddenly the heavens were opened to him. And a voice from heaven said, "This is my Son, the Beloved with whom I am well pleased."

Heavenly God, knowing how our hearts ache when a child is taken home, I can only imagine the heartache and turmoil you went through to find the answer to the conundrum of what it would take to save your people. Jesus was born to teach the 'way, the truth and the light' to people who had lost their way and to fulfill the prophecy, thus Jesus was born to die in order that we might be saved, our sins forgiven and by that act, we might go boldly and free from guilt. Thank you Lord God, for the wisdom and gift of Jesus Christ. Lord, I pray your words and you will for us will be carried forth forever more. Help us to discern your will in response to any and all circumstances or adversities. Through you, all things are possible. May we always honor the sacrifices made in our names. Your love and faith comfort and embolden me to pray and help others find their faith in you. Be with us this day and all of our days. We ask you to forgive our sins and save us in your Holy name, I pray. Amen.

APRIL 18

JOHN 13:1-5, 12-15, 18-20

Now before the festival of the Passover, Jesus knew that his hour had come to depart from this world and go to the Father. Having loved his own who were in the world, he loved them to the end. The devil had already put it into the heart of Judas son of Simon Iscariot to betray him. And during supper Jesus, knowing that the Father had given all things into his hands, and that he had come from God, got up from the table, took off his outer robe, and tied a towel around himself. Then he poured water into a basin and began to wash the disciples' feet and to wipe them with the towel that was tied around him. He came to Simon Peter and said to him, "You will never wash my feet." Jesus answered, "You do not know now what I am doing, but later you will understand.

And after he washed their feet, had put on his robe, another had returned to the table, he said to them, "Do you know what I have done to you: You call me Teacher and Lord— and you are right, for that is what I am. So if I, your Lord and Teacher have washed your feet, you also should wash one another's feet. For I have set you an example, that you also should do what I have done to you.

I am not speaking of all of you, I know whom I have chosen. But it is to fulfill the scripture, "The one who ate my bread has lifted his heel against me.' I tell you this now, before it occurs so that when it does occur, you may believe that I am he. Very truly, I tell you, whoever receives one whom I send receives me; and whoever receives me receives him who sent me."

———

Lord God, thank you for sending your beloved Son into the world. What a great teacher he was. It is said, "timing is everything," we are reminded how Jesus demonstrated in thought, word and deed, he truly was your son. Jesus' love for you and those who followed him, had no beginning nor ending. Thank you, Lord of All, for the life, death and resurrection of your son. Thank you for his loving ability to teach the people, your people. Jesus fulfilled the expectations of your power and love. His message, all are welcome and through grace, we are pardoned, our faith in you is certain. I pray today for a "closer walk" with you and Jesus. May my words and love for you, impart to others just what a special moment in time Jesus' life and death was. Those who have lost a loved one, know just how painful it must have been for you and Mary, Jesus' mother. It seems almost like nothing has changed. Too often people deny you, God, their lives pass with little or no faith. By faith, Lord God, I have felt your love and gentle touch. I write prayers, trying to be a "voice" for others. May they learn acceptance and just how great knowing your love is. Your words, Lord God have brought me through the trials and turmoil that is part of my life, my story. I believe I have been called to serve you and pray that others might be persuaded to follow, and learn they are not alone. May we all draw closer as we move from a trial to a cross, to a resurrection. Be with us these days and forgive our sins, in the name of your son, Jesus the Christ. Amen.

APRIL 19

1 CORINTHIANS 11:23-26
INSTITUTION OF THE LORD'S SUPPER

For I received from the Lord what I also handed onto you, that the Lord Jesus on the night when he was betrayed took a loaf of bread, and when he had given thanks, he broke it and said, "This is my body that is for you. Do this in remembrance of me." In the same way he took the cup also, after supper, saying, "This cup is the new covenant in my blood. Do this as often as you drink it, in remembrance of me." For as often as you eat this bread and drink the cup, you proclaim the Lord's death until he comes.

———————————

Holy Lord God, we hear the words of institution each time Holy Communion is offered. Thank you for giving us the symbols associated with communion. I know as I approach the table, I come secure in the knowledge that you love me and you love all who are prepared to take the bread and drink from the cup. We leave the table charged with having a compassionate heart. We are to follow the example of your son, Jesus by giving voice to those who would be silent, and strength to the weak. Lord, we will be a church family that will listen to and care for one another. Lord God, we promise to love one another as we love you. Thank you for giving your son. His words were a powerful tool of communion. I struggle sometimes, Lord, but I know that I am not alone, we are not alone. We know our brothers and sisters in Christ will come to care and comfort those in need. Be with us Lord as we prepare prepare to live a live pleasing to you. I ask for the forgiveness of my sins, and that you save me through your grace. Amen.

APRIL 20

PSALM 53:1, 2, 4

Fools say in their hearts, "There is no God." … God looks down from heaven on humankind to see if there are any who are wise, who seek after God. …When God restores the fortunes of his people, Jacob will rejoice; Israel will be glad.

God, we remember Jesus was born to die for the forgiveness of our sins. Holy Father, your son's death had to be, just as it was. In essence, Jesus' death was hideous, the fulfillment of the prophets. There would not be a more gut-wrenching death of any other human than that of your beloved son, which was and is a glaring lesson to all. Holy God, I have learned by your example what it means to pass into your kingdom, as a place where pain and suffering are no more. I am thankful for the life, death and resurrection of your beloved son. I acknowledge that death signals relief from pain and suffering. I have suffered the pain of loss, with a thankful heart, and with peace and calm as You have called home many of your "children." For them, pain and suffering are no more. My heart and mind are at peace, knowing these children of God, have been released to your care. I have felt your presence, love and Holy Spirit. The pain of personal loss reminds me of my love for each one, the life they led. I knew each one had gone to a better place; a place you created for "believers." I am eternally thankful and pray those who mourn, may be comforted in the sure knowledge, they are now with You. Be with me now and for ever, saving me from all sin. Amen.

APRIL 21
PSALM 126:1-6

When the Lord restored the fortunes of Zion, we were like those who dream. Then our mouth was filled with laughter, and our tongue with shouts of joy; then it was said among the nations, "The Lord has done great things for them." The Lord has done great things for us, and we rejoiced. Restore our fortunes, O Lord, like the watercourses in the Negeb. May those who sow in tears reap with shouts of joy. Those who go out weeping, bearing the seed for the sowing, shall come home with shouts of joy, carrying their sheaves.

———————————

God of all creation, I give thanks for your son, mesus Christ. That's all, Lord. Jesus' message was heard and believed. The song about in the Psalm foreshadowed what was to come. In fact, Holy God, you have done great things, for all of humankind. Thank you for the hard work and faithfulness of those who have gone before. Each generation is entrusted with buidling on the past. Sometimes, Lord, our buildings and ideas were sin filled. We are working to "get it right" and make something for which you will be pleased. Help us each day, Lord, to do your will and to remember to offer you our very best. We are not always successrul in our efforts to "get it right," and make something for which you will be pleased. Help us, each day, Lord, to make something for which you will be pleased. Lord, help us to find the way by heeding your teachings and following by eaxmple. Help us forget arbitrary things, like the color of one's skin. Be with us this day and please forgive our sinful ways. With faith and love. Amen.

APRIL 22

PSALM 5:1-12

Give ear to my words, O Lord; give heed to my sighing. Listen to the sound of my cry, my king and my God, for to you I pray. O Lord, in the morning you hear my voice; in the morning I plead my case to you and watch. For you are not a God who delights in wickedness; evil will not sojourn with you. The boastfull will not stand before your eyes; you hate all evildoers. You destroy those who speak lies; the Lord abhors the bloodthirsty and the deceitful. But I, through the abundance of your steadfast love, will enter your house, I will bow down towards your holy temple in awe of you. Lead me, O Lord, in righteousnes because of my enemies; make your way straight before me. For there is no truth in their mouths; their hearts are destruction; their throats are open graves; they flatter with their tongues. Make them bear their guilt, O God; let them fall by their own counsels; because of their many transgressions cast them out, for they have rebelled against you. But let all who take refuge in you rejoice; let them ever sing for joy. Spread your protection over them, so that those who love your name may exult in you. For you bless the rigthteous, O Lord; you cover them with favor as with a shield.

Holy God, the psalmist has prayed almost in angst, knowing you will hear a sincere petition. Your love and faithfulness to those who pray faithfully indicates a faith-filled person, someone whose petition you would not ignore. During this time of pandemics and systemic racism, I ask for your undersanding and guidance.. Help the caregivers and parents care for the children suffering the Covid-19 virus. Lord, I also pray for a peaceful solution to the country's racist past and pressent. There seems to be rebellion by those who have been mistreated. Be with the law enforcers and help them take a step back from aggressive resolution to a situatop. Be with them as they try to be safe while addressing the situation. Too many innocent people of color have lost their lives by police tactics. We need to learn how to use services to help domestic situations and how to address peaceful demonstrations, which have been provided for in our constitution. Children are hurt by rash actions that could be solved peacefully. Lord, why the color of one's skin remains an issue in this day and age, I do not know nor understand. Soften the hearts and minds of each person and help us end the racist practices of our land. Be with each one seeking answers to difficult questions. Lord, you teach us love, may we learn to love our neighbor as ourselves. Be with me this day, and forgive my sins, I pray in the name of Jesus. Amen.

APRIL 23

PSALM 8:1-4

Lord, our Sovereign, how majestic is your name in all the earth! You have set your glory above the heavens. Out of the mouths of babes and infants you have founded a bulwark because of your foes, to silence the enemy and the avenger. When I look at your heavens, the work of your fingers, the moon and the stars that you have established; what are human beings that you are mnidful of them, mortals that you care for them?

Holy God, the psalm of David is a beautiful one, filled with praise and love for all you have provided us on Mother Earth: the stars and planets, on earth majestic mountains, rivers and lakes and minerals below the surface to provide sustainability for all of the inhabitants on this earth. May our footprint be no more than is necessary. May we live in harmony with nature and our environment. Lord, may we be mindful of plants and animals with whom we share the land. May we be good stewards of the earthly gift you have provided. Be with us Lord God, as we live our lives in ways that are pleasing to you, forgive us our sins and save us, I pray in the name of Jesus. Amen.

GALATIANS 1:1-5 SALUTATION

Paul an apostle—sent neither by human commission not from human authorities, but through Jesus Christ and God the Father, who raised him from the dead—and all the members of God's family who are with me.

To the churches of Galatia

Grace to you and peace from God our Father and the Lord Jesus Christ, who gave himself for our sins to set us free from the present evil age, according to the will of our God and Father, to whom be the glory for ever and ever. Amen

———————

Loving Lord, your faithful servant Paul, wrote to many, including to the ones from the churches of Galatia. It took all of one sentence to greet the recipient(s) of the letter and to tell them or perhaps to reassure them of exactly what had happened to Jesus Christ and why. God, how do we persuade the people of the world you sent your son, Jesus, to set us free from the present evil in our world? Turns out, Lord, we could say the same now! The good news is that there are many Christian leaders who are carrying forth your will. As we celebrated the Risen Lord this past weekend, I pray that you will fill our leaders with patience and love. May they be rejuvenated from the outpouring of people everywhere who flooded churches across the world to hear again the story of Jesus Christ. I pray those who accepted the invitation to come to church will become regular attendees and they will bring their children in order to facilitate education about Jesus and Christianity. I pray, Loving God, the children will joyfully participate in the opportunities churches make to enrich their understanding of who you are, and learn where they may choose to participate in helping others to learn about Jesus and his ministry. Be with all caretakers of your will, may they become joyful Easter People, loving and teaching others about you and Jesus. Be with those who seem to have lost their way. Help them to find You. Be with the clergy who worked diligently to bring your word to the communities they serve. Be with each of us, forgive our sins and save us, in your sacred name, I pray. Amen.

APRIL 24

PSALM 88:1-2, 13

O Lord, God of my salvation, when, at night I cry out in your presence, let my prayer come before you; incline your ear to my cry.

But I, O Lord, cry out to you; in the morning my prayer comes before you.

"Are you there God, it's me ...." Sometimes life seems unfair, too hard. Sometimes, we are in such a hurry, we do not take time to listen, we get absorbed in the issues of any moment, any day. Jesus' example was just the opposite. When he was troubled, he withdrew and went into prayer. Why Lord, do humans today insist on quick fixes and immediate answers or resolutions to the issues on their minds? This day I pray for those who have what might appear to be mountains of worries. I pray that those who pray for resolution of problems will go into a quiet place and seek your guidance. Be with us when it seems as though our plates are too full and our faith in you seems to be slipping. Help us face the challenges of each day with faith and grace. I pray for all who are finding their ways through problems which seem to be insurmountable. May the initial worries we have, be tempered by your love. Sleeping on problems, often gives the body and mind time to rest and when we awaken, a way to move forward seems possible. There are times Lord, when issues seem to take over, help us slow down, take a deep breath and quiet our minds. While the answer to petitions we receive may not be the ones prayed for, help us to recognize and evaluate. I pray for faith and time to resolve challenges. Lord, you know what is on our minds and in our hearts, I ask that you help lift our burdens and calm our worries. Give us this day a feeling of calm and strength. May our resolve be settled after soul-searching and listening to you. Be with all who struggle with difficult issues, may your love comfort each one. May we remember the teachings of Jesus, and become people who spend daily time in prayer. I am thankful to have finally learned to slow down and listen for your guidance and loving ways. I come to you in prayer and say, "Holy God, it's me ...., hear my prayer..." Amen.

APRIL 25

PSALM 101:1, 2

I will sing of loyalty and of justice to you, O Lord, I will sing. I will walk with integrity of heart within my house

MICAH 6:8

He has told you, O mortal, what is good; and what does the Lord require of you but to do justice, and to love kindness, and to walk humbly with your God?

Lord God, around this land a political season has divided our country and made enemies of neighbors. I pray for those who seem to be haters of all that is good, and just for our changing world. May each of your children feel your love and hear your joy of people who truly follow Christ. If we are following "What God Requires;" then why patient God, is our world struggling with showing you loyalty and justice? I feel both have taken a back seat to bullying and disrespect. The abandonment of values has changed people into becoming people whose hearts are "anti" many values, including doing justice and loving kindness, while walking humbly with you, Lord God. So today, Savior God, I pray for civility in our dialog with others who disagree with a particular religious, social or legal norm. May we seek to find common ground that acknowledges our differences in healthy ways. Be with our changing world, without abandoning acceptable societal norms. Help the opposing factions' ' listen and respect the differences of our neighbors throughout the world and in particular in the United States. May your peace, Lord help us to find a way to be together, honoring and even celebrating our differences in peaceful and joy-filled ways. When we do this, I know you will rejoice. Be with each of us this day as we all seek to embody the Risen Christ in this season of joy. In your holy name I pray. Amen.

APRIL 26
JOHN 14:27

Peace I leave with you; my peace I give to you. I do not give to you as the world gives. Do not let your hearts be troubled and do not let them be afraid.

———————————

L oving God, I know you are in my heart and mind. Loving your teachings, your spirit and you son calms my emotions which seem to overwhelm me. Sometimes, Lord God, I am overwhelmed with emotions that seem to come out of nowhere: a favorite song is playing, a memory that demonstrates a deep love, a task a loved one used to do, which now I must do. I'm minding my own business and suddenly, I am feeling profoundly sad or lost. I feel the loss of a dear one and just need to reconnect and have my private time. Remembering a happier time that perhaps brought me great joy will reaffirm the essence of a loved one who has gone home to you. Thank you Holy One, for the beautiful and painful memories, for they both live in my heart and mind. Embracing the pain is reaffirming. The pain validates the relationship and love between me and those dear ones I am missing. Holy God, I pray your loving grace will continue to walk with me. Thank you for protecting those memories and for helping to calm my wounded spirit so that I may rejoice in you and them. Heavenly Lord, be with us this day and every day, give peace to those who perhaps are at war with their memories, be with all who have not yet realized that your's are the footsteps walking next to them, in their darkest hours. Be with me, forgiving my sins and and save us, I pray in the name of Jesus Christ. Amen.

APRIL 27

PSALMS 1:1-3, 6

Happy are those who do not follow the advice of the wicked, or take the path that sinners tread, or sit in the seat of scoffers; but their delight is in the law of the Lord, and on his law they meditate day and night. They are like trees planted by the streams, which yield their fruit in its season, and their leaves do not wither. In all that they do, they prosper. ... for the Lord watches over the way of the righteous, but the way of the wicked shall perish.

Gracious and loving Lord, thank you for the wisdom of the psalmist. The clear message is to carry you inside our hearts and minds. You have saved me from myself and I am thankful you have. In dark hours, you were my saving grace. You were there when I might have become inconsolably lost. I remember sitting alone in a church without a single person to turn to, when I turned to you. Be with those who are struggling and help each one to know your love and wisdom and may they find you waiting to help them. May your love open the hearts and minds of each one. Help us to always turn to you in good times and in challenging times. You are the way, the truth and the light. Be with us each day and save us, I pray in your sacred and steadfast love. Amen.

APRIL 28
JOB 21:1-7; 42:2

Then Job answered: Listen carefully to my words, and let this be your consolation. Bear with me, and I will speak; then after I have spoken, mock on. As for me, is my complaint addressed to mortals? Why should I not be impatient? Look at me, and be appalled, and lay your hand upon your mouth. When I think of it I am dismayed, and shuddering seizes my flesh. Why do the wicked live on, reach old age, and grow mighty in power?

"I know that you can do all things, and that no purpose of yours can be thwarted."

Patient Lord, sometimes things happen and I do not understand why they did. Job felt that way, too. Instead of leaning into your love, sometimes I become impatient and judgmental. At times, when I expect a certain outcome and if fails to happen, I become indignant. Forgive me for acting as though I am 'in charge.' Your patience Lord, brought Job to a better place, and I pray that you will have patience with me, as well. I give praise and glory to you for the example of Job. When one follows you, we are promised the greatest reward ever. Patience is not easy, nothing worthwhile is. Help us when we feel alone, forgetting you are always with us. Through your teachings, help us live the life expected. May your words bring a calm resolve; to follow your teachings and to live a life that is pleasing to you. I pray that each of us will consistently resist imposing our will on others. Lord, there are many in our world who are truly needy. Help those with much to share, to do what we can to help those less fortunate. Be with us this day and every day and save us. I pray. Amen.

APRIL 29
MATTHEW 6:25-30, 34

...*"Therefore I tell you, do not worry about your life, what you will eat, or what you will drink, or about your body, what you will wear. Is not life more than food, and the body more than clothing?" Look at the birds of the air; they neither sow nor reap nor gather into barns, and yet your Heavenly Father feeds them. Are you not more valuable than they? And can any of you by worrying add a single hour to your life span? And why do you worry about clothing? Consider the lilies of the field, how they grow, they neither toil nor spin, yet I tell you, even Solomon in all his glory was not clothed like one of these. But if God so clothes the grass of the field, which is alive today and tomorrow is thrown into the oven, will he not clothe you—you of little faith?*

"So do not worry about tomorrow, for tomorrow will bring worries of its own. Today's trouble is enough for today."

Lord, taking a step toward not worrying can be terrifying. Sometimes, I worry about family and friends, sometimes, many times, I worry about trying to be a healthier person. My resolve focuses on something I never pray for...I just realized that! I have never prayed for you to help me improve my health by selecting appropriate food. What a revelation. I have prayed for many things, but never for help in making wise decisions that will bring improved health. Lord, give me the strength to follow an important food and fitness plan, for I know by following it, I will have fewer aches and pains and I will be a better, healthier me. I pray for all who carry worries about their lives, too. For instance, I pray for what will happen to a child, a parent, a friend, meeting personal needs and not to mention how will the bills get paid? So this day I pray for assistance in becoming a healthier me, and for all who struggle with personal issues, help us to take better care of our physical and mental health. Forgive us our sins, and be with us this day and each day, in your holy name I pray. Amen.

APRIL 30

PSALM 23

The Lord is my shepherd, I shall not want. He makes me lie down in green pastures; he leads me beside still waters; he restores my soul. He leads me in right paths for his name's sake,

Even though I walk through the darkest valley, I fear no evil, for you are with me; your rod and your staff—they comfort me.

You prepare a table before me in the presence of my enemies; you anoint my head with oil; my cup overflows. Surely goodness and mercy shall follow me all the days of my life, and I shall dwell in the house of the Lord my whole life long.

Savior God, I give thanks to the psalmist for the assurance that my God, our God has a place in our very souls This is the Psalm I pray most often when I feel as though I am lost, in a 'valley,' all alone. Always reminding me that I can come to You, is a great comfort and helps me reconcile your love even when 'bad' things happen. God, thank you for always being present, for your steadfast love and guidance. Holy God, sometimes I have prayed for a miracle and when the miracle I prayed for does not happen, I know that it is because the miracle you provided was the miracle that needed to happen. I shall be eternally thankful for the miracles you have provided "and I shall dwell in the house of the Lord, for ever. Amen

MAY 1

ISAIAH 42:10-13

Sing to the Lord a new song, his praise from the end of the earth! Let the sea roar and all that fills it, the coastlands and their inhabitants. Let the desert and its towns lift up their voice, the villages that Kendra inhabits; let the inhabitants of Sela sing for joy, let them shout from the tops of the mountains. Let them give glory to the Lord, and declare his praise in the coastlands. The Lord goes forth like a soldier, like a warrior he stirs up his fury; he cries out, he shouts aloud, he shows himself mighty against his foes.

Warrior God, your mighty powers have not gone unnoticed. In fact, we see them everywhere we are. Spring time yields new growth and warmer climates, following a darker time of winter when all vegetation appears to be dead. What a glorious showing of the colors you have mixed into the fabric of this earth. So too, Holy God, you have taken summer as a time for warming the earth, yielding foods that are gathered and prepared for later sustenance, preparing for a period of rest. The foliage erupts in glorious colors and then releases the leaves from their branches as winter comes. Thank you God for all you have provided. May we rejoice in the beauty of your land and take steps to keep the natural beauty of this planet. We need to work on preservation of natural resources. Be with us as we move from home to school/work safely and help to make our lands better off than they were when we arrived. Be with the people who care for our environment and help us, even if it is in a small way, to make the beauty of our earth, lasting. Be with us this day and help us to make decisions that leave a smaller footprint. Forgive us from our sins and save us, I pray. Amen.

MAY 2

MATTHEW 5:1-5

When Jesus saw the crowds, he went up the mountain; and after he sat down, his disciples came to him. Then he began to speak, and taught them saying: Blessed are the poor in spirit, for theirs is the kingdom of heaven. Blessed are those who mourn, for they will be comforted
Blessed are the meek, for they will inherit the earth.

Teacher, I pray this day for all whose spirits seem to be broken; for those who have lost a loved one; and for those who are easily imposed upon or submissive. Be with those who are suffering and feel "lost." We see them, our brothers and sisters, who are unable to do anything. Some carry signs, many of them, asking for money, for help; others living inside themselves in their own places. When you look into their eyes, there is no effect. They are broken people, many living in one of the wealthiest countries in your world. Holy God, please lift the veil of those who suffer in silence for their days and nights without connection to humanity and to you. Bless each one and help them to "find their way" to you and to a place where their bodies and spirits may be renewed, and their spirits lifted. Be with those who mourn a profound loss, may they lean in to your love and to their faith which has been shaken with the loss. May they be comforted and loved. Help those who are unable to express their truths and because of that, others take from them. These people, some of the least of your people need your love and care and they need our love and care. May we be leaders in finding ways to help these "lost souls." Thank you teacher, for all you have done for me, I pray you will forgive my sins and save us, this day. Amen.

MAY 3

MATTHEW 5:1, 6-8

When Jesus saw the crowds, he went up the mountain; and after he sat down, his disciples came to him. Then he began to speak, and taught them saying: Blessed are those who hunger and thirst for righteousness, for they will be filled. Blessed are the merciful, for they will receive mercy. Blessed are the pure in heart, for they will see God.

Lord, God, Teacher, you have charged your people, the "believers," to be morally right. You have called on us to protect religious freedoms and to respect one another. Your instructions call on us to check our piety and to be mindful of what is morally right, and justifiable. Help us Lord, to be a kind and forgiving people. Your son, Jesus Christ was a great teacher. His words and deeds demonstrate how people are to be: generous, loving and yes accepting. We pray for those who use their "faith" to harm others, to governments who insist on extinguishing faiths that are incompatible with those in power. Melt the cold hearts of those who claim to be acting according to your teaching, when really they are not following your teachings at all. Lord, there is room for everyone regardless of faith, skin color, gender or sexual orientation. May we set aside prejudices and learn to live in a way that honors and pleases you. I pray this day for the parents and children who have been separated by a leader whose head and heart seem to have forgotten your son's teachings. Be with each one, parents and children, and help them to be strong and safe until our leaders set aside the politics that were the impetuous for such intolerance. May our nation seek a merciful solution that will find parents and children reunited. Holy God, be with us as we work to follow your teachings, we pray your words and love for each one, will live in our hearts and minds. Be with us and save us, I pray in your name. Amen.

MATTHEW 5:1, 10-12

When Jesus saw the crowds, he went up the mountain; and after he sat down, his disciples came to him. Then he began to speak, and taught them saying: Blessed are the peacemakers, for they will be called children of God. Blessed are those who are persecuted for righteousness' sake, for theirs is the kingdom of heaven. Blessed are you when people revile you and persecute you and utter all kinds of evil against you falsely on my account.
Rejoice and be glad, for your reward is great in heaven, for in the same way they persecuted the prophets who were before you.

God, your teachings to the disciples were clear. You want "peacemakers" to carry out the basic tenets of Christianity. What a "tall order" for the times, then and now. I give thanks for those who have carried out your vision through the ages. Currently, our nation is in "disarray" which is causing discussion and rift between friends and family, as well as within our government. I am praying for a peaceful resolution to our differences, may the leaders try compromising. I pray that certain "rights" granted to citizens and those who are seeking political asylum be found quickly. There are children of varying ages: toddlers to high school aged who have been separated from their parents or family members. They may be forever scarred by the separation and lack of compassionate guards that are unable to communicate and care for them. The executive branch of our government created this problem without provocation, and has not stepped up to help them, Lord I pray that you will be with the persecuted minors and adults and that you will soften the hardened hearts of those who have caused this travesty. I pray for the legislative branch to find a common ground on which the migrant issues can be addressed and resolved. Be with them as they fight against any one solution. Our nation is counting on leaders to do the right thing for the persecuted who fled their home country in order to escape certain death. Be with the peacemakers and grant them the courage to "do the right thing" for the children and parents or guardians. A former President once said, "Mr. Gorbachev, tear down that wall." Shouldn't the President realize that a wall is not the answer? May our leaders come together to have an honest and spirited debate regarding those "imprisoned" for fleeing a regime that threatened their lives? At the end of the day, soften the hardened hearts, and Lord, I pray they will together resolve the issues that are tearing apart our democracy. The immigrants who stumbled into "the land of the free and the home of the brave," are counting on us. May it be so. Amen.

MAY 5

ACTS 2:24-25, 32-33

But God raised him up, having freed him from death, because it was impossible for him to be held in its power. For David says concerning him,

I saw the Lord always before me,
for he is at my right hand so that I will not be shaken.

This Jesus, God raised up, and of that all of us are witnesses.

Being therefore exalted at the right had of God and having received from the Father the promise of the Holy Spirit, he has poured out this that you both see and hear.

Lord God, the promise you made to your son, Jesus was truly amazing. You placed him at your right hand reassuring him by saying "until I make your enemies your footstool", thus making Jesus both Lord and Messiah. Peter, a beloved disciple told those around him they needed to "repent, and be baptized in the name of Jesus Christ." The promise made was not only for those gathered, but for all who are yet to be born. Lord God, thank you for those first converts and your promise to forgive our sins, and to save them and us from a corrupt generation. Help us Lord, to live a life according to your teachings. May our lives be pleasing to you. Be with those who are sick and dying and also with those caregivers, loved ones, who mourn. Please, Lord, help us all to be people of faith. Lord there are so many who are suffering, physically, emotionally and economically, please comfort them. I pray for the forgiveness of sin, and to receive your holy blessings. Amen.

LUKE 20:30-31

Now Jesus did many other signs in the presence of his disciples, which are not written in this book. But these are written so that you may come to believe that Jesus is the Messiah, the son of God, and that through believing you may have life in his name.

———————————

Omnipresent God, how mighty is your power and love! I give thanks for your son, Jesus Christ, who following your instructions provided a way that today, all might learn of you through the deeds and words Jesus spoke. He showed love and compassion and also his strength and determination and at times anger or impatience. Because of Jesus, I have learned that what is done in his name, your name is the way to live my life. I have learned about advocacy for what Jesus called "the least of these" and Lord, I am so thankful to look beyond myself to see the needs of others. I pray that my walk through this life will be pleasing in your sight. I have felt you with me when I felt I was alone. Be with those who have yet to learn of your teachings and your love. Help all who are struggling to reach out for services that can change their lives and keep them safe. Be with those who are sick and facing the day when you shall call them home. Bring comfort to the families and friends who are suffering a loss. Be with us each day and save us, I pray in your name, Lord God. Amen.

MAY 7

ISAIAH 55:1-3
AN INVITATION TO ABUNDANT LIFE

Ho, everyone who thirsts, come to the waters; and you who have no money, come, by and eat! Come, buy wine and milk without money and without price.
Why do you spend your money for that which is good, and delight yourselves in rich food. Incline your ear, and come to me; listen, so that you may live. I will make you and everlasting covenant, my steadfast, sure love for David,

---

Lord God, your invitation to all the people is to have abundant life from the everlasting covenant. I pray that your people who are perhaps unsure of their faith take time to see your glory. May those who put their trust in you, demonstrate ways that are pleasing to you that their ways may help those who are searching for you, find you. May they Help me, Lord to live a life that praises you. Be with those who have suffered loss; for the family of Kishore Carey and Rachel Held Evans may you bring peace. I pray you are with them as you welcome these two who have recently passed. Comfort all who are mourning and give them comfort in the sure knowledge that their loved ones are with you. As you shine on me, may the sunshine this morning bring more light and life for those who have accepted your invitation to abundant life. Be with us this day and every day, forgive our sins and save us. I pray. Amen.

MAY 8

JEREMIAH 8:4-6
THE LORD'S DISPLEASURE
WITH THE NATION

When people fall, do they not get up again? If they go astray, do they not turn back? Why then have these people turned away in perpetual backsliding? They have held fast to deceit, they have refused to return. I have given heed and listened, but they do not seek honestly; no one repents of wickedness, saying, "What have I done!" All of them turn to their own course..."

Loving God, your displeasure with the nation of Israel, for they refused to return to you was clear. I read your words and know how incredulous you became when the nation began to backslide into old habits. You expect that when we fall down, we will get back up. Your will is that we will learn from our mistakes. Your will is that everyone, no matter their position, will cease stepping on or over others for personal gain. Rather you expect that we will learn from our mistakes. I pray Lord, that when I ask for forgiveness of sin, that I will make an honest attempt to keep my promise to you. Values or accepted norms of leading a proper life will help me to be true to my words. These values came directly from you, the 10 Commandments are clear about your expectations and how your children are to live. Just as we pick up toddlers when they fall, you will pick us up when we fail and learn from our transgressions. In the name of your son, Jesus Christ who gave his life on the cross that we might be saved for our sins. Amen.

PROVERBS. 15:1, 4

A soft answer turns away wrath, but a harsh word stirs up anger.
A gentle tongue is a tree of life, but perverseness breaks the spirit.

All knowing Lord, the world seems to be spinning out of control. Every day our news cycles are filled with people fighting with each other and getting nowhere, but angry. Please help our nation's leaders learn to listen to one another and seek solutions for the common good, especially for the leaders who cannot decide on a policy to save lives. Another life has been lost by a shooter's well-placed aim, others injured and yet no solution to take guns off the streets is forthcoming. I pray that a plan to address the problem with assault weapons being sold in our land to "hunters' ' be stopped. I pray for peaceful solutions for people who are unable to act rationally against perceived foes. One loss is too many and yet the numbers grow all too quickly and more school-age children, teachers, administrators and volunteers fall victim to an assassin's gun. Lord be with those dealing with their senseless loss.

And Lord, our community is being assaulted by those who do not tolerate people of differing religious practices, skin color, etc. Help us find a way to celebrate our differences and turn away harmful acts by the prejudices of those who are defaming houses of worship and graffiti spread throughout neighborhoods. Today, I especially pray for one of the most perverse actions, there are those who lure or kidnap females into sex trafficking. The problem is great and the help needed is underfunded and rarely discussed. Be with the females who have been trafficked, keep them safe and help them to get away from their "handlers." Lord God, I know through you, all things are possible and I just pray you will help us with these problems. Please be with us and save us as we continue to work to eradicate the problems of violence and sex trafficking, in your name, I pray. Amen

*Blessed are those who hunger and thirst for righteousness'
for they will be filled.*

MATTHEW 5:1-3

*When Jesus saw the crowds, he went up the mountain, and
after he sat down, his disciples came to him. Then he began
to speak, and taught them saying:*

*Blessed are the poor in spirit, for theirs is the kingdom of
heaven.*
Blessed are those who mourn, for they will be comforted.

Lord, what a blessing you gave the world, your beloved son, Jesus
Christ. He embraced the purpose and why you created him.
Jesus' disciples, and all who were with him, those who were bold
enough to follow, received Jesus' words of instruction for the living
of one's life. In essence, Jesus fulfilled your expectations, his teaching
ministry succinctly proclaimed what characteristics and behaviors
are expected, if one is to be given eternal life. Your gift of Jesus to
the people gives all hope for all of our days. Thank you loving God
for teaching us how to live a blessed life. Spiritually the disciples
and followers had much to learn, your people have much to learn,
too. Jesus more than fulfilled that purpose. He made certain his
disciples and those who joined in, believed in him, and they would
also come to know the "kingdom of heaven". The first goal for all
believers then and now is to recognize and accept God as King. Be
with each of us on our unique journeys accepting God as our King,
our Savior. Amen.

MAY 11

MATTHEW 5:1

Blessed are those who mourn, for they will be comforted.

Lord God I give praise and thanks for sending your son, to "take away the sins of the world." Jesus showed believers the way to receive eternal life. One must become free from sadness over sin in order to receive forgiveness and to have life eternal. Please Lord, forgive my sins and save me. I pray so that one day I too may have everlasting life, joining those who have gone before me. In the blessed name of your son, Jesus Christ, I pray. Amen

MATTHEW 5:5-6

Blessed are the meek, for they shall inherit the earth.
Blessed are those who hunger and thirst for righteousness'
for they will be filled.

———————————

Lord, your son speaks of qualities that are pleasing to you. I humbly pray each day as Jesus commanded, as people with a penchant for kindness and humility. Being meek, we understand You have high expectations. Jesus taught us to follow our hearts, living lives following your commandments. Lord, may our words and deeds seek to be an outward reflection of one who is humble, one who has an awareness of spirituality. Jesus teaches us that the meek are not prideful nor boastful. Lord God, I pray when your judgement comes, the inner peace in my heart will be pleasing to you.

God, you have commanded those who hunger and thirst for righteousness' sake will be filled. You are patient. Lord, help us realize our desire to follow Jesus' teachings by having a hunger and thirst to follow. You expect righteousness will be a "work in progress" throughout our entire lives. Just as we need food and water to survive, we also need to nourish our souls. Holy God, you provide righteousness to all who follow your words. I pray that I will nourish my soul, learning and sharing that faith each day. I pray you will forgive my sins and save me, in the name of Jesus I pray. Amen.

MAY 13

MATTHEW 5:7

Blessed are the merciful, for they will receive mercy.
Blessed are the pure in heart, for they will see God.

Holy Lord, your mercy is never ending. Thank you for the way you have shown me kindness, sitting in the pews, no one there knew, but you knew and you gave me courage to accept the things that I could not change. Not only that, but Lord, your compassion told me that I am never alone, for you are with me always. You simply ask us to help those who are in need from life's realities that make victims feel alone. Your mercy to those who are sick is a demonstration of your power and love. Help your children learn how to be kind to others, especially those who may be brutalized or bullied. Help all remember your gifts of mercy and grace which we receive from you.

Lord God, the commandment to bless the pure in heart is the essence of how believers are welcomed into your house, forever. Your teachings are clear, to have a pure heart, one must follow the path that you set for them, for us is an outward demonstration of what you expect. Holy God, your amazing grace in the community of believers throughout the world is humbling. Be with your flock, blessing each one as they seek forgiveness for their sins. Comfort them as they learn what it means to be merciful and pure in heart. I pray in your holy and sacred name, Lord, be with me, forgive my sins and save me, I pray. Amen.

MAY 14

MATTHEW 5:9-12

Blessed are the peacemakers, for they will be called the children of God.
Blessed are those who are persecuted for righteousness' sake, for theirs is the kingdom of heaven.
Blessed are you when people revile you and persecute you and utter all kinds of evil against you falsely on my account.
Rejoice and be glad, for your reward is great in heaven, for in the same way they persecuted the prophets who were before you.

L oving God, I know when one struggles with faith, you expect that person to lean into what the Bible has to say. The Beatitudes recenter me and provide me an outlet for my struggle. I am blessed to be able to share your words and my thoughts through Bible study and prayer. I am focused on the lessons of the Bible, Lord as a way to share what you had to say about how to lead a life with values and virtue. Today's world finds "peacemakers" struggling with differing opinions about what is"right `` and"just." The words, your words, help me to be what my faith is calling me to be, by helping others find inner peace. Your unconditional love affirms my faith and beliefs. Peaceful congregations and protestations help those who are being persecuted for righteousness' sake find a way to have their voices heard. There is such "intolerance" in the world which is often hurtful and violent. Help me to be more mindful of your words and how to help people who cannot speak for themselves. I pray especially for the young females snared into human trafficking. I pray in Jesus' name that these young women will be freed. My prayer is for others, that they might come to know you, love you, and lead a life following your values. Forgive our sins, give us the peace and grace to follow your teachings all of our days. Amen.

MAY 15

PSALM 18:1-3

I love you, O Lord, my strength . The Lord is my rock and my fortress and my deliverer, my God, my rock, in whom I take refuge, my horn and the shield, and the horn of my salvation, my stronghold. I will call upon the Lord, who is worthy to be praised.

Dear Prayer Partners,

I was sent the following story from a friend who thought I would be moved by it. I've been praying for a time to share it, and just following prayers of praise to the risen Lord, I feel today is the day. Peace, Love and Joy,

Marcia

From: "The Daily Encourager"
    <thedailyencourager@harrisburgonline.org>

Subject: The Empty Egg
Reply-To: thedailyencourager@harrisburgonline.org

The Empty Egg

Jeremy was born with a twisted body and a slow mind. At the age of 12, he was still in second grade, seemingly unable to learn. His teacher, Doris Miller, often became exasperated with him. He would squirm in his seat, drool, and make grunting noises. At other times, he spoke clearly and distinctly, as if a spot of light had penetrated the darkness of his brain. Most of the time, however, Jeremy just irritated his teacher.

One day she called his parents and asked them to come in for a consultation. As the Forresters entered the empty classroom, Doris said to them, "Jeremy really belongs in a special school. It isn't fair to him to be with younger children who don't have learning problems. Why, there is a five year gap between his age and that of the other students."

Mrs. Forrester cried softly into a tissue, while her husband spoke. "Miss Miller," he said, "there is no school of that kind nearby. It would be a terrible shock for Jeremy if we had to take him out of this school. We know he really likes it here." Doris sat for a long time after they had left, staring at the snow outside the window. Its coldness seemed to seep into her soul. She wanted to sympathize with the Forresters. After all, their only child had a terminal illness.

But it wasn't fair to keep him in her class. She had 18 other youngsters to teach, and Jeremy was a distraction. Furthermore, he would never learn to read and write. Why waste any more time trying?

As she pondered the situation, guilt washed over her. Here I am complaining when my problems are nothing compared to that poor family, she thought. Lord, please help me to be more patient with Jeremy.

From that day on, she tried hard to ignore Jeremy's noises and his blank stares. Then one day, he limped to her desk, dragging his bad leg behind him.

"I love you, Miss Miller," he exclaimed, loud enough for the whole class to hear. The other students snickered, and Doris' face turned red. She stammered, "Wh-why that's very nice, Jeremy. N-now please take your seat."

Spring came, and the children talked excitedly about the coming of Easter. Doris told them the story of Jesus, and then to emphasize the idea of new life springing forth, she gave each of the children a large plastic egg. "Now," she said to them, "I want you to take this home and bring it back tomorrow with something inside that shows new life. Do you understand?"

"Yes, Miss Miller," the children responded enthusiastically - all except for Jeremy. He listened intently; his eyes never left her face. He did not even make his usual noises. Had he understood what she had said about Jesus' death and resurrection? Did he understand the assignment? Perhaps she should call his parents and explain the project to them.

That evening, Doris' kitchen sink stopped up. She called the landlord and waited an hour for him to come by and unclog it. After that, she still had to shop for groceries, iron a blouse, and prepare a vocabulary test for the next day. She completely forgot about phoning Jeremy's parents.

The next morning, 19 children came to school, laughing and talking as they placed their eggs in the large wicker basket on Miss Miller's desk. After they completed their math lesson, it was time to open the eggs. In the first egg, Doris found a flower. "Oh yes, a flower is certainly a sign of new life," she said. "When plants peek through the ground, we know that spring is here." A small girl in the first row waved her arm. "That's my egg, Miss Miller," she called out.

The next egg contained a plastic butterfly, which looked very real. Doris held it up. "We all know that a caterpillar changes and grows into a beautiful butterfly. Yes, that's new life, too." Little Judy smiled proudly and said, "Miss Miller, that one is mine."

Next, Doris found a rock with moss on it. She explained that moss, too, showed life. Billy spoke up from the back of the classroom, "My daddy helped me," he beamed.

Then Doris opened the fourth egg. She gasped. The egg was empty. Surely it must be Jeremy's, she thought, and of course, he did not understand her instructions. If only she had not forgotten to phone his parents. Because she did not want to embarrass him, she quietly set the egg aside and reached for another. Suddenly, Jeremy spoke up. "Miss Miller, aren't you going to talk about my egg?"

Flustered, Doris replied, "But Jeremy, your egg is empty." He looked into her eyes and said softly, "Yes, but Jesus' tomb was empty, too."

Time stopped. When she could speak again, Doris asked him, "Do you know why the tomb was empty?" "Oh, yes," Jeremy said, "Jesus was killed and put in there. Then His Father raised Him up."

The recess bell rang. While the children excitedly ran out to the schoolyard, Doris cried. The cold inside her melted completely away.

Three months later, Jeremy died. Those who paid their respects at the funeral home were surprised to see 19 eggs on top of his casket, all of them empty.

Lord, thank you for all of the "Jeremys". I pray this message will give hope to those who may feel hopeless. Help them and all who learn of these stories to feel renewed in the spirit of the empty tomb and our response. I will praise Jesus. Amen

To receive The Daily Encourager FREE each weekday, click on the following link: http://go.netatlantic.com/read/all_forums/subscribe?name=thedailyencourager

MAY 16

PROVERBS 2:1-5
THE VALUE OF WISDOM

My child, if you accept my words and treasure up my commandments within you, making your ear attentive to wisdom and inclining your heart to understanding: if you indeed cry out for insight, and raise your voice for understanding; If you seek it like silver, and search for it as for hidden treasures—then you will understand the fear of the Lord and find the knowledge of God.

All knowing God, I pray seeking to find relevance in today's world. Thank you for providing insight into concerns one might have. I have wanted to find a way to learn more about you, to have inner peace, to have time each day to pause, to find ways to foster learning, and embrace your purpose for me. Have we not learned anything? Lord God, it continues to baffle me how cruel the world was in Jesus' time and now. Jesus taught us to seek your love and to accept your grace. The relevance of "In God we Trust", is challenged by governments who embrace the separation of church and state to the detriment of learning and living one's faith. I pray, Church and State will move forward with your love in their hearts. Help leaders all over the world make wise decisions, remembering that no matter the religion, following you in thought, word, and deed is paramount. Help us peacefully speak our truths, loving our neighbor and helping those whose life is a daily struggle. Be with us this day and save us Lord God, in the name of the Risen Son. Amen.

MAY 17

DEUTERONOMY 28:1-3
BLESSINGS FOR OBEDIENCE

If you will only obey the Lord your God, by diligently observing all his commandments that I am commanding you today, the Lord your God will set you high above all the nations of the earth; all these blessings shall come upon you and overtake you, if you obey the Lord your God: Blessed shall you be in the city and blessed shall you be in the field.

Teacher, thank you for your servant, Moses. He was faithful to you and your teachings. Moses might have been a bit frustrated to have to constantly remind the Israelites what was expected of them prior to entering into the Promised Land of Canaan. And yet Moses remained faithful. Lord God, in today's world, some find difficulty in embracing your words, deeds and love. I pray for all who want to know and follow your teachings. Be with those who are teachers of the Word. Be with all of your children each day as they live out their faith as an example for those around them to see what loving you means. Your spirit is at work in our lives and may we be reminded of that when we are faced with challenges that seem hopeless. I am so grateful that your Spirit found me and has continued to lift me up when I have felt lost. I am honored to have found a way to share a faith that you have given to me. I pray for all who seek you, may they find you and that each one will find the courage to face their tomorrows and any barriers in their paths. Be with us Lord, receive our petitions of sin and forgive us, I pray in the name of your beloved son, Jesus Christ. Amen.

MAY 18

Selah - Into My Heart/Fairest Lord Jesus ~ With Lyrics
https://youtu.be/XBR0QpQYKdw

MATTHEW 5:17-20
THE LAW OF THE PROPHETS

"Do not think that I have come to abolish the law or the prophets; I have come not to abolish but to fulfill. For truly I tell you, until heaven and earth pass away, not one letter, not one stroke of a letter will pass from the law until all is accomplished. Therefore, one who breaks one of the least of these commandments, and teaches others to do the same, will be called least in the kingdom of heaven; but to whoever does them and teaches them will be called great in the kingdom of heaven. For I tell you, unless your righteousness exceeds that of the scribes and Pharisees, you will never enter the kingdom of heaven."

Fairest Lord Jesus, all honor and praise to you for following the teachings of your father in heaven. Your faith and teachings honor not only God, but also the law of the prophets. Sometimes it is challenging to embrace change. You, Lord God made acceptance of the prophecies live in today's world. Your son, Jesus Christ was the perfect foil to bring the teachings of the Old Testament into today. So, God, what I love is when Your people embrace you with certainty. Jesus brings your words into my heart and soul, therefore what was old, is now a melding of the essential tenants for all to live by, for me to follow. Please Lord, help those who do not know you, or perhaps have lost their way, to carry their faith for all of their days. I give thanks for the lives of those who have gone home to you, in the sure knowledge of their love and life devoted to you. Knowing that they are with you in Heaven warms my heart and helps me have joy, that one day I will be together with you and them. I ask that you forgive my sins, and help me find grace. Be with those who are ill and who have special needs. Be with them and all your people, I pray in your holy name. Amen.

MAY 19

REVELATION:21:1-6

Then I saw a new heaven and a new earth; for the first heaven and the first earth had passed away, and the sea was no more. And I saw the holy city, the new Jerusalem, coming down out of the heaven from God, prepared as if a bride adorned for her husband. And I heard a loud voice from the throne saying, "See the home of God is among mortals. "See the home of God is among mortals. He will dwell with them; they will be his peoples, and God himself will be with them; he will wipe every tear from their eyes. Death will be no more; mourning and crying and pain will be no more, for the first things have passed away."And the one who was seated on the throne said, "See, I am making all things new." Also he said; "Write this, for these words are trustworthy and true." Then he said to me, "It is done! I am the Alpha and the Omega, the beginning thirsty I will give water as a gift from the spring of the water of life."

Dear Lord, thank you for John, one of the twelve apostles of Jesus. John's message in Revelation was one of hope and newness. Thank you for the clarity you gave John, who wrote of a new heaven where you and your son live. We also learn of your creation of a new earth. Your gift fulfilled the prophecy in the Old Testament and clarifies the gift of a new earth, filled with hope for your people. Your gift Lord God was better than good, it was amazing! I pray today for your gift to generations and for the hope we enjoy because of you. It is that hope, Creator God we cling as earthly people try to live a peaceful and faith-filled life. Be with those who are finding life difficult, shine your love on them. I pray for those who have broken lives and families, help them to find peace and joy. Strengthen those whose faith is tested, be with the sick and those who have lost a loved one. May your light of love be with all. Be with us and save us, in your name I pray. Amen.

MAY 20

JOHN 6:63-65

It is the spirit that gives life; the flesh is useless. "The words that I have spoken to you are spirit and life. But among you there are some who do not believe." For Jesus knew from the first who were the ones that did not believe, and who was the one that would betray him. And he said, "For this reason I have told you that no one can come to me unless it is granted by the Father."

Holy creator, sometimes I wonder why people spend enormous amounts of money tending to their outer shell, their skin. The message from Jesus is all about the spirit, the life-giving affirmation of what is unseen. Seeking 'perfection' on the outside, while perhaps putting my 'best foot forward' would be nothing without my soul, filled with love for you and faith freely given to me and to all who desire it. Thank you for the gift of the Holy Spirit, Lord God. Thank you for helping me use my voice in prayer and praise of all the ways you have carried me through life. I pray for each one to be comforted and uplifted and for some, to learn to love and trust in you, again. Be with me and save me, in your name I pray. Amen.

MAY 21

JOHN 8:12-13, 15

Again Jesus spoke to them saying, "I am the light of the world. Whoever follows me will never walk in darkness but will have the light of life."..."My testimony is valid because I know where I have come from and where I am going, but you do not know where I have come from and where I am going, but you do not know where I come from or where I am going. You judge by human standards; I judge no one."

———————————

Loving and patient God, I give you praise and glory for your son who shines the light on whoever follows him. He gave me hope, when I was losing mine. Your watchful grace has been a comfort not only to me, but to countless others. Jesus speaks of one of humankind's flaws, that of judging others based on human standards. Jesus judges no one. The message Jesus spoke was He is the light of the world, He and he alone is the spiritual light for those who demonstrate their good works for others. Humans reflect the light of Jesus Christ, allowing others to see Jesus' light in us. Our good deeds are performed in faith and through the power of the Holy Spirit. Help me Lord and all people who seek to shine the light of goodness on others, that they might be saved when they come into your light. Be with us this day and save us, I pray. Amen.

MATTHEW 6:33-34 DO NOT WORRY

"Strive first for the kingdom of God and his righteousness, and all things will be given to you as well. So do not worry about tomorrow for tomorrow will bring worries of its own. Today's trouble is enough for today.

Gracious and loving God, help me bring the issues weighing heavily on my heart to you, on the front end of worry. I know I should turn to you first with my worries or concerns, and yet I find myself trying to "fix it" on my own. Today Lord, I am making a deliberate attempt to hand off the things that I need help with or that I cannot change. I often feel overwhelmed and frankly, lost over issues weighing heavily on my heart and mind. Friends are worrying and I feel their pain as well. Help us all to turn to you and give up our worries. It is easier said than done, Lord. There is a peace that passes all understanding when we bring our concerns to you, and yet, when life complicates our "normal" ways, it is hard to give our pain away. We struggle and feel guilty about things we are powerless to change. Be with those who are worried, no matter what the issue. Help the troubled find their way to you, be with them as they struggle for meaning and understanding, please keep them safe. Be with the sick and grieving. Lord, please help the "lost" ones who are contemplating taking steps to harm themselves. Help those who are contemplating ending their lives. Be with and comfort those who are terminally ill. Help the caregivers and professionals to ease the pain and suffering of the patient and his/her loved ones. It is such a stressful time, knowing a loved one's days on earth are numbered, making it hard not to worry. In all instances, Lord, I pray we might set aside the things that we cannot change and give courage and help to those in need. Be with us all, and save us, I pray in your name, Amen.

ECCLESIASTES 1:13, 11:5-6
THE FUTILITY OF SEEKING WISDOM

The Value Of Diligence

I applied my mind to seek and to search out by wisdom all that is done under heaven: it is an unhappy business that God has given to human beings to be busy with.

Just as you know how the breath comes to the bones in the mother's womb, so you do not know the work of God, who makes everything. In the morning sow your seed, and at evening do not let your hands be idle; for you do not know which will prosper, this or that, or whether both alike will be good.

Holy Provider, God, there are limitations to what we can understand, we do not know how or why you center the universe. Knowledge is a component of those limitations when it comes to the faith. We do not know particular ways in which you, Lord God, miraculously work on this planet. People cannot predict specific outcomes, therefore, determining results is not possible. Today, Lord, we learn that there will be "dangerous weather" but we do not know the specifics of exactly where or even if the tornados will touch down, what buildings will be ruined nor whose life will be ended because of the storm. We do not know everything, and that lack of knowledge is humbling. I pray, All-knowing God that you will sharpen our minds so that we might be open to what has been written in the Bible, your Holy book and that our "blind" faith in you will sustain us. I pray for all who may be impacted by today's storms, may their lives be spared. Give us patience as we attempt to discern the meaning of the scriptures. May the words of the wise, written in the Holy Bible guide our ways. Be with us this day, forgive our sins and please help us to do works that are pleasing to you. Amen.

ISAIAH 6:3-5
A VISION OF GOD IN THE TEMPLE

....."Holy, holy, holy is the Lord of hosts, the whole earth is full of his glory.

The pivots on the thresholds shook at the voices of those who called and the house filled with smoke. And I said, "Woe is me! I am lost, for I am a man of unclean lips, and I live among a people of unclean lips; yet my eyes have seen the King, the Lord of hosts!"

———————————

Heavenly Lord, your servant, Isaiah tells of a 'God moment." Isaiah saw you and was quick to proclaim your 'glory'. I have heard from people who have experienced a "God moment." They tell me, the moment came at a time of great stress and that you, caring Lord, came to them and reassured them. Others report "God moments" at times when one feared an illness would be fatal, and God spoke saying, "its not your time." I give thanks to you, Lord God. You have shown how you want us to speak and live our lives, and you show your love and compassion when it was needed it most. I pray for all to live their lives serving you and helping humankind. May we use personal "God moments" and share them in loving ways, in service of those who need comfort and assistance. May we seek to serve those in need by loving and supporting them and their petitions for help. I pray our actions will help the needy and glorify your holy name. Amen.

MAY 25

CORINTHIANS 9:11-13

If we have sown spiritual good among you, is it too much if we reap your material benefits? If others share this rightful claim with you, do not we still more?

Nevertheless, we have not made use of this right, but we endure anything rather than put an obstacle in the way of the gospel of Christ. Do you not know that those who are employed in the temple service get their food from the temple, and those who serve at the altar share in what is sacrificed on the altar. In the same way, the Lord commanded that those who proclaim the gospel should get their living by the gospel.

Generous provider, your expectation for believers is to lead by example. At an early age I felt "the call to serve." The parallel life I lived through my profession and my faith in you, led me to teach and to be faithful to your expectations of me. Sometimes, I certainly did not realize it was a "calling," but I know that now. The "service" to the many I taught also enhanced my faith in you. I give thanks to all who lead lives in service to you and their unique professional choices. When our professional lives meet the needs being served and build up the "body of Christ" a powerful combination exists. I give thanks to all whose work and faith impacts others in significant ways. The glory of the work we do to help others while living out our faith is rewarding. Thank you Lord God, for steering me and other Christians into serving you as well as our fellow humans. Be with your servants who live and work by their faith in you. Be with us each day and save us, I ask in the name of your son, Jesus Christ. Amen.

ACTS 16:11-15

We set sail from Troas and took a straight course to Samothrace, the following day to Napoli's, and from to Philippi, which is a leading city of the district of Macedonia and a Roman colony. We remained in this city for some days. On the sabbath day we went outside the gate by the river, where we supposed there was a place of prayer; and we sat down and spoke to the women who had gathered. A certain woman named Lydia, a worshipper of God, was listening to us; she was from the city of Thyatira and a dealer in purple cloth. The Lord opened her ear to listen eagerly to what was being said by Paul. When she and her household were baptized, she urged us, saying, "If you have judged me to be faithful to the Lord, come and stay at my home." And she prevailed upon us.

Holy Lord of all, thank you for showing how you led "your people" in such a way that they were able to accomplish all you required. Jesus gave the command to go into the world, making disciples, baptizing, and teaching. Lydia listened to what Paul had to say, realizing that baptism is a holy sacrament. As a faithful person to you Lord, Lydia opened her home. Lord, throughout time, I have heard stories of other Lydias and how their hearts were softened and how they opened hearts and minds to you Lord. I pray their stories of you and your son may bring a calming peace and abiding faith. Be with those who do not yet know you. Help Christians set an example in the places they live of your messages of faith and hope for all of our tomorrows. May we live in service to all of Jesus' teachings, and help others to turn toward you. Be with those who are suffering in the world, show them a way to move forward, recovering from whatever malady or disaster may have touched their lives and shaken their faith. May the Lydias give strength and courage to spread the good news that your son, our savior lives within each of us. Be with us and save us, I pray. Amen.

MAY 27

ISAIAH 66:12-13

For this is what the LORD says: "I will extend peace to her like a river, and the wealth of nations like a flooding stream; you will nurse and be carried on her arm and dandled on her knees. As a mother comforts her child, so will I comfort you; and you will be comforted over Jerusalem."

God of the heavens and earth, I am learning the piano which is another way to focus on my faith. This week the song is "Peace Like A River" and the song is in my head and in my heart. As I practice, it calms me. When the practice is over, I realize my mind is perplexed and fearful. I watched a beautiful Memorial Day tribute to honor all who served in any capacity in the United States military. Scenes at Arlington National Cemetery, Lord broke my heart and at the same time I saw hope for those that were bowing in reverence for a lost loved one. Their mourning formed a bond with others who also had a loved one buried in Arlington. The reverence and love the entire evening was juxtaposed by our national reality. I pray for all who have served and are serving and for those who may be called into service. I pray that our government will lower the volume on the discussion about sending our troops into harm's way. Be with our executive and legislative branches, I pray you will help them see peace like a river, is much preferred to the loss of lives whose river is bloody. Comfort those caught and held in cages on our southern border and may they be returned to their parents. Be with us all as we travel and seek comfort with loved ones and save Us, I pray in the name of Jesus Christ. Amen.

I saw the following prayer for Memorial Day and thought I would use it instead of writing my own. My heart was called to prayer. This is also a beautiful one that was in Presbyterian USA Outlook.

———————————

Lord God, until there is war no more and you wipe every tear from every eye, we will remember. We will remember those who have served and died for the sake of something greater than themselves. We will remember and give thanks for the men and women who knowingly put themselves in harm's way so that others might be safer. We will remember the families who grieve this day and every day for brothers and sisters, mothers and fathers, daughters and sons, friends and spouses, who lost their lives while wearing the uniform of our country.

Lord God, until you beat swords into plowshares and the ox and lamb lie down together, we will remember. We will remember that peace doesn't happen without peacemakers and violence won't cease unless we stand in the breach and begin to repair it. We will remember that war is costly, the price paid in priceless lives cut short.

Lord God, until the Prince of Peace returns and death and crying are no more, we will remember. We will remember those who made the ultimate sacrifice in service of their country. We will support those left bereft in their absence. We will remember to seek reconciliation, knowing that while we cannot control the ways of the world, we can seek to work for peace in our own lives and communities.

Lord God, until there is no need for men and women to place themselves in harm's way, we will remember and give thanks for those who did and died.

In the name of the One who grants us the peace that passes understanding, we pray. Amen.

– by Jill Duffield

MAY 29
ACTS 16:16-18

One day, as we were going to the place of prayer, we met a slave girl who had a spirit of divination and brought her owners a great deal of money by fortune-telling. While she followed Paul and us, she would cry out, "These men are slaves of the Most High God, who proclaim to you a way of salvation." She kept doing this for many days. Put Paul, very much annoyed, turned and said to the spirit, "I order you in the name of Jesus Christ to come out of her." And it came out that very hour.

Heavenly God, how often do slaves serve their masters evil ways? Do they do their owner's will out of fear of repercussions? What happens to slaves when they disobey? The strange thing is her words had an air of truth. And yet as a petulant child the slave repeats and repeats things any parent would find themselves responding harshly to such an annoyance. Paul knew this slave was not speaking with knowledge, she was "possessed." The spirit coming out of this "girl" who was earning money fortune-telling was a demon. The evilness of her owners had planted the hoax for the sole purpose of their own profit. Gracious Lord, help us to listen and follow your teachings. Help all who seek to serve you, no matter where that place may be. Be with each of us as we go about our days, serving and praising you. I pray you will forgive our sins and save us, I pray in your holy name. Amen.

MATTHEW 11:28

"Come to me, all you who are weary and burdened, and I will give you rest."

Loving God, the "simple truth" that Matthew got, is one that is oftentimes is not the upper most thought in my mind, if I am anxious or worried. Your servant Matthew reminds all of us that you will ease my tiredness and what worry is on my mind or in my heart. Thank you Lord, for calming my fitful sleep and racing mind, so that I may rest. Sometimes when I am too busy, I let the cares of the day interrupt my sleep and prayers to you. Thank you for bringing calmness, so that I might sleep. Lord others are suffering, too. Be with them and with your gentle and loving way remind them that you will give them rest. I pray this day for all who are in harm's way from fierce storms, tornados and other 'natural' disasters. Be with those who are traveling and those who are anxiously awaiting a loved one who is. Thank you God for the words of C. S. Lewis, when he wrote "God doesn't want something from us, he simply wants us." That is the essence of your teaching. Be with us this day and save us, I pray. Amen.

MAY 31

ISAIAH 1:18

The Book of Isaiah is the first of the Latter Prophets in the Hebrew Bible and the first of the Major Prophets in the Christian Old Testament.

"Come now, let's settle this," says the LORD. "Though your sins are like scarlet, I will make them as white as snow. Though they are red like crimson, I will make them as white as wool."

———————————

L ord of all, I am reading about your words in Isaiah with renewed interest. You are forgiving, Lord God. I am moved by your willingness to listen to me as I pray. We reason matters together which makes me feel closer to you. I sometimes go to sleep at night with unresolved petitions to you and when I awaken, I know that my petitions were heard and I have a sense of your will for me. I ask for forgiveness of my sins evident as the brightest of colors, and thankfully you have forgiven me. I too, shall receive your grace, the greatest gift I will ever receive. I pray today Lord God that others may come to know you and to love you. Be with those who are sick or dying, and with the hungry and homeless. Show each one the purity of your forgiveness. Be with us and save us, in your holy name I pray. Amen.

JUNE 1

2 CORINTHIANS 5:17

"Therefore if any man be in Christ, he is a new creature; old things are assed away, behold all things have become new."

H ear my prayer Lord. What a blessing the words of your servant Paul provided. Reading his words to the people is just as timely today as it was hundreds of years ago. It was such a comfort to those who have become Christians by the holy sacrament of baptism. Christians are and were able to continue their lives starting over as their sins were washed away. Through baptism, all or their sins were "washed away". What a powerful and loving message it is to know all had been forgiven and for Lord I am thankful baptism isn't the only way to start over in my walk with you! I admit Holy God things in my past I am not proud of and honestly petition your forgiveness. Each of us has the hope of new life both on earth and in heaven. By an honest petition I ask you to forgive me and you have forgiven my sin by your grace. Thank you seems like a simple word, I know you only expect me to ask and your forgiveness shall be forgiven. How amazing your grace is to me and to all who seek to live a more rld and help all of your "children" live a life pleasing to you. Be with me and all "new creatures" this day. I pray you will be with me and save me, this day and for all the days of my life. Amen.

PRAYER FOR VIRGINIA BEACH

Loving God, we defy your goodness and deny your character of kindness in the violent acts we inflict upon each other. Why, Lord, why? What drives your children to kill their colleagues and then themselves? How can we break this cycle of desperation, despair and murder? We struggle with what to do, what to say, how to help those whose lives are forever changed in an instant of senseless slaughter.

How do we heal our communities and our country so riddled with bullets that tear apart the fabric of our life together?

In this moment, all we know to do is cry out to you in lament and recommit to work tirelessly for your promised peace. Comfort those who mourn, strengthen those who minister in body, mind and spirit to those devastated by this tragedy, grant wisdom and courage to all of us who yearn for the day when swords are beaten into plowshares and all people rejoice in the abundant life you wish for the whole of your beloved creation. Amen. by Jill Duffield

JUNE 2

REVELATION 22:17

"The Spirit and the bride say, "Come." Let anyone who hears this say, "Come." Let anyone who is thirsty come. Let anyone who desires drink freely from the water of life.

Gracious and forgiving God, your open invitation to join "believers" in worship is a powerful one. All who "hunger and thirst for righteousness sake" are welcome to join the new church. Everyone, all peoples, no exceptions. And so God waits for those who do not yet know what it is to be saved, and like a wedding couple, moving forward in a new life. Those who seek a new life with you, I pray they will find an open door and a warm welcome. Sometimes, Lord, those who have lost their way, need a little more time to realize they are meant to be part of a worshipping community. You are a patient Lord, waiting for each of us. May all who seek you find their way into your house where your church instructs us on various ways Christians are meant to live. Today I pray especially for those who seem to have lost their way. Guide them back to you as they repair their lives, be with those who have been affected by natural disasters and give them hope that the "stuff" of their possessions become less important than their very life itself. Let all who seek, find you and help them start anew. I pray today that those who are too young to know you, follow and find their way to you. I pray especially for the boys and girls who have been abducted and are enslaved by deprived people. My they escape the bondage and depravity of human trafficking and re-join a society. Heal them and give them new life. Be with us and save us, I pray in the name of Jesus Christ. Amen.

JUNE 3

GALATIANS 2:20

"I have been crucified with Christ, and it is no longer I who live, but Christ lives in me. So the life I now live in the body, I live because of the faithfulness of the Son of God, who loved me and gave himself for me."

God of the universe, your servant Paul wrote powerful words of faith to those Jesus wanted him to convert to Christianity. The symbolism of using the words "I have been crucified with Christ" is the most dramatic way how Paul led this tribe to what Jesus' death on the cross means to believers. When I think of how those powerful words were received by a Jewish nation, I understand how those who have not been led to you must be perplexed. The symbolic words tell me of your plan for all humanity. I know "Christ lives in me" and the path "believers" follow is how one is made right with God. The believer is saved, by the life, death, and resurrection of Jesus. I pray for those whose walk with you is fraught with uncertainty of Paul's powerful message. Making myself "right" with you means that I have given up myself to you, Lord God. Accepting your love simplifies life in so many ways. Christians have the love of Jesus in their hearts. As Jesus was nailed to the cross, so too were the sins of the world, my sins, and the sins of all believers. Thanks be to you, Savior God. Be with us everyday as we acknowledge how special our lives are made knowing your son "loved me and gave himself for me." The resounding love Lord God, you gave to all who would hear the message, determines a "right path" for life on earth. Be with us and save us, I pray in your blessed name. Amen.

JUNE 4

1 CORINTHIANS 6:9-10

"Or do you not know that wrongdoers will not inherit the kingdom of God? Do not be deceived: Neither the sexually immoral nor idolaters nor adulterers nor men who have sex with men nor thieves nor the greedy nor drunkards nor slanderers nor swindlers will inherit the kingdom of God."

Forgiving God, the people of Corinth were faithful to your teachings. I am thankful that in today's world, many wrongdoers have attempted to corrupt the world, and "she" resisted. Sometimes Lord God, it is difficult to live in a world of "saved" peoples when the incidences of evil cross our paths so frequently. Throughout our country, unspeakable events have continued to kill and alter our way of living or peaceful coexisting, celebrating our differences. Wrongdoers assaulted the city of New York, Virginia and Pennsylvania, causing my country to be more intentional about safety. And yet, intolerant people continue to spread hateful language in an attempt to irradiate the citizenship and freedom of religion, causing in many cases more hatred and vitriol. I pray that those who are strong and use their voices and deeds for good, will prevail. Be with our leaders, local, state, and national as we work to find peaceful ways to coexist in this chaotic world. Give us strength and the courage to continue to follow your will. Be with your people and forgive us our sins, I pray in your holy name. Amen.

JUNE 5

1 CORINTHIANS 6:9, 11

"Do you not know that wrongdoers will not inherit the kingdom of God? Do not be deceived. And this is what some of you used to be. But you were washed and you were sanctified, you were justified in the name of the Lord Jesus Christ and in the Spirit of our God.

Patient Lord, forgive our sinful and stubborn ways. Please keep us on a right path to you and the Kingdom of Heaven. Lord, I have strayed and at times I am filled with remorse, even though I have asked for forgiveness. I know better, we know better and yet sometimes I feel as though my transgressions, some of them are not worthy of forgiveness. I am thankful to your calming words and your promise to believers. You were baptized and died on the cross for all who believe in you. Help me to do what you have done for me. I want to forgive myself as you have forgiven me. And Lord, help each of us to have the sensibility to be the Christians we are meant to be. Be with those who do not yet know you, or those who pray for your mercy and due to life's situations, mercy has not come. Lord, I pray for all who are in need of basic necessities: food, clean clothing, medical care and a place to call their home. Please watch over those in great need of your mercy. Melt our stubbornness and keep us on the path you have chosen for us. May your spirit ever dwell with me, forgive our sins and save us. I pray in your name. Amen.

JUNE 6

ROMANS 12:1-2

"I appeal to you therefore, brothers and sisters, to present your bodies as a living sacrifice holy, acceptable unto God, which is your spiritual worship. Do not be comforted by this world: but be transformed by the renewing of your minds, so that you may discern what is the will of God—what is good and acceptable, and perfect."

(Excerpts of the prayer written by President Franklin D. Roosevelt and delivered on the evening of D-Day, June 6, 1944.)

Almighty God: Our sons, pride of our Nation this day have set upon a mighty endeavor, a struggle to preserve our Repbulic, our religion, and our civilization and to set free a suffering h umanity. Lead them straight and true; give strength to their arms, stoutness to their hearts, steadfstness in their faith. They will need Thy blessings. Their Road will be and hard. For the enemy is strong. He may hurl back our forces. Success may not come with rushing speed, but we shall return again and again; and we know that by Thy grace, and by thy righteousness of our cause, our sons will triumph. . . .

With Thy Blessing, we shall prevail over the unholy forces of our enemy. Help us to conquer the apostles of greed and racial arrogancies. Lead us to the saving of our country, and with our sister Nations into a world unity that will spell peace a peace invulnerable to the schemings of unworthy men. And a peace that will let all of men live in freedom, reapng the just rewards of their honest toil. Thy will be done, Almighty God. Amen.

JUNE 7

COLOSSIANS 3:9-10, 12

"Do not lie to one another seeing that you have stripped off the old self with its practices and have clothed yourselves with the new self, which is being renewed in knowledge according to the image of its creator."

As God's chosen ones, holy and beloved, clothe yourselves with compassion, kindness, humility, meekness, and patience.

Lord of all, I pray this morning for all who seek to follow you, praising your servant Paul. May the seekers find you through the leadership of believers. Paul dedicated himself to teaching the supremacy of your beloved son, who died that we might live and have new life in Christ. Lord, I pray for those who tell the truth and affirm the "new ways" according to the teachings of your son. Paul's message resonates. Your people, Lord God are supposed to follow your teachings as Paul related. I ask for your help so I may harness my love for you in ways that help share the "good news" of Jesus. I pray also to be compassionate towards those who have yet to learn of your power and grace. Forgive us our sins, be with us in our daily lives and save us, I pray in your glorious name. Amen.

JUNE 8
ROMANS 12:6-8; 10

We have gifts that differ according to the grace given to us: prophecy, in proportion to the faith; ministry, in ministering; the teacher in teaching; the exporter, in exhortation; the giver in generosity; the leader, in diligence; the compassionate; in cheerfulness. Let love be genuine; hate what is evil, hold fast to what is good; love one another with mutual affection; outdo one another in showing honor.

Lord, this morning I pray for your mercies and wisdom. Your words transmitted through have such a loving tone for those who would hear them. Grace is the best gift you have given to calm worries and fears. It is sometimes hard, Lord God to "get it right all of the time" and yet, you knew a request for forgiveness would be given, thus providing a "do over". When you mention "gifts" I feel humbled and a bit embarrassed knowing there are times when I have not been as compassionate with my reactions to what others say or do. I pray for less intolerance and a more understanding demeanor. May I invest in a tempered response and do what I can to be gracious when inside I am irked. Taking the easier route, anger in situations where political and social injustice prevail. Lord, I seek to be a catalyst for change and not just another negative voice that falls on deaf ears. Be with those who are joyful and those who weep. Be with me this day and forgive my sins, I pray in your beloved and holy name. Amen.

JUNE 9

PHILIPPIANS 2:2-8

"...make my joy complete: be of the same mind. Do nothing from selfish ambition or conceit, but in humility regard others as better than yourselves. Let each of you look not to your own interests, but to the interests of others. Let the same mind be in you that was in Christ Jesus, who thought he was in the form of God, did not regard equality with God as something to be exploited, but emptied himself taking the form of a slave, being born in human likeness. And being found in human form, he humbled himself and became obedient to the point of death—even on a cross."

O Lord, I give thanks for your servant Paul. He continued to follow your laws and to emulate the teachings of your son. Help me to put others before self and to walk through life honoring your blessed son. I humbly ask you to lead me where you would have me go. I pray for those who are ill, may they find healing and comfort. Be with those who lack the means to access medical attention, I pray health professionals will go to them. Lord I especially pray for parents and their children who are separated from one another in the south. The children are receiving inhumane treatment simply because of race. The irreparable psychological harm the separation has caused is only exasperated by many being restricted in hot vans with no services that were once part of their incarceration. The government has now denied them educational and recreational services. May this new policy be reversed. I pray for those who feel despondent and need to feel your love. May we never forget the call to live a more Christ-like life. Be with us and save us, I pray. Amen.

JUNE 10
COLOSSIANS 1:9-10

"For this reason, since the day we heard it, we have not ceased praying for you and asking that you may be filled with the full knowledge of God's will and all spiritual wisdom and understanding, so that you might lead lives worthy of the Lord, fully pleasing to him, as you bear fruit in every good work and as you grow in the knowledge of God."

———————————

Praise to you, Lord most high. Your servants Paul and Epaphras brought your "good news" to Colossae in accordance with your holy word and the teachings of Jesus Christ. Paul heaped praise on the people because of their love of the heavens, God and the son, Jesus Christ. May we, Heavenly Teacher, love you and follow you and your teachings. I pray for your people throughout the world, t they might have the faith to turn to you in times of need and in times of plenty. Lord, I pray for the churches throughout the world who acknowledge you and seek to follow your teachings. Be with the houses of worship who see their numbers diminish. Show them the way to renew their efforts to meet the needs of all people and at the same time help those who do not know you to become followers. Help those who are ministers of the word and teachers of children to rekindle in each, ways to bring the promises,of life everlasting. Our world has many needs, may they be filled by the Holy Spirit and dedicated ministers, priests, teachers, and elders. Many of the holy buildings are suffering from decaying infrastructures, which is a sign that money is not flowing into the churches to help maintain the buildings and especially carry out your plan for us. Help us Heavenly God, to bring your people back into the churches, teaching, preaching, and caring for the needs of your flock. Lord, if it is your will, please help us see the houses of worship an answer to the world problem of racism. Our world has been rocked by the senseless devotion by white people to hate their brothers and sisters with skin of a different hue. Help us Lord to show love to our brothers and sisters without regard to ethnicity. Lord, I pray for all of the families who are hurting this day because of the senseless loss of life at the hands of evil prejudice. Make this world reflective of all colors, genders and faiths. It is time for arbitrary prejudices to end. Make it so, Lord. Be with us this day and every day, forgive us our sins, in your name I pray. Amen.

ROMANS 6:1-3

"What then are we to say? Should we continue in sin in order that grace may abound? By no means! How can we who died to sin go on living in it? Do you not know that all of us who have been baptized into Christ Jesus were baptized into his death?

Holy God, thank you for the life and teachings of your beloved son. Jesus lived his adult life organizing and putting into place a way for Christians to live and to be saved. His miracles, teachings, death and resurrection was for us. If I stop right there and think about what you and Jesus did for me, for you, for all who believe I get an overwhelming love for how much you loving father have for humanity. We walk in the newness of life and in the sure knowledge of your plan for me and for all believers. Our "do over" is replicated by one requirement... we must go to God in prayer and repent our sin. What a precious gift! As I think about it and how unworthy I feel, your love comforts me. Jesus would be tortured, nailed to the cross and be crucified to take away the sins of the world. Lord God, help your family of believers by making time each day to reflect on how that day was spent and to consider any words or actions that would not have been pleasing To you. May we learn from our sinful deeds and help us keep from repeating them. Sometimes it is really hard to break a bad habit, but you are right there with me, helping me to move to a life that is pleasing to you. I pray for your patience as I work on those bad habits. I know, by your loving grace, my sins will be forgiven. We must consider ourselves dead to sin and alive to God in Christ Jesus. May it be so. Amen.

Healing God, be with all who are suffering serious illness. Cancer is such a frightful word and when that word is applied to one of our children, our hearts break. Be with the parents who are waiting for a miracle and live in fear for their beloved children. And loving God, be with those whose battle ends when you call some home. I pray especially today for one, who is fighting hard to be released from disease. I pray for parents, like Rob, Dave and Paula, Sherry, Miranda, Malinda and Terry. Each has a child who has gone home to you. Lord, today I pray for those who need your healing powers. Be with all who are recovering from illnesses. I pray for your grace and love for all those mentioned and those not mentioned. Be with us, and them as we nurture, and love each one. Bless all professionals and those who care for loved ones. Comfort them and give them strength to minister to each one. In your blessed name I pray. Amen.

JUNE 12

JUDE 1:4

"For some men, who were designated for this judgment long ago, have come in by stealth; they are ungodly, turning the grace of our God into promiscuity and denying Jesus Christ, our only Master and Lord."

Lord, the words of Jude are chilling. Your teachings indicate what is just and right and how through grace we may be saved. Doubters deny your words and continue to live a life that is unacceptable. The 'ungodly' exhibit behavior that is contrary to all that is good, and just, and right. The senseless killing of black men and women has sparked an abundance of disdain for prejudice. People throughout theworld are holding peaceful protests, hoping and praying an end to systemic racism will be the outcome. Many today find such deeds as repugnant as ever, while others deny you and your teachings, as their salacious behavior continues. Denying your commandments seems to be a way of life for many. Lord God, temptation is ever-present and I pray your words and guidance will continue to inform us on what is right, just and the way to live in eternal life. I pray all men and women may seek your countenance. May each learn of your glory and find the way, the truth and the light. Christians know that your son, Jesus was crucified to take away the sins of the world. I pray all people will find their way to you, Lord God and to accept your teachings and those of your son. May believers, offer help to the petitioners who repent and seek to turn away from sin and toward your light. Be with us, loving God, and save us. I pray. Amen.

JUNE 13
LUKE 14:27

"Whoever does not carry his own cross and follow me cannot be my disciple."

———————————

Dear Lord, teacher of the Messiah, how do we begin to thank you for such a loving and unselfish gift? Through the brilliance of Your divine plan, Jesus came to us to bring a reformed church into the world. His life was not easy, but His focus was filled with a plan to teach, to preach, and to heal, in obedience with your desire to make the world a better place. Let those who love you, Lord God, devote ourselves and our lives to your teachings and the love of Jesus Christ. While the cross we carry may not be in the same form, nor our death be on a cross, we do go forth with Jesus' love in our hearts and minds. That love emboldens us to do brave and wondrous deeds in the name of our Lord and Savior. Be with us this day, forgive our sinful ways and help us to march boldly into each day, praising you and doing acts of kindness to those in need. In your Holy name I pray. Amen.

JUNE 14

"Flag Day is an annual celebration of the flag of the USA. The celebration commemorates the adoption of the national flag in 1777 by the Continental Congress. In 1916, President Woodrow Wilson proclaimed June 14 as Flag Day, and in 1949, Congress passed legislation establishing it as a day of observance."

PHILIPPIANS 3:20

But our citizenship is in heaven, and it is from there that we are expecting a Savior, the Lord Jesus Christ.

Holy Lord God, I often hear people talking about our flag as though it is something "holy" and to be worshipped. It is an important symbol of our country but is not to be considered as an object to worship. Americans have national pride, almost all countries have national pride. The flag of each country is merely a symbol. Christians worship you and sometimes wear jewelry as a silent reminder of their love for you. Lord, help me to keep an ever present knowledge of you and your great promise. May we always put our faith in you first. On this day, I pray for all who are homeless and hungry, may they find a safe haven to rest and a warm meal to soothe their growling bellies. I pray each will receive adequate dental and medical care and for children who have never known what it is to see a doctor or a dentist and for that matter, do not know what it is to have a home with a roof over their heads, and safety behind a closed door. Our nation is a wealthy one, by comparison, Lord. Help us to provide for your displaced people. I send special prayers for those who have fled their home countries, fearing their safety, only to be turned away or "incarcerated" on the southern border. Help us Lord God by finding humane accommodations and ways to include these desperate people. Be with them as they come needing a myriad of services and personal health care. Lord, may you continue to guide my ways and forgive my sins. Be with me each and every day, I pray in your name. Amen.

JUNE 15

We must leave our life of darkness behind.

1 PETER 4:3-4

"For you spent enough time in the past doing what the gentiles like to do, living in sensuality, sinful desires, drunkenness, wild celebrations, drinking parties, and detestable idolatry. They insult you now because they are surprised that you are no longer joining them in the same excesses of wild living."

Wise and wonderful Lord, you have taught us well. It is more blessed to give than to receive. In our abundance, Lord God, help us to give freely and share our bounty with others. Help us to feed the hungry, clothe the naked, and provide medical care for those in need. Lord, in the world most of us live in, we have plenty to share. May we be cheerful givers and teach our children the same. Be with those who, due to circumstances too horrific for us to imagine, like a woman who flees a life with a spouse abuser, and end up living in shelters or on the streets. Give her courage and a new life of hope. May her example of survival be an inspiration to other women so that their children will grow up strong and know how toxic abusive relationships are and they will avoid them. Be with those who abuse their families, guide them to a life changed by your life and teachings. Be with each of us Lord, and save us from all ill, I pray in the name of the Son. Amen.

JUNE 16

HEBREWS 12:1

Therefore, since we are surrounded by so great a cloud of witnesses, let us also lay aside every weight and the sin that clings so closely, and let us run with perseverance the race that is run before us.

———————

Lord, ruler of all, thank you for once again making your intention for those who believe in your word, your promise. Sometimes doubt and sin, seem to sneak in when I least expect. Am I running this race called life with you foremost in my heart and head? I must set the record straight. Of course I am, and so are you! Think of the people who have gone to 'the house of the Lord, forever." You know the believers you used to hang with who have gone to a better place. So stop the doubts. Jesus said, "Do not let your hearts be troubled. Believe in God, believe also in me. In my Father's house there are many dwelling places. If it were not so, would I have told you that I go to prepare a place for you?" (John 14: 1-3). Praise God from whom all blessings flow! With a song in your heart and a head full of confidence, lead the life you have chosen. May it be so, Lord. In the name of your beloved son, I pray you will be with me and save me. Amen.

JUNE 17

2 TIMOTHY 2:22-23

Shun youthful passions and pursue righteousness, faith, love and peace, along with those who call on the Lord from a pure heart. Have nothing to do with stupid and senseless controversies, you know that they breed quarrels.

Loving God, through forgiveness of sins, you have freed me to pray to you with a grateful heart. I pray for peace and understanding in a world that seems lacking. The world I live in, mimics what must have been occurring centuries ago. Paul's letter to Timothy was to encourage the people to live a simple life, free from useless arguments. Lord, help me find ways to keep from senseless controversies. And yes, I know that indulging in word battles will prove fruitless to solutions and cause unnecessary inner turmoil. Sometimes I feel I just have to respond. I pray for your guidance to keep my eye on what is most important and not insipid responses to nonsense. As lives are negatively impacted by senseless quarrels I pray My voice will be a voice for the voiceless. I pray to focus on important societal matters in order to inform and perhaps let those suffering know there are people praying for a resolution to the injustices they suffer. May we follow the rule of law that you have taught, to seek justice, to love mercy and to walk humbly with you, my Lord. On this Father's Day I give thanks to all the loving fathers. I pray for those who have lost loving fathers and are especially grieving for them today. May those who miss their dads today be comforted knowing what a role model they were and seek to live their lives in honor of them. Be with us and save us Father God. Amen.

JUNE 18

PSALM 51:1, 10, 12
PRAYER FOR CLEANSING AND PARDON

Have mercy on me, O God, according to your steadfast love; according to your abundant mercy blot out my transgressions. Wash me thoroughly from me iniquity, and cleanse me from my sin.

Create in me a clean heart, O God, and put a new and right spirit within me.

Restore to me the joy of your salvation, and sustain in me a willing spirit.

———————————

Gracious and forgiving God, you are always with me, with us in times of trouble or angst. Thank you for the certain understanding that through you our sins are forgiven. Help us to be better people by remembering to spend time thinking and praying about how words and actions that might be objectionable in your sight. Be with each of us as we sincerely repent our sins and help guide us to a better way to think, act and speak. Lord, you know our sins before we speak them, and yet, when we do, your mercy is granted. Thank you God for the gift of salvation. In your holy name, I pray. Amen.

JUNE 19

PSALM 68:4-5

Sing to God, sing praises to his name; lift up a song to him who rides upon the clouds—his name is the Lord—be exultant before him.

Father of orphans and protector of widows is God in his holy habitation.

———————————

Compassionate Lord God, your ministry to the vulnerable is reassuring. I pray you are there where children are essentially caged and alone. Be there for them Lord, help them to keep their spirits up as they face each day without mothers and fathers. Lord, they do not know what is happening to them and why they feel abandoned. Calm their fears and give them hope. A portion of the wedding vow is, "til death do us part." We say those words and we mean them. We know you have prepared a place for our spouse who has died, and yet it is so hard to wrap our minds and hearts around the very idea that one is living without a beloved spouse. Great loves seem to be shattered in a moment. Help those who are left behind to make wise decisions and to feel your compassionate love. Be with all who are suffering and vulnerable. Be with us and save us I pray, Amen.

Lord, I pray this day for a dear one who is suffering following surgery. Be with her and her family as she struggles to regain health. And I pray for one who has medical challenges. Be with each as they struggle with health issues and also those who love them. Amen.

JUNE 20

EXODUS 20:1-6

Then God spoke all these words: I am the Lord your God, who brought you out of the land of Egypt, out of the house of slavery; you shall have no other gods before me. You shall not make for yourself an idol, whether in the form of anything that is in heaven above, or that is on the earth beneath, or that is in the water under the earth. You shall not bow down to them or worship them; for I the Lord your God am a jealous God, punish children for the inequity of parents, to the third and fourth generation of those who reject me, but showing steadfast love to the thousandth generation of those who love me and keep my commandments.

Creator God, your strength, love and leadership brought not only the people of Israel out of the house of bondage, but to this very day you bring hope to those who would hear. Your words clearly establish who you are and all that you have done to save us. Your sovereignty is as clear as our obligation is to obey you. The "moral" codes of how you expect your people to live via your messenger Moses establish your expectations. The setting, Mount Sinai, was dramatic. Lord God, you sent Moses to clearly lay out the laws which have existed from the time of Adam and Eve. The norms of your expectations are universal and part of the footprint we carry in our hearts and minds. The penultimate expectation is the sovereignty of you, Lord. Your words to Moses leave no room for idol worship in the kingdom. There will be no idol worship nor will the norms of an earlier time be valued. May each one be mindful of your steadfast love for us which shall endure forever. Be with us and save us, I pray. Amen.

JUNE 21

EXODUS 20:7

You shall not make wrongful use of the name of the Lord your God, the the Lord will not acquit anyone who misuses his name.

Holy God, the prayerful people utter your name in reverence and in adoration. Often your name is used in prayer and to instruct those who do not yet know you. The supplications of believers fulfills your expectation of how one is to use your name. Hypocrites who speak your name outside of prayer in disparaging ways, have been warned. Lord God, help those who utter your blessed name, making promises on the sure strength of your name and yet, neglect to actually take action. When your name is used, it must not be for any other purpose, rather, may it be the practice of achieving the goal expressed. You alone, Lord will be the ultimate judge. Misuse of your name, God, denies the fact, you will be the one who has the final say regarding vain promises. I pray in your blessed name for forgiveness of the sin, by uttering your name inappropriately. Help your people pay more attention to the words we use. The shock value of misusing your name has almost become accepted by our society. Help your people find ways to stop this abhorrent and sinful practice. Today Lord, I also pray for all who are suffering. Help them find a way to resolve the pain or inner turmoil that threatens their lives. Be with those who are homeless and those who have arrived in our country, only to be threatened and have their children separated from them. May we make better use of our grateful nation, by taking in and helping those who seek asylum and those whose very lives are threatened. Help our government find ways to lead and to care for the downtrodden, and help us stand on solid ground with you, blessed savior. Be with us, each one and save us, I pray. Amen.

JUNE 22

"Faith is taking the first step even even when you don't see the whole staircase."

– Martin Luther King Jr.

PHILIPPIANS 4:6-7

Do not worry about anything, but in everything by prayer and supplication with thanksgiving let your requests be made known to God. And the peace of God, which passes all understanding, will guard your hearts and your minds in Christ Jesus.

I pray this day, O God, for those whose burdens weigh heavily on their hearts and minds. May they turn to you, with home, school, or work issues. Although our troubles might seem insurmountable, it is through you, our troubles will find answers. Each one of us faces seemingly insurmountable issues, God has a plan to comfort our anxiousness. I know, Lord God the answer I get may not be the one sought after, you know what is best, although it may take time for me to embrace the solution you provide. When this happens, I have to search to find out what the answer means and know your response is sure. When I feel overwhelmed, I pray about it, trying not to offer a solution, but to listen for your answer. Be with all who are not at peace about something, may you show them the way. Be with us this day and each day, forgive our sins and save us, I pray. Amen.

JUNE 23

Longing for God and His Help in Distress

PSALM 42:6-8

Hope in God; for I shall again praise him, my help and my God. My soul is cast down within me; therefore I remember you from the land of Jordan and of Hermon from Mount Mizar. Deep calls to deep at the thunder of your cataracts; all your waves and your billows have gone over me.

God of all creation, sometimes my mind is so absorbed in just getting ready for a new day, when I find myself too self-absorbed to go to you in prayer. And then the miracle happens, I forget what pains my heart and remember you, merciful Lord. As I pray, saying your prayer, the deepest storms of my heart and mind begin to be washed over me and my despair is comforted. Thank you God for those moments when I feel lost and panic takes over my thoughts. When you come to me, my panic begins to move out of my thoughts. You help me to bask in the silver glow of the moon and turn my darkness into the beautiful sound of waves pounding on the beach. The affirmation you are with me, allows me to feel your blessing and to feel something more powerful than my grief and fears. I know that you, holy God, are with me in my waking and sleeping and your mercy, power and truth, is with me always.

Lord, today I pray for those who cannot set aside their worries and fears because their world has been turned upside down. Those who have fled political oppression need to feel your comfort and love. I pray you will be with them and help keep them healthy and safe. Lord, be with those who are suffering from unspeakable oppression at the hands of evil. Send your love and guidance to them until they are free from their captors. Help those who are searching for a safe place to sleep and food for their rumbling stomachs. Help the leaders do what is humane, without regard to political opposition. Lord, make the nightmare of those who fear for their very lives, find a welcoming home and safety.

You are my refuge in a raging storm and salvation for all of our tomorrows. Be with my mind and heart as I head into another day, save me from my transgressions and be with each one as the new dawn brings clarity and purpose to all of our days. Amen.

JUNE 24

PSALM 5:4-5, 8, 11-12 TRUST IN GOD FOR DELIVERANCE FROM ENEMIES

For you are not a God who delights in wickedness; evil will not sojourn with you. The boastful will not stand before your eyes; you hate evildoers. You destroy those who speak lies; the Lord abhors the bloodthirsty and deceitful.

Lead me, O Lord, in your righteousness because of my enemies; make your way straight before me.

But let all who take refuge in you rejoice; let them ever sing for joy. Spread your protection over them, so that those who love your name may exult in you. For you bless the righteous, O Lord; you cover them with favor as with a shield.

———————————

Supreme Lord, throughout the universe there are people who are disrespectful to one another and to your teaching, your words. You teach us to love one another as ourselves, and yet the world seems to spin out of control with vitriol and hatred. Today, I pray for peace and the end of "war-like" practices and evildoers. May oppression and the hungry drive to step on and over others be abdicated in favor of peace and harmony. When leaders control people the ones who are most in need of help are imprisoned by the laws that are created to control them. I pray for everyone throughout the world to be set free from bondage and helped to have a fresh start, a "do over." Be with those who take advantage of the most vulnerable, turn their evil ways into good. Lord, teacher, continue to show the way to live in this world singing songs of hope and joy. Protect your children, teach them of your abundant love. Be with all who are hungry and devoid of basic needs. Feed and clothe them as your word finds a home in their hearts. And Lord, please warm the cold heart of oppression turning it to love and protection. Be with us and save us all, in your holy name, I pray. Amen

JUNE 25

Most people believe that following Jesus is all about living right.

Not true. Following Jesus is all about living fully. Listen.

– Michael Yaconelli
Dangerous Wonder (1998)

———————————

L ord of all, your wisdom and countenance never cease to amaze. How many times in the past have I felt you with me, heard you speaking to me? I treasure the moments when I am closer to you. Today, I pray for those who do not know you, to listen for your wisdom and learn of your mighty power. I pray for those who are in need of mental or physical healing, that they might be restored and comforted by you. I also pray for the powerful, may they listen to you and apply their learning to those who are the most needy. Be with our elected leaders across the land. May you lead them to make wise decisions on behalf of the oppressed. Lord God, be with parents and family members. I pray they will teach their children about your mighty power, love, and tell the story of Jesus Christ. In this chaotic world may the love of you and your son melt the hearts of the doubters and warm the hearts of those who already know of your great love. I give thanks for the life of Michael Yaconelli, a pastor and author whose influence is still being felt, although he is with you in heaven. Be with us and save us, I pray. Amen.

JUNE 26

Jesus and the woman of Samaria

1 JOHN 4:7-10

A Samaritan woman came to draw water, and Jesus said to her, "Give me a drink." (His disciples had gone to the city to buy food.) The Samaritan woman said to him, "How is it that you, a Jew, ask a drink of me, a woman of Samaria?" (Jews do not share things in common with Samaritans.) Jesus answered her, "If you knew the gift of God, and who it is that is saying to you, 'Give me a drink,' you would have asked him, and he would have given you living water.'

Savior, thank you for sending your beloved son. Jesus was wise and a compassionate teacher. You sent Jesus to the well in order that all would learn an important lesson. God, you sent your only son to live among the people as a gift. Jesus was your gift to the world. He came to take away the sins of the world, and to forgive all or our sins so that we might live through him. When my mind settles into the very thought of such a gift, I am humbled and I feel your love. Even the woman at the well, a sinful lady by Jesus' comments, even she was to have her sins washed by the 'living water.' Savior, your love for humanity and us was the reason for Jesus. You loved us and gave us a human gift. I have felt your presence and your love and realize what a precious gift you have given me. What a loving sacrifice! I pray you will be with me, and forgive my sinful ways. Thank you Lord God, for the precious gift of your son and the tangible way the lesson of forgiveness is freely given. Be with your "flock" and save them. I pray in the name of the one who was sent to take away the sins of the world, a savior, Jesus Christ. Amen.

JUNE 27

ROMANS 16:17, 20

I urge you, brothers and sisters, to keep an eye on those who cause distention and offenses, in opposition to the teaching you have learned; avoid them.

The God of peace will shortly crush Satan under your feet. The grace of our Lord Jesus Christ be with you.

———————————————

L ord of our minds and hearts, the conclusion of Paul's letter to the people of Rome urges the people to watch out for trouble-makers who would upset life and cause the people to perhaps question your authority. Paul warns the Roman people about false teachings. Paul's words are intended to comfort and reassure, just as we reassure our children about our love and our statements of expectations: "Be safe, call me if you …". Like Paul, we find it difficult to send our children off into a world that perhaps is contrary to our expectations or does not mimic what we expect of our children. Therefore, Paul reminds the Roman people to avoid people who oppose the teachings Jesus modeled throughout his life. Lord God, you gave us many gifts, but the most precious is knowing when we stand in the grace of God we are saved. What more could one desire, but to walk faithfully and confidently in the certain shadow of your loving grace? Be with us and save us, Lord. Amen

JUNE 28

MATTHEW 19:13-15
JESUS BLESSES LITTLE CHILDREN

Then little children were being brought to him in order that he might lay his hands on them and pray. The disciples spoke sternly to those who brought them; but Jesus said, "Let the little children come to me, and do not stop them; for it is to such as these that the kingdom of heaven belongs. And he laid his hands on them and went on his way.

Lord, your faithful servant and son, Jesus was such a loving and compassionate man to everyone he encountered (I know, he wasn't so nice to the money changers in the temple), Jesus knew the value of speaking to and loving everyone. We learn from the beginning that all lives matter to you and to your son. Our pastors today, serve children in much the same loving way. Our pastors nourish all, including making sure programs to teach and love children. My friend, Pastor Stan used to have such a loving and chaotic Christmas Eve children's message that showed them God's love and how important playful learning about our savior and the grace of God truly is. Lord, I thank you for special people: pastors, Christian educators, lay leaders, elders, deacons, Sunday school and youth leaders. Your flock is working diligently to "grow up" the next generation of faithful servants and believers. Be with them as they seek to educate our young. Lord be with us all and save us, I pray. Amen.

JUNE 29

PSALM 62:1-2

For God alone my soul waits in silence; from him comes my salvation.

He alone is my rock and my salvation, my fortress; I shall never be shaken.

Loving God, all praise and glory I give to you. As we continue our journey through life, sometimes I feel a tug-of-war between what is expected of me and doing what I feel called to do. Help me make decisions that please you. Be with us Lord God, as we seek ways to trust in your teachings. When we turn to you in prayer, may we find ways to hear you and to be patience. We know of your great love for each one. You support and forgive our impatient ways. Help us to listen and pray for continued guidance, fully trusting in you. By your grace, you have washed away the sins of the world. Help us to have confidence in the biblical teachings as we strive to do your will. May the song in our hearts always be "On Christ the solid rock I stand, all other ground is sinking sand." Holy Lord, be with our friends and neighbors. May we afford them and the stranger with respect and joy. Be with those who are away from their homes, serving in far-away lands to free the oppressed from evil doers. Be with all who are representing our country, and those friends and family members who are left to run the households. May the soldier return home safely to a loving home that awaits them. Lord, be with the sick and dying. May they know your love and grace. Be with each of us and forgive our sins, in your glorious name I pray. Amen.

JUNE 30

PROVERBS 2:3-8
THE VALUE OF WISDOM

*If you cry out for insight, and raise your voice for
    understanding;*
*If you seek it like silver, and search for it as for the hidden
    treasures—*
*Then you will understand the fear of the Lord and find the
    knowledge of God.*
*For the Lord gives wisdom; from his mouth comes
    knowledge and understanding; he stores up sound wisdom
    for the upright; he is a shield to those who walk blamelessly,
    guarding the paths of justice and preserving the way of his
    faithful ones.*

Faithful and teaching God, often I seek wisdom and understanding from those whose writings give an indication of how to understand and live a life which is pleasing to you. Many followers seek to understand and love you, its value is greater than any precious ore we might own. You, Lord God are the source from which we receive wisdom and peace. Heavenly one, I treasure your teachings and wisdom. They continue to be a source of comfort and a pathway to my tomorrows. I shall never forget those who have gone before me and how often they were described as "saints" or "angels" who are now with you. In hindsight, Lord, I know now what the elegies were really saying. The saints are justified because they followed your commandments. And so again patient teacher, we come full circle back to your expectations. Thank you Lord for those who helped shape my faith and ways, especially I give thanks for 'finding' you and not a way out, but a way into your love and grace. May my words and understanding love be a way to share your love and grace with those near and dear and those who may still be searching. And so today, Lord, I give thanks for Wilmer

Blankenbaker, Stan Wherry, Christian and Emma Clemens, Lois and Wendell H. Kline, Edith Stover, Cleta White, Betty Jo Dickson, and Dorothy McKinney Wright. These faithful servants are in your dwelling place and fill my heart with faith, hope and peace. Lord I pray also today for those who have not yet found a faith in you. May your love and peace help them to find the way. Be with those who are sick, and those whose mental capacity has placed a veil over their being. Be with them and each one as we ask for forgiveness of our sins. May you be with us this day and all the days of our lives, I ask in the name of your son, Jesus. Amen

JULY 1
PROVERBS 1:7-10, 15-16

The fear of the Lord is the beginning of knowledge; fools despise wisdom and instruction. Hear my child, your father's instruction and do not reject your mother's teaching; for they are a fair garland for your head, and pendants for your neck. My child, if sinners entice you, do not consent.

...my child, do not walk in their way, keep your foot from their paths; for their feet run to evil.

———————————

All knowing Lord, your servant Solomon, (the son of David, King of Israel) offers affirming words in support of your teachings. Parents are expected to instruct their children acceptable behavior and knowledge. The world today is fraught with disconcerting powers and pitfalls. The evils of long ago are similar to the evils of today, only the methodology is a bit more sophisticated. Sinners continue to recruit young people, making the words of Solomon, even more relevant today. I pray to the Lord, that those who would prey on our youth shall be thwarted by "the adults in the room." Gangs and other types of evil constantly place pressure on the most vulnerable. It falls to parents and adult leaders to be vigilant in keeping children safe. Especially vulnerable are children who do not seem to have adult leadership to keep them from joining gangs and from adults who gain the confidence of impressionable youth and turn boys and girls into human trafficking. I pray for wisdom and rational behavior for the parents, family members and guardians of all children. May they watch over impressionable children, keeping them safe and secure. The enticement of evil-doers can be overpowering when parents are not present in their children's lives. May parents be forever vigilant keeping their children mentally and physically safe. I pray for the lessons being learned by the children in the 'migrant' camps set up to harm their parents for seeking asylum in our country. Shame and dishonor on those who ordered the irrational and the disgusting habit of separating children from the adults who brought them to our borders. I pray also, for the children of disengaged parents, who turn to evil people seeking love or approval. Be with each one, forgive our sins holy God, and save us, I pray. Amen.

JULY 2

1 PETER 5:10-11
TENDING THE FLOCK OF GOD

And after you have suffered for a little while, the God of all grace, who has called you to his eternal glory in Christ, will himself restore, support, strengthen, and establish you. To him be the power forever and ever. Amen.

———————————

Lord, "your loving grace is amazing, because you are.*" I do not know why so many struggle with faith. Reading your words in 1Peter and throughout the Bible the reader is given a road map showing humans how to develop their faith. Help those who do not know you, loving God, to be in community with believers and to grow their faith in you. Lord, I pray for those who have 'rejected' your teachings and do not find relevance in your words. Be with them and help to awaken their slumbering faith. Working in community with those who have accepted you as our Lord and Savior has been vital to my survival in a family and in a world that often behaves in ways I cannot fathom. You saved me and walked me through a tumultuous family life and adopted me into a family who did know of your love and your light. Your faith in me gave me the courage to step up and help those whose lives mirrored my own. I am thankful that you were there to help me find a way and to save me when I stumble. Lord, I pray that you will melt the cold hearts that 'imprison' children and separate families who have fled to the United States, seeking a safer life. My government is unrecognizable when it comes to human rights for the oppressed and I pray for your grace to shower the suffering ones with your grace and your love.

———————————

* Quotation from John Piper. Piper is founder and teacher of Desiring God. org and chancellor of Bethlehem College and Seminary. He served as pastor of Bethlehem Baptist Church, Minneapolis, Minnesota for thirty three years. He is author of more than fifty books.

Lord, I pray for those who are sick and dying, and for their families and loved ones. May your love comfort each one. Be with those who are traveling this summer. May each journey be filled with love and renewal and may they return to their homes enriched by your peace and love. God of hope and peace and grace, I pray that you will melt cold hearts and minds. To God be the glory, this day and all the days to come. Amen.

JULY 3

JAMES 2:14-16, 24, 26

What good is it, my brothers and sisters, if you say you have faith but do not have works? Can faith save you? If a brother or a sister is naked and lacks daily food, and if one of you says to them, "Go in peace; keep warm and eat your fill," and yet you do not supply their bodily needs, what is the good of that? So faith by itself, if it has no works is dead.

You see that a person is justified by works and not by faith alone.

For just as the body without the spirit is dead, so faith without works is also dead.

———————————

"Jesus Christ calls us to love our neighbors and to welcome those in need. The Bible calls us to do justice, and to love kindness, as we walk humbly with our God. Carolyn Winfrey Gillett has written words to a hymn in celebration of God's love for the stranger." The quotations that follow are her words:

Lord of all, another day has passed without humanitarian assistance to those in need on what has been called our 'southern' border.' "We have made their journey harder..." Why is this so Lord of all? "When your children are in danger, will we love them, or concede?" So far, it seems like we shall turn a blind eye. What will it take to soften the cold hearts of those who have been imprisoned "Yet we place them in detention, far from loved ones, scared and worn." Heavenly God, some of our brothers and sisters have 'visited' one of the detention centers and found over one hundred frightened children and adults, huddled together on a concrete floor, with one toilet and no source of water! Help Americans to empower immediate assistance from heartless treatment. Today I give thanks to you Lord God, for the words of Ms. Gillett. May each of us find a way to demonstrate peacefully over this unnecessary and sad saga in American history. Lord, I pray we can find a way to welcome the strangers who are suffering unnecessarily. Be with us as we pray on this disaster and seek a resolution sooner. How can we celebrate July 4th, Independence Day under such a stain occurring in our homeland? I pray our Congress will cancel all the celebrations and the Presidential plans and use that money for those in need. Forgive us our sins, Holy and Just God, and this particular one of neglect and meanness. I pray in your holy name, May it be so. Amen.

JULY 4

We celebrate American Independence Day on the Fourth of July every year. We think of July 4, 1776, as a day that represents the Declaration of Independence and the birth of the United States of America as an independent nation.

PSALM 33:12-22

Happy is the nation whose God is the Lord, the people whom he has chosen as his heritage. The Lord looks down from heaven; he sees all humankind. From where he sits enthroned he watches all the inhabitants of the earth—he who fashions the hearts of them all, and observes their deeds. A king is not saved by his great army; a warrior is not delivered by his great strength. The war horse is a vain hope for the victory, and by its great might it cannot save. Truly the eye of the Lord is on those who fear him, on those who hope in his steadfast love, to deliver their soul from death, and to keep them alive in famine. Our soul waits for the Lord; he is our help and our shield. Our heart is glad in him, because we trust in his holy name . Let your steadfast love, O Lord, be upon us even as we hope in you.

Holy God, you are the parent of all. While around the world, nations celebrate their nation's 'birth' on different days, those are not the most important days to be celebrated each year. That day, Holy God, is reserved for you. May every head bow down and every heart open wide to your authority. We place our trust in you, Lord God and set aside a portion of each day to honor your mighty deeds and sovereignty over all. For some, today is another special day without a loved one. I pray for those who mourn a loss. Today, I give thanks for all who are in your heavenly care and calmly recall their names through their joyful and playful loving ways; one who loved this country and parades, one who always set a beautiful table to celebrate, one whose laugh was infectious, one whose bear hugs I can still feel, one whose twinkle in the eyes signaled a child-like prank that was oft repeated and yet always made us laugh, one who loved to entertain us with backyard fireworks, and great stories. They are with you now, loving God and I pray their loving laughter and joy has made them forget the agony of passing and rejoice in living with you, for ever. I pray those reading this prayer, will finish it with their own silent memories. Be with us all this day, forgive us our sins, save us and Lord, bring a moment, no matter how fleeting, to laugh and recall one who fills a special place in our hearts. May your steadfast love be with us all the days of our lives, in your blessed son's name, I pray. Amen.

JULY 5

PSALM 30:2, 4, 11-12

O Lord, my God, I cried to you for help, and you have healed me.

Sing praises to the Lord, O you his faithful ones, and give thanks to his holy name.

You have turned my mourning into dancing; you have taken off my sackcloth and clothed me with joy, so that my soul may praise you and not be silent. O Lord, my God, I will give thanks to you forever.

Faithful God, I turn to the words the authors of Biblical tomes recorded. The psalmist has captured my thoughts and what is held dearly in my soul. There are hurting people who are turning to you for strength and courage to carry on after suffering the loss of a loved one. There are those so impacted, they have turned away from you. Help them all, loving God. You have taught us well, Lord, we know that our joy is conjoined with your grace and love. I pray for those who have lost a dear one and may find the loss insurmountable and yet, the consequences of the loss itself has presented countless obstacles. The lives of survivors are stressful to endure, they may become mired in the minutiae of paperwork and all sorts of requirements resulting since the passing of a beloved. Be with us this day after our national celebration, as we pray for those who have lost a dear one who gave his/her life in service of our nation. They would want us to remember what our country stands for and to celebrate their efforts on our behalf. Help us all to love and honor the efforts to carry on. Loving God, remind them you are walking with them. I pray that details like health care, bill paying, sorting of stuff and taking care of children will not consume them as it is difficult at any time. Bless and love them and help them give thanks. You, Lord, know the ache of losing a beloved. We rejoice in your holy walk and sacrifice. Be with each one and save them from their despair. Lord, help us to be thankful for what we have, not for what we have lost. Show us the way to help those in need and to be gracious to those who need our love and support. God, I will give thanks to you forever and humbly ask you to forgive my sins and shortcomings. Save me and all who seek to live in one with you and your beloved son. Be with us this day and each day. In your holy name I pray. Amen.

JULY 6

1 JOHN 4:20-21 GOD IS LOVE

Those who say, "I love God," and hate their brother or sisters, are liars; for those who do not love a brother or sister whom they have seen, cannot love God whom they have not seen. The commandment we have from him is this: those who love God must also love their brothers and sisters also.

———————————

Teacher, you speak the truth as learned from our Lord God. The commandment is to love one another as God also loves us. Who could deny such an edict? The words are not a challenge, although some might find them challenging. God asks us to love one another as ourselves. And so, today Jesus, I pray for those who have loving relationships with their fellow brothers and sisters, in Christ. Help us learn to work through our disagreements, while maintaining our love and respect for one another. While our discussions may be spirited, may they be honest, allowing us to work out any disagreement we may have. Be with your people this day and every day as we strive to walk in faith with your grace and love in our hearts. I pray for those who may be hateful with a brother or sister in Christ, may their differences lack the substance to sustain an estrangement. May all we do and say be to praise and glorify you. Loving teacher, be with us this day and each day as we walk in your light. Forgive us our sinful ways and save us, I pray in the name of the Father and the Son. Amen.

JULY 7

1 CORINTHIANS 12:13
ONE BODY WITH MANY MEMBERS

For in the one spirit, we were all baptized into one body—Jews or Greeks, slaves or free—and we were all made to drink of one Spirit.

Heavenly Teacher, we learn from your servant, Paul just how unique each member's contributions to the church are. You recognize just how precious and welcome our talents are. Lord the unique appreciation of the spiritual gifts each member contributes to the quality of the ministry has sustained the church. Each person's spiritual gifts and your grace contributes to the idea we are one in Christ. We are all members of the same church body and through baptism we are embraced by the Holy Spirit of Christ into one body - the Church. In times of discontent, help us to celebrate our differences for the singular purpose of building a great church. May our efforts glorify you. Be with us each day as we use our time and talents for your church and your people. Lord, I pray your spirit will empower each one as our life and our faith grows. Be with us and save us Lord as we endeavor to learn your will for us. May all that we do and all that we say glorify your church. Amen.

JULY 8

EPHESIANS 4:17-24
THE OLD LIFE AND THE NEW

Now this I affirm and insist on the Lord: you must no longer live as the Gentiles live, in the family of their minds. They are darkened in their understanding, alienated from the life of God because of their ignorance and hardness of heart. They have lost all sensitivity and have abandoned themselves to licentiousness, greedy to practice every kind of impurity. That is not the way you learned Christ! For surely you have heard about him and were taught in him, as truth is in Jesus. You were taught to put away your former way of life, your old self, corrupt and deluded by its lusts, and to be renewed in the spirit of your minds, and to clothe yourself within the new self, created according to the. likeness of God in true righteousness and holiness.

Lord, this morning I am praying for your children who are being mentally and physically abused. I continue my personal attempt to help women and young girls who are being abused by predators who have lost all sensitivity and have adopted unspeakable impurities. Several years ago I became aware of Human Trafficking Initiative and those who seek to help those most vulnerable. The news is filled with salacious details of a case originating in Florida. Women and children are the most vulnerable to the deviant behaviors forced upon them. You saved me from a predator and I pray you will help those who need your love and care to also be saved. I learned of a loving Christ who is the way, the truth and the light. Soften the hardened hearts of those who are living lives without you. Help trafficked servants of deviant people to escape and have their hearts and minds turned to you and your love. Lord, your children want to be with you and to be safe, make it so. Lord, I pray for the forgiveness of sins and for the suffering of the oppressed. Be with us as we try to find a way to help your children. Save us as we continue on this journey with you in our hearts and minds. In your blessed name I pray. Amen.

JULY 9

1 SAMUEL 16:7

But the Lord said to Samuel, "Do not look on his appearance or on the height of his stature, because I have rejected him; for the Lord does not see as mortals see; they look on the outward appearance, but the Lord looks on the heart."

Wise and loving Teacher, your words make 'simple' what sometimes feels so hard to grasp. As a child, I heard "you can't judge a book by its cover." Talk about jolting the conscious from complacency. Your words Lord, are ice water in the veins of those who would seek to deny you. The lesson learned is we should probe deeper and find what the heart and soul of a person really represents. "Be aware of the wolf in sheep's clothing." Wise and merciful Lord, again and again your teachings have urged us to look at "the heart" of a person to know what a person really is. The glitz of newspapers and magazine covers represent the political "wolves" in our society. Today we are bombarded by "many, who are good people" and encouraged to support them as leaders of our society. The parade of those whom you would reject due to the evil in their hearts include an elected official in Alabama who preyed on young girls and was pardoned by another, one who received a 'sweetheart' settlement more than a decade ago as at least one US attorney allowed a man his freedom to continue abhorrent behavior; more than one US President whose personal behavior was complicit in taking advantage of young females. Recently a deplorable man was scooped up by authorities and I pray your "will be done." Justice can never erase the scars evil behaviors have left on their victims. Human Trafficking is slavery on innocent, young girls and boys. Lord help us to right the wrongs and stop the abuse inflicted on the most vulnerable in society. Help us to find, Lord, the kind and loving "adults in the room" to fix societal problems. Help our world leaders to remember your rule, the Golden Rule, ("do unto others..."). We have societal issues and Lord I pray we will look into the hearts of leaders and potential leaders to fix the issues related to Human Trafficking. Be with each of us as we focus on this abhorrent issue today. Our children deserve our very best love and care. Help us find ways to 'save' them. Lord, by your love and grace, we are saved. I pray for the forgiveness of my sins and that you will continue to walk in my heart and in my head. I pray my words will be a voice for those whose voices are rarely heard and yet ones that need to be heard and saved. In your wise and blessed name, I pray. Amen.

JULY 10

1 TIMOTHY 5:21
DUTIES TOWARD BELIEVERS

In the presence of God and of Christ Jesus and of the elect angels, I warn you to keep these instructions without prejudice, doing nothing on the basis of partiality.

Lord God, for centuries your people have struggled with the issue of superiority, particularly of feeling and acting better than others. We avoid discussion of this issue and often hold ourselves apart from the discussion of prejudice by our silence and by looking away. Help us Lord to be more like your son, who showed us the way. We learned many parables spoken by Jesus that point to believers, and how they are instructed to live. The gospel of Matthew (13:34-35) explains why Jesus spoke in parables. Jesus understood the need to directly connect his message in order to fulfill what the prophets had spoken. Linking teachings we find from the Old Testament to the New Testament, consistent and specific ways we are expected to live and treat fellow humans. Today I give thanks to your wisdom, Lord. It is painful to think of the way you planned to save us by the life, death, and resurrection of your son. Your unselfish devotion to us and the hope that all might live together harmoniously, ridding the world of the evils of prejudice continues to be illusive in your world. And yet, we continue to struggle with the very thought of all being equal. Help us Lord, we want our society to be one that follows your teachings. Open our hearts and minds, may we love our neighbors as ourselves. I pray, Lord, you will forgive our sin of prejudice today. Forgive me Lord for harboring the teachings of my parents and taking so long to realize the teachings learned from birth were abhorrent. I became an educator to teach and love the children, especially those who needed my help the most. Be with all of us this day and each day, I pray in the name of your son, Jesus Christ. Amen.

JULY 11

ACTS 17:22-25, 29

Then Paul stood in front of the Areopagus and said, "Athenians, I see how extremely religious you are in every way. For as I went through the city and looked carefully at the objects of your worship, I found among them an altar with the inscription "To an unknown, this I proclaim to you. The God who made the world and everything in it, he who is Lord of heaven and earth, does not live in shrines made by human hands, as though he needed anything since he himself gives to all mortals life and breath and all things.

Since we are God's offspring, we ought not to think that the dirty is like gold or silver, or stone, an image formed by the art and imagination of mortals. While God has overlooked the times of human ignorance, now he commands all people everywhere to repent...

Creator God, your servant, Paul, spoke in Athens to reach the people in ways that were inclusive. He tells the people he has seen things in the archives that seem consistent with what one might find in Christian churches today. He specifically mentions an altar with an inscription. Lord God, you live in the minds and hearts of people, not the things, the stuff. However, inside the holy spaces where worship takes place, one might find such items. What is important Lord, is what is in the hearts and minds of the worshippers and each person's intimate relationship with you. There can be no such relationship with God, without repenting one's sins. And so this day, and every day, all people everywhere are commanded to repent. The forgiveness of sin is secured by the act of repentance. In essence Lord, what comes between birth and death is you. It is not a dash on the tombstone noting birth and death, it is not the job, the house, the cars, the things. It is you, period. You sent your son, Jesus Christ to help secure our future. He died on the cross for our salvation and freedom. Help us Lord to put all the other "stuff" aside and humbly, honestly walk with you as though you are holding our hands with every step. Forgive me Lord, help me to be the Christian you want me to be, may the words come from my heart be caring, loving and in praise of you. I am so thankful that you found me and saved me even before I realized I needed your guidance and love. The impressive thing, Lord, is that you do the same for every person who repents. Be with us Lord, in your name, may we be ready to guide, to lead, and to comfort. As needy people tend to be, you know Lord how to reach us, to save us. I pray each person will know that what comes between the moment of birth and death is your abiding faith and love. May it be so. Amen.

JULY 12

GALATIANS 3:22-28

But the scripture has imprisoned all things under the power of sin, so that what was promised through faith in Jesus Christ might be give to those who believe.

Now before faith came, we were imprisoned and guarded under the law until faith would be revealed. Therefore the law was our disciplinarian until Christ came, so that we might be justified by faith. Now before faith came, we were imprisoned and guarded under the law until faith would be revealed. Therefore the law was our disciplinarian until Christ came so that we might be justified by faith. But now that faith has come, we are no longer subject to a disciplinarian, for in Christ Jesus you are all children of God through faith. As many of you as were baptized into Christ have clothed yourselves with Christ. There is no longer Jew or Greek, there is no longer male or female; for all of you are one in Christ Jesus.

Thank you God for your wisdom and teachings. Your son, Jesus had a great and faithful disciple in Paul. The writings of Paul have helped me to understand in specific and concrete terms what your intentions were and are for all who are walking in the faith. Sometimes, Lord God, the "law of man" does not conform to your expectations. Nations have been guilty of laws that discriminate against one's skin color, gender, faith, etc. It is hard to 'conform' or follow the laws of humans when they are in conflict with your teachings and those of your son, Jesus Christ, for we are "one in Christ Jesus." Help your faithful people to prayerfully work with countries, municipalities, and locales that discriminate against any person for any reason. Lord, I pray that discrimination against women and children in particular be stopped. The most vulnerable of your children lose themselves when they fall victim to human trafficking, sexual abuse and battery. Love them a little more and help them to find their way to safety. The scars will be hard to live with, Lord and I just pray that each one is able to escape the bonds of abuse through your love and their faith. Be with each of us this day and help us to make courageous choices. Lord be with those who are suffering illness or mental issues. Love them and help them to remain strong. Save us in the name of your son, Jesus Christ, I pray. Amen.

MATTHEW 7:1-5 JUDGING OTHERS

"Do not judge, so that you may not be judged. For with the judgement you make, you will be judged, and the measure you give will be the measure your get. Why do you see the speck in your neighbor's eye, but do not notice the log in your own eye? Or, how can you say to your neighbor, 'Let me take the speck out of your eye?' You hypocrite, first take the log out of your own eye, and then you will see clearly to take the speck out of your neighbor's eye."

Heavenly God, I cannot tell you how many times I heard the first line from my mother and her family! I think I heard the word "ye" instead of "you." I thought it meant "shut up!" The full measure of Jesus' ideas about judging others has more to do with what is in our hearts. Think about it, how often have we passed by seeing without "seeing" a person in need? I remember when a hungry, homeless person came to our door. My father went to some lengths to make bacon and egg sandwiches for the person. As the years have progressed, our hungry and homeless populations have grown. Our food closets and generous school children lead the way with clothing and food drives. In recent years, efforts for adequate warm clothing for the winter months has begun. I have seen hats, mittens and scarves adorning the courthouse fencing, free for those in need. It seems like some people care. I cannot imagine what I would not have done to take care of my family. I can imagine people so in fear of their lives, they leave their homes taking only their children as they flee persecution and certain death from heartless and cruel dictators and gangs. I pray for all who need to feel your love and compassion. I pray for those who are helping to welcome the stranger. May we find ways to assist the desperate ones, care for the broken, the homeless, and for their children. Be with those in need and with those with plenty. May we find ways to embrace one another with compassion and love. Lord, be with us this day, forgive our sins and soften our hearts. In your name, I pray. Amen.

MATTHEW 7:6 PROFANING THE HOLY

"Do not give what is holy to the dogs; and do not throw your pearls before swine, or they will trample them underfoot and turn and maul you."

Wise and all-loving God, we live in a world that seems to be empowered to use language that not only is not pleasing to you, it is down right defaming. I am guilty of this disgusting habit, Lord. Help me continue to work hard to break a habit I do not believe in and one I do not want to participate in any longer. Let the words of my mouth and the meditation of my heart be an inspiration in your sight and not an embarrassment. Forgive me this day Lord, of the sin of using profane language to express disapproval. Help me find better ways to express myself when I have negative reactions to situations. Be with me this day and every day and help me be a better person from the inside out. I pray today Lord, for all who are suffering illnesses: physical or mental. I pray for your loving care for those who live alone and who need your watchful eyes, and I pray for those who suffer pain, anguish or fear in their present situation. Help us Lord to be more thoughtful and generous to our brothers and sisters who go to bed in conditions that are unhealthy and cruel. May they find a shelter from the heat and humidity and conditions that make their days and nights even more complicated. Lord, let my words and actions be used as an instrument of love, faith and ones that glorify you. Help me to find ways to resolve difficulties and injustices when I encounter them. May my words and deeds be helpful and positive. Be with us Lord and save us, I pray in your blessed name. Amen.

JULY 15

MATTHEW 7:7-11

"Ask, and it will be given you, search, and you will find; knock and the door will be opened for you. For everyone who asks, receives, and everyone who searches finds, and for everyone who knocks, the door will be opened." Is there anyone among you who, if your child asks for bread, will give a stone? Or if the child asks for a fish, will he give a snake? If you then, who are evil, know how to give good gifts to your children, how much more will your Father in heaven give good things to those who ask him!"

———————————

G ood morning Lord! I am praying this morning for those who have been enjoying nature and the beautiful lakes and oceans. They sometimes find your glory there when the sunrise or sunset reminds them of you. Today I pray for those who know your majesty but who may have stepped away from the church. Help them make their hearts yearn for more. Lord be with each person who perhaps does not know what they are seeking, but knows something is missing. Help your people find an open church door with a faith-filled community. May they and their families find "it" in you. Be with those today who are facing stressful choices about loved ones. I pray you will be with each one. Be with the caretakers of the sick and those who are most vulnerable to evil choices. Show them the way, Lord. And Lord, I am praying for those whose voices have been silenced. Help them find a way to you and to safety. Be with those who need to feel cool air on these hot and humid days. I pray you will let your love be a beacon of forgiveness and love for those whose needs are great. Be with us this day and every day, Lord and forgive us our trespasses. In your blessed name I pray. Amen.

JULY 16

MATTHEW 7:12 THE GOLDEN RULE

"In everything do unto others as you would have them do to you; for this is the law and the prophets."

Lord of heaven and earth, your law, the law of the prophets, too, lays out how people are to live. Our country and the people in the world need to embrace the "golden rule." We hear of cruel comments from leaders that are divisive and filled with hate. The actions of many are fueled by almost hourly media replay. We are living in a time where comments of our leader and his supporters stir up visceral reactions and feelings. Please Lord God, help us to end divisive behavior. Help us to end harmful separatist ways. May we treat our brothers and sisters with love and kindness. Empower our leaders to calmly and definitively have honest dialogs about policies that impact the welfare of your people, for that is the law, your law. Lord, I know that sometimes I have unintentionally and sometimes in anger disparage others. I have felt such shame for my words. They were not what is in my heart nor how I truly feel. Words can hurt and I am truly sorry for each one. Please forgive me. Help me make sure my words reflect my love for you, brothers and sisters and a desire to be a leader in an inclusive, caring society. May my words and actions be supportive of all people. We must find words to cease the racist dialog and speak in comforting words backed up by positive actions. Help all people live the lives all are capable of living. The problem of racism must be tamped down and forever silenced. Be with us as we struggle with the issue of racism throughout the world. Save us as we work to do your will. In your name I pray. Amen.

JULY 17

MATTHEW 7:13-14
THE NARROW GATE

"Enter through the narrow gate; for the gate is wide and the road is easy that leads to destruction, and there are many who take it. For the gate is narrow and the road is hard that leads to life, and there are few who find it."

———————————————

Holy God, as we maneuver our way through life, we encounter speed bumps, potholes, and fresh, beautifully paved highways. Life's road sometimes is full of curves, potholes and yes, heartache. I felt that when my dear friend died last November, when my son suffered a subdural hematoma and more recently a nasty dog bite. I felt so very joyful when I completed the hard journeys without skipping a single moment, or missing a single narrow gate. The challenges God lays down for us, yes, even the hard ones bring the biggest rewards. They are the best, for at the end of the journey Lord, we are promised a heavenly reward. I know that it is so. I pray all will find the gate that leads to abundant life and our great reward, life eternal in your heavenly house. I also pray that we do not skip the curves, but lean into them, hang on and enjoy the ride! I pray each day Lord, be with me and save me. (I know it will be so, and I pray you do, too.) Amen.

MATTHEW 7:15-20

"Beware of false prophets, who come to you in sheep's clothing but inwardly are ravenous wolves. You will know them by their fruits. Are grapes gathered from thrones, or figs from thistles? In the same way, every good tree bears good fruit, but the bad tree bears bad fruit. A good tree cannot bear bad fruit, nor can a bad tree bear good fruit. Every tree that does not bear good fruit is cut down and thrown into the fire. Thus you will know them by their fruits."

———————

Teacher, help us this day to refocus. What is it you want us to do? Perhaps there is nothing new…but so what? All the glitz and glamour eventually fades and then what, Lord? In my thoughts right now I am thinking about how you want others to know you. Do you know we all have monikers with goals? Baby Boomers, Generation X, Millennials, etc. Just like you, the list never ends. There is actually a site recommending the care and treatment of Millennials! I think you've got this, wise and capable Lord:

1. Understand who they are
2. Help them learn and grow
3. Establish clear goals
4. Make them part of a team
5. Give them a sense of purpose
6. Keep in mind their strengths & weaknesses
7. Inspire them to be brand ambassadors
8. Provide flexibility

So if we follow the playbook, written for the Millennials, we have authenticity from the beginnings of time, until the end of our lives. As they say, "I'm down with that!" Social and environmental issues are on "the list," and you know what…it is on your list, too, Lord God! So perhaps we put the fruit that isn't so tasty out for the animals, and if we recycle our unwanted, re-purpose and save a tree, right? It's fair to say, God, your teachings are taking hold in a new way. We are working God to keep you in our hearts and minds and to find a way to "use" what once was thought of as "useless." You, Lord, will never fall into that category. Our "fruits' ' collide with your love and teachings. The qualities expressed in the beatitudes give us a snapshot of the unique people in your kingdom and the qualities of those who are true, good and ready to receive the promise Jesus left with us. He died to take away the sins of the world and to save each one of us. Be with us this day, Teacher, forgive us for our sins and save us, I pray in the sure and true name of your blessed son, Jesus Christ. Amen.

JULY 19

MATTHEW 7:21-23
CONCERNING SELF-DECEPTION

"Not everyone who says to me, 'Lord, Lord,' will enter the kingdom of heaven, but only the one who does the will of my Father in heaven. On that day many will say to me, 'Lord, Lord did we not prophesy in your name, and cast out demons in. your name, and do many deeds of power in your name?' Then I will declare to them, ' I never knew you; go away from me, you evildoers.'

Lord God, you gave us your son to take away the sins of the world. Words and deeds are not the pathway to heaven nor a seat at your feet. Jesus did that for us, through your loving grace. He took it all on and paid a price some might consider too high. Through your love and the actions of Jesus we are forgiven, "but only the one who does the will" of you Heavenly Father may enter that kingdom. We are saved by grace from you, not by the deeds we do. While some may say, "faith without works is dead," that is putting false expectations on the road to your kingdom. When people lose sight of your will and interpret their actions as "good works or deeds" they have crossed over the line. They never asked, "God show me the way, the truth and the light." The answer to that Teacher, is those who are not doing what you would have them do, shall not be welcomed into life eternal. You know what is in our hearts and minds. Lord, help us to translate those thoughts and our love for you until we draw our final breath. At that moment Lord, we shall rejoice for we know Jesus has gone to prepare a place for us in your majestic kingdom. Be with us every moment of our lives and save us, I pray. Amen.

JULY 20

MATTHEW 7:24-27
HEARERS AND DOERS

"Everyone then who hears these words of mine and acts on them will be like a wise man who built his house on rock. The rain fell, the floods came, and the winds blew and beat on that house, but it did not fall, because it had been founded on rock. And everyone who hears these words of mine and does not act on them will be like a foolish man who built his house on sand. The rain fell, and the floods came and the winds blew and beat against that house, and it fell—and great was its fall!"

I recently read a new book, Enabled, authored by Ceci & Lucy Sturman. (This is a wonderful poignant story of two sisters and is available on Amazon.)

The following was written by Lucy and reflects wisdom and faith. Where did that come from you may wonder, I do not. It came from a firm foundation of love for the Lord and Jesus Christ. (Used with permission from my dear friends, Cici and Lucy Sturman.)

Advice for people with Down Syndrome and their families members:

1. Inspire as many people as you can
2. Be a team with your community
3. Advocate for yourself and become your own self-advocate
4. Share with the world you were meant to
5. Speak up for yourself
6. Be informed
7. Stand up for inclusion
8. Band together
9. Don't lose hope

A rchitect of the universe and all there is, thank you for your son, also a carpenter. Jesus spent some time articulating what is expected and how to get to it. The thought-provoking stories from Jesus during The Sermon on the Mount, and recounted by his disciples makes use of analogies to which people from all ages can relate. Thank you Jesus for bringing clarity and wise teachings to all people, young and old. You tell us how irrelevant it is to disconnect the foundation of a physical building or the foundation upon which one builds life. The concept is the same. What you put into your foundation shall determine the strength and quality of it. Quality of materials or for that matter, the cost only matters if the house built on sand is unable to stand the test of nature and time. We have learned from time to time one has to tend to the house to keep it fully functional. So it is, also with one's faith. Lord God, help us to understand how vital it is that we not only have a "firm foundation" but that we also impart that knowledge and your teachings to our children. Help us to set aside the "foundation shaking" busy lives and make teaching our children the importance of learning about loving and worshipping with you. I pray for the children and grandchildren who struggle to fit everything into busy lives. May we be intentional in prioritizing putting you first on the "to do" lists. Let the lessons of life we learn be lessons that will prepare children to stem into their tomorrows as Christians, believers and strong in their faith practices so that their children will be strong leaders who will lead lives that are pleasing to you and a blessing to the world, just like Lucy and Ceci. Amen.

Holy God, I pray for all of the youth of your Church. Give them passion and joy as they find you and follow Jesus. May their faith be real, vibrant, joyous, and triumphant! Give them a sense of your glory. Sustain them through their later years with a deep assurance of your presence, victory, and grace. In Jesus' name. Amen.

JULY 21
MATTHEW 7:28-29

Now when Jesus had finished saying these things, the crowds were astounded at his teaching, for he taught them as one having authority, and not as their scribes.

———————————

Holy Father of Jesus, thank you! Your beloved son did so much to bring a new order of worship and clarity to a people who were without a road map and lost. And how amazed they were! Lord God, your son seemed "regular" in many ways, after all he was a carpenter! So the multitudes were amazed at how Jesus spoke to them, healed them and instructed them. Jesus' teachings demonstrated his leadership and they were convinced he had the authority to teach, preach and heal. There was not doubt in their minds, Jesus was the beloved and accepted Messiah! Help us to continue the story and to be faithful servants. Lord, be with each of us as we work to honor you in a world that seems in chaos. Help us to be part of the solution and not enhance some of the challenges we face. May all that we say and all that we do be to glorify your holy name. Amen.

JULY 22

MATTHEW 8:18-21
WOULD-BE FOLLOWERS OF JESUS

Now when Jesus saw great crowds around him, he gave orders to go over to the other side. A scribe then approached and said, "Teacher, I will follow you wherever you go." And Jesus said to him, "Foxes have holes, and birds of the air have nests; but the Son of Man has nowhere to lay his head."

Holy God, Jesus the mortal had thoughts we all have had. Jesus left his home and his craft as a carpenter to advance the bold prophecy, arriving as the long awaited Messiah. Thank you God for the gift of your son. He was a man who gave everything to everyone and at the end of the day...he did not even have his own bed to sleep in each night. Jesus was constantly beholden to his "handlers' ' for finding a place for him to eat and to sleep. He gave everything, personal possessions to demonstrate his love and advance a new form of religion, Christianity. There may never be another person so unselfish. Thank you God for the gift of your son who lived and died to take away the sins of the world, my sins, too. Be with us this day and every day, even when we know where we will be sleeping tonight, while many do not. Help us to be more accepting of strangers, to spread the word of your beloved son and to be the people you want us to be. Thank you for pastors, ministers of the word, and all who are bold enough in this "politically correct world" to show "they are Christians by their love." Lord forgive our sins, knowing we are imperfect and yet still love you and your teachings, Jesus' teachings. Be with us in our hearts and minds. I pray in the blessed name of the Savior, Jesus the Christ. Amen.

JULY 23

MATTHEW 9:9-13
THE CALL OF MATTHEW

As Jesus was walking along, he saw a man called Matthew sitting at the tax booth; and he said to him, "Follow me." And he got up and followed him.

And as he sat at dinner in the house, many tax collectors and sinners came and were sitting with him and his disciples. When the Pharisees saw this, they said to his disciples, "Why does your teacher eat with tax collectors and sinners?" But when he heard this, he said, "Those who are well have no need of a physician, but those who are sick. Go and learn what this means, 'I desire mercy, not sacrifice.' For I have come to call not the righteous but sinners."

Dear Lord, today I pray for the wisdom of the people. May we learn the lessons of your son, Jesus as he lived his life walking among sinners. Sinners, the very ones you sent him to save. Thank you Lord for the Savior who worked tirelessly to bring salvation and Christianity to the world. We have been blessed to learn what it means to be "called" by you. Your love and teachings help us to see what a "calling" looks like for each person. In the simplest of terms, being "called" means to follow what you, Lord God, want us to be and to do. We are most at peace with ourselves when we know in our hearts and in our minds what it is that we are supposed to do. Some people run away from the "calling" while others embrace it. Lord, help us all learn to embrace and enhance the pathways you would have us go, so that we too might receive your mercy at the end of our life's journey. Be with us and save us this day and each day, I pray in your holy name. Amen.

JULY 24

MATTHEW 9:14-17
THE QUESTION ABOUT FASTING

When the disciples of John came to him, saying "Why do we and the Pharisees fast often, but your disciples do not fast?" And Jesus said to them, "The wedding guests cannot mourn as long as the bridegroom is with them, can they? The days will come when the bridegroom is taken away from them, and then they will fast. No one sews a piece of unshrunk cloth on an old cloak, fir the patch pulls away from the cloak, and a worse tear is made. Neither is new wine put into old wine skins; otherwise, the slings burst, and the wine is spilled, and the skins are destroyed but new wine is put into fresh wineskins, and so both are preserved."

———————————

Loving God, you opened the eyes of the blind with your vision. Thank you Lord, for your son, Jesus. He saw things in a more gentle and loving way. Imagine thinking that your son was well contemporary and filled with what 'old timers' might have called 'new fangled ideas!' What pleased Jesus was not sacrifices nor the dogma of decades before. Your vision was a savior who would radically transform religious dogma and teach a new and compassionate way ... filled with mercy, acts of benevolence and kindness. Jesus, the man you sent to take away the sins of the world, had no need nor interest in sacrifices (much less the brutal and bloody killing of animals) which were offerings made as a result of sin. He represented a radical transformation of the Jewish faith which collided with what people knew and had grown to accept. There was a certain external or face forward, superficial going through the motion to please the Lord God, but clearly missed the mark. The Pharisees had much to learn and for that very reason you sent Jesus. It was Jesus who was associated with sinners, for the purpose of transforming their actions and very beings into good. May your vision be translated into our action, too! In today's world, what does that look like? I think Jesus wants us to represent sacrifices like we do...save up to give to those less fortunate, help our children learn to know and to love you, and to celebrate your gift to us. We must celebrate the birth and yes the death of your son, our Savior. For without both, we would not move past sacrifices and fasting to a life where the forgiveness of sin is but for the heartfelt petition to you. Thank you faithful God, for the life and death of your son, who died that we may live and have life abundant. Help us to be generous and to share that gift. Thanks be to God, there is no need to fast. Be with us this day, forgive our sins and save us, I pray in the name of Jesus. Amen.

MATTHEW 10:40-42 REWARDS

"Whoever welcomes you, welcomes me, and whoever welcomes the one who sent me. Whoever welcomes a prophet in the name of a prophet will receive a prophet's reward; and whoever welcomes a righteous person in the name of a righteous person will receive the reward of the righteous; and whoever gives a cup of water to one of these little ones in the name of a disciple—truly I tell you, none of these will lose their reward."

———————————

Heavenly Planner, we have heard stories how Jesus welcomed the "little children" and recognized that each of us is welcome in your kingdom. Your mandate is to care for one another as we would care for Jesus himself. Jesus said this over and over, "whatever you do for the least of these, you do it unto me." You created us and you want us to "love one another" as we "love ourselves." How is it possible in today's complicated world? Is it just the pattern of being welcoming? Just as your son had many disciples to spread the word and care for your people, we look to preachers of the word to move the mission of your church forward. And not just any preacher, but Jesus taught us to hear preachers of the truth. A true preacher is a disciple who continues the teachings in word and deed of Jesus. I am thankful your realm continues beyond the ministry of Jesus. Thank you God for the gift of your beloved son and the lessons taught by parables, sermons and most importantly, deeds. Quite simply, he saved the world, he saved me. I am thankful also, Lord, to be in community with you in a faith-filled, caring community. Your vision continues and I pray it shall continue. Be with us as we continue to love one another and share Jesus' "good news," and save us I pray. Amen.

JULY 26

MATTHEW 11:25-27
JESUS THANKS HIS FATHER

At that time Jesus said, "I thank you, Father, Lord of heaven and earth, because you have hidden these things from the wise and the intelligent and have revealed them to infants; yes, Father, for such was your gracious will. All things have been handed over to me by my Father; and no one knows the Son except the Father, and no one knows the Father except the Son and anyone to whom the Son chooses to reveal him."

———————————————

Good morning God! Thank you for blue skies, green trees, and rolling oceans. You have set quite a magnificent world on its axis and provided all that I have ever needed. Praise God, from whom all blessings flow... is a song sometimes referred to as the offertory in many churches. Truly, clearly, certainly, it is not all about the money. I give thanks for the monies our churches use to proclaim the greatness of you, Lord God and your son, Jesus and for the use of monies to help those in need. From the outset, you two modeled how Christians are to live..."thy will be done on earth as it is in heaven." And you have instilled a great sense of family in each. Jesus, the best son ever, followed your words and taught us a prayerful family is vital. Further, the family unit was tight, they hung together. Family conversations were not shared nor discussed outside the intimate, closed circle. Some things have changed with the family dynamic as our civilization has changed and while that is not necessarily a "bad" thing, the changes have, in many ways, fractured the family. When the family ceases to function, members are often broken and seem to be searching for understanding. Your world, Lord, has changed and your children often find themselves without both parents living under the same roof. Circumstances pull families apart: jobs that require one parent to be apart from the family for work, divorce, illness and death. Lord, I thank you for the strength and courage to seek out healthy relationships and for families who teach their children the important things in life, and most importantly, to love you. Help those families who do not yet know you that they may be enfolded into your love and care. Jesus has taught me well and I so thankful to have your love and guidance when there were so many times I felt alone. You were / are there for me, and for all. I pray Lord God, for those who are seeking you, and yet do not know you and especially for the children of the world who are hungry, frightened or homeless. May they find comfort in your love and safety in a world that overwhelms them and perhaps is evil. May the sunshine warm their hearts and melt the fears away and may the majesty of the world you have created keep them safe, healthy and content. Be with each of us this day, forgive our sins, save us, and know that we feel your precious spirit and love. Amen.

JULY 27

*Faith isn't about having everything
figured out ahead of time; faith is about
finding the quiet voice of God,
without having everything figured
out, ahead of time.*

– Rachel Held Evans

MATTHEW 11:28-30

*"Come to me, all you that are weary and are carrying heavy
burdens, and I will give you rest. Take my yolk upon you and
learn from me, for I am gentle and humble in heart, and
you will find rest for your souls. For my yolk is easy, and my
burden is light."*

Hear my prayer O Lord. Your invitation to answer the SOS we send gives assurance that you, compassionate and loving God will give us rest, further, we are told your "burden is light." I cannot think of anyone who might say those words! And God... really? Your burden is light? I am humbled and embarrassed to think of the times I have whined about "poor me" and "how weary I am." Your people, fully human, have to have faith in your willingness to be there for each one of us. You know the best wise Lord, and when we ask for you to help us, you always answer, in your time and with the best answer, which may not be the exact one we have prayed to you, hoping to receive. In the long run, most often I have learned that your wisdom and love is paramount and that I must have the patience and faith in the answer you have provided. Help guide us Lord God to pray to you and to patiently open our minds and hearts to ascertain what is to be. There is nothing that we cannot tell you and what a comfort that is. I have seen inquisitive children cower in the face of an angry parent, fearing the question would be answered with a smack. I learned quickly not to ask a question of my parents if I thought the answer would be, "no." I have learned not too worry, because of your promise to listen with a gentle and loving heart. Be with others who fear the asking, give them courage and enfold your love around them. I feel your saving grace and have accepted the answers to my prayers. Be with all of your children Lord and help them to learn of your love. Traveling mercies for those who are out and about this summer, may they return safely. Be with those facing illness, loneliness, and with the children who do not understand what is happening to them nor why. Please comfort the lonely and grieving. On this day in 2019 another of your beloved flock will be memorialized, Pastor David. Be with his wife, children and family and the family of Vienna Presbyterian who also mourn. Loving God, thank you for the gift of your son and the promises he made when he gave his life for us. Be with us and save us, knowing we are imperfect, but striving to do your will. In your name I pray. Amen.

JULY 28

MATTHEW 12:14-21
GOD'S CHOSEN SERVANT

But the Pharisees went out and conspired against him (Jesus), how to destroy him. When Jesus became aware of this, he departed. Many crowds followed him, and he cured all of them, and he ordered them not to make him known. This was to fulfill what had been spoken through the prophet Isaiah:

"Here is my servant, whom I have chosen,
my beloved with whom my soul is well pleased.
I will put my Spirit upon him, and he will proclaim
Justice to the Gentiles.
He will not wrangle or cry aloud,
nor will anyone hear his voice in the streets.
He will not break a bruised reed or quench
a smoldering wick until he brings justice to victory.
And in his name the Gentiles will hope."

Beloved God, the thanks one has when an instant of clarity appears brings such joy. Your love and guidance sustains us. When your people Lord, hear you, feel your presence and love, overwhelming emotions profoundly pour forth. I have heard and felt what that is like, even just yesterday when loved ones gathered to celebrate a profound loss. What a comforting time it is to miss and love someone so much and to share that heartache knowing he is in a better place. The time it takes to understand and recognize that truth is often agonizing. In another way, we agonize over the way people try to harm others, like the Pharisees sought to destroy Jesus. It is hard to make sense of it and I give thanks that you hold the key. Help us to keep searching. Your son has taught us to love one another as you, Lord God, love us. Why then do we try to best others? Your justice does not speak loudly nor carry a big stick. And yet, the sound of the 'clanging bell' can still be heard, like we heard it in Charlottesville. We have examples of love and kindness to follow. Help us to be our better selves and learn from the example of your son. Jesus simply tried to go quietly about the work he was sent to do. Help us Lord to proclaim justice through your love and abiding faith in us. Let us gently and faithfully teach our brothers, sisters and children to love their neighbors and to not step over those who need our help. When crowds gather, may their actions be peaceful and give hope to the oppressed. May we be people who seek to build up and help those in need. Lord, be with us this day as we enjoy the love of family time, remembering those who have gone before us with joy, knowing they are in your dwelling place. Keep our children safe and be with those who suffer mental or physical illness or pain. Be with us this day and all of our tomorrows, and save us, I pray. Amen.

JULY 29

MATTHEW 12:46-50
THE TRUE KINDRED OF JESUS

While he was still speaking to the crowds, his mother and his brothers were standing outside, wanting to speak to him. Someone told him, "Look, your mother and your brothers are standing outside, wanting to speak to you." But to the one who had told him this, Jesus replied "Who is my mother, and who are my brothers?" And pointing to his disciples, he said, "Here are my mother and my brothers!" For whoever does the will of my Father in heaven is my brother and sister and mother.

Lord, your beloved son, spoke and led your people. When there was a distraction, and not just any distraction, but a family distraction, Jesus responded to the person who made known to him that his mother and brothers were present and wanted a word with him. How could that happen? Interrupt the Savior, didn't they know he was busy and that tomorrow is not ours? The Son of God was preoccupied with his work, knowing his days were numbered. Lord, do we walk around with blinders on? Are we so oblivious to our surroundings that we lose sight of you and what is right? Or is it just easier not to look? Today, upon learning of yet another senseless exhibition of gun violence, several paid a price they should not have had to pay. Let no duty disrupt our focus on you, but help us embrace the duty of what it is that You expect from your people. Sometimes that takes courage and a willingness to stand up for what is just and good. Your son knew that his tomorrows were numbered and so his focus was on what brought him into being. He taught us how to be one with you, with what is just and right. Everything else was a lesser duty, following Christ's example, may we be brothers and sisters to all, not constrained by familial ties. We must love, respect and be kind to those in need. Be with us Lord, these times are trying and some feel heavy burdens from oppressive controls. Melt cold hearts and closed minds, may they live a kinder and more humane life. Help those who hunger and thirst, the weary, broken-hearted, and frightened wherever they may be. Lord, I pray especially today for those who have lost loved ones and who perhaps find each day overwhelming, confusing, depressing, grant them peace and may their tomorrows be filled with the joy you and their loved ones desire for them. Be with us, each one, friend or otherwise, and save us I ask in your holy name. Amen.

JULY 30

MATTHEW 13:34-35
THE USE OF PARABLES

Jesus told the crowds all these things in parables; without a parable he told them nothing. This was to fulfill what had been spoken through the prophet;

> *"I will open my mouth to speak in parables;*
> *I will proclaim what has been hidden from the*
> *foundation of the world."*

Wise and wonderful teacher, you knew how to make all who heard your message truly understand. Thank you for reminding those during your time on earth the depth of your mission. You words, reiterated through your chosen disciples clearly sets forth the way Christians are encouraged to act, to live their faith-filled lives. The father in the parable of the Prodigal Son teaches the message of redemption. The answer, so simple and yet so hard for others to hear... ask for forgiveness, and you shall receive it. (Luke 15: 31 - 32). And he said to him, "Son, you are always with me, and all that is mine is yours. It was fitting to celebrate and be glad, for this your brother was dead, and (now) is alive; he was lost, and is found." Again, in the parable of the Salt and Light, (Matthew 5:14-16) "You are the light of the world. A city set on a hill cannot be hidden. Nor do people light a lamp and put it under a basket, but on a stand, and it gives light to all in the house. In the same way, let your light shine before others and give glory to your Father who is in Heaven." I am thankful today that Jesus' spoken words and messages were recorded in meaningful, concise ways. Knock and the door will be open, seek and you shall find. All we have to do is pray to our Lord, asking for forgiveness of our sins, and we too shall be forgiven. Help us Lord, to let go of our misgivings, trust in you and live a life where redemption warms our hearts and fills our minds with joy. We shall love the way your beloved son brought your message to us, for each one enlightens us and lays open the path we are to follow and the way to be closer to you. Be with us and save us in your name I pray. Amen.

MATTHEW 13:51-53
TREASURERS NEW AND OLD

"Have you understood all this?" They answered, "Yes." And he said to them, "Therefore every scribe who has been trained for the kingdom of heaven is like the master of a household who brings out his treasure what is new and what is old." When Jesus had finished these parables, he left that place.

———————————

Holy God, how unburdened Jesus must have felt, having assurances from his disciples that they understood the parables he used to teach them. It meant that after Jesus was gone, the training he provided was sufficient for the disciples to lead and to teach the gospel of the ancient traditions in ways that all could comprehend, endorse and follow. As his days were soon to be ended, Jesus knew he had done his best to teach his chosen ones in ways that would be everlasting. Loving Lord God, the parables reassure us and grant us glimpses of your kingdom and the parables we meet in everyday life ensure our faith in you and your teachings, will be renewed. Give us courage as we seek to love others as you have loved us. No matter the cost, the gift of the "good news," and the treasures of long ago, have become new again in our lives. We have learned that Jesus paid the ultimate price involved in your dominion God, but ultimately the good news is priceless and for that we are filled with thanks and love. Lord, I pray for all who are searching for meaning in their lives, may they find their answers in your words and those of your son. Give courage to those who are hesitant to delve into your teachings, be a comfort to those who are suffering in any way, and share your love and compassion for those suffering under oppressive conditions and in need of basic necessities. Loving God, help us all to share the good news of your teachings and the parables of Jesus in our lives in thought, word and deed. I pray for the church, may those around us "know we are Christians by our love." Be with us and save us. I pray in the strong and loving name of the one who saved me, Jesus Christ. Amen.

AUGUST 1

MATTHEW 16:1-4
THE DEMAND FOR A SIGN

The Pharisees and Sadducees came and to test Jesus they asked him to show them a sign from heaven. He answered them, "When it is evening you say, 'It will be fair weather, for the sky is red.' And in the morning, 'It will be stormy today, for the sky is red and threatening.' You know how to interpret the appearance of the sky, but you cannot interpret the signs of the times. An evil and adulterous generation asks for a sign, but no sign will be given to it except the sign of Jonah." Then he left them and went away.

Lord of all, your son's lessons to the Pharisees and Sadducees who tried to test him is a lesson for all of us today. Are we looking at the world around us with open and objective eyes? Do we see people seeking you? Are our lives "too busy" to follow you? Are we drifting aimlessly away, always searching but never really seeing? Are we blessed to follow the faithful teachers of our time? Can we discern the signs of the times? Can we mark what is evil from what is of Christ? Do we even care? I believe we do care and we are able to ascertain what is fundamentally good. The political times have brought a stark contrast of the differences between what your son saw at the time: tax collectors living fat and happy and the needy. Our world today is fraught with divisions Jesus worked hard to heal. Poverty vs Wealth in America today has found a line drawn. Which will it be? Why in a wealthy country have we slipped back into the "haves" and the "have nots?" Help us find ways to help one another without stepping on and over each other. Where there is hate, let us seek peace, where there is abundance, let us share with those who hunger and thirst. Let us be an example, Lord to the world that we can be stronger together and while raising up the sick, the needy and people of all ages, faiths, and socio economic backgrounds. Help us to love our neighbors as ourselves and may we never turn our backs on those who perhaps have fallen on hard times. Lord, help us to clean up our world, preserving it for future generations and to learn what the little children know instinctively: what matters most is the respect and love one has for another. "We are one in the spirit, we are one in the Lord, and I pray that all unity will one day be restored... and they'll know we are Christians by our love." Give us courage to lead and treat each one with dignity, respect and love. Help us Lord, as we strive to be the people you want us to be. I give thanks for the blessings you have given us. Be with us and save us, I pray. Amen.

AUGUST 2

MATTHEW 16:13-17
PETER'S DECLARATION ABOUT JESUS

Now when Jesus came into the district, of Caesarea Philippi, he asked his disciples, "Who do people say that the Son of Man is?" And they said, "Some say John the Baptist, but others Elijah, and still others Jeremiah or one of the prophets." He said to them, "But who do you say that I am?" Simon Peter answered, "You are the Messiah, the Son of the living God." And Jesus answered him, "Blessed are you, Simon, son of Jonah! For flesh and blood has not revealed this to you, but my Father in heaven.

———————————

Loving and wise God, Peter learned the lessons Jesus taught via and loving deeds, and when prompted by Jesus, this disciple responded with a clear and certain mind. He answered Jesus' questions, without hesitation. Jesus, "You are the Messiah, the Son of the living God." One's "faith" is the key to knowing God and Jesus. I pray for those who do not yet feel the confidence in loving and knowing you Lord and your son, Jesus. May those who celebrate the virgin birth of Jesus, the tumultuous end on the cross, followed by Jesus' resurrection give their minds and hearts to the faith displayed by Peter. History documented the supernatural and spectacular glory of your power and love. Jesus came that we might all know and love you, Lord. Some times, things happen and we do not know why. Humans have evolved, please be with each one today and every day as faith-filled people. Lord God, I feel blessed to have felt your love and care for me as a young teen and throughout my life. You gave me courage and most importantly assurances that I am a child of God. You helped me then and now, You gave me the faith and courage to pray and help others to know you and to feel your love, peace and grace. Feeling you there with me, when I felt alone and when family members and friends lives were ending was not only calming, but beautiful. I was saved and spared for a purpose and I pray that you are pleased with most of my choices and how I have brought your words to others. The journey continues and I pray to be faithful to you and help others to also love and be faithful to you. May our eyes and hearts know you and your son, just as surely as Peter. Lord, be with us always, forgive us our sins and save us I pray. Amen.

AUGUST 3

MATTHEW 17 :20-21

He said to them, "Because of your little faith. For truly, I say to you, if you have faith like a grain of mustard seed, you will say to this mountain, 'Move from here to there,' and it will move, and nothing will be impossible for you.

Holy and all-knowing God, Jesus' teachings to his chosen twelve were almost complete when he said "If you have faith the size of a mustard seed...," you beloved son was referring to the faith each one had in themselves. By definition, Jesus is also empowering us to have faith in ourselves, and in our own growing love and understanding of what divine Power we possess. Jesus is telling them (and us) that we can master the challenges of our life experiences and be faithful, faith-filled people. When I think of lessons learned, I hear the song "This Little Light Of Mine, I'm Gonna Let It Shine" and in particular the line "Hide it under a bushel, no, I'm gonna let it shine." Your will is for believers to conduct their lives and their faith out in the open. Help us all, knowing creator, to embrace the challenges of life knowing that our abundant life comes from our oneness with you and the result of our abundance is an infinite Source within each one of us. May the source grow and shine in me and each of us as we teach our children and live our private and professional lives. While the public or professional lives we live may not be receptive to proselytizing, in the specific ways we treat one another and conduct our business, people will recognize there might be a certain something missing in their lives. May they find You, in us, Lord. May the words of our mouths be an inspiration to others while pleasing to you. Holy One, thank you for your grace and for loving me. Be with me this day and each day and save us all. I pray in your glorious name. Amen.

AUGUST 4

MATTHEW 18:1-5 TRUE GREATNESS

At the time the disciples came to Jesus and asked, "Who is the greatest in the kingdom of heaven?" He called a child, whom he put among them, and said, "Truly, I tell you, unless you change and become like children, you will never enter the kingdom of heaven. Whoever becomes humble like this child is the greatest in the kingdom of heaven. Whoever welcomes one such child in my name welcomes me.

Lord God, sometimes our faith in you, like our lives in general, is immature. We struggle with trying to be the "top dog" or the best. Jesus teaches us to be "good" which is quite different from trying to be better than others. The goal is to be unencumbered by "acting like someone you think you want to be" and be more like an innocent child, waiting for God to enter your head and your heart. The world to children is just what they see. Their world is unencumbered; it is what they see which is quite different from the expectations (barriers) adults place in front of themselves. Like the twelve, sometimes I am confused. Jesus likened the gifts of the children: innocence, honesty and humility, as an indication of true greatness. Who sees an adorable child who knows they are loved and loves back, right? We all do! It is that unencumbered love Jesus wants us to cultivate and embrace. Translating that to adults, Jesus wants us to give up claims to power and status. He wanted the disciples and each of us to know a dependence on God, then we shall know greatness in the kingdom of heaven. We have learned, Holy God, how Jesus humbled himself and taught the disciples and us we to seek the powerless, needy and marginal. Help us to embrace all just as they are and to sow the seeds of love for our neighbor everywhere we go. Be with us and save us, each one, warts and all! I pray in your blessed name. Amen.

AUGUST 5

MATTHEW 18:21-22 FORGIVENESS

Then Peter came and said to him, "Lord, if another member of the church sins against me, how often should I forgive? As many as seven times?" Jesus said to him, "Not seven times, but, I tell you, seventy times seven times."

———————————————

Jesus, you want me to what? Forgive? Forgive? Forgive? The number seems unreachable and yet it must be part of the plan. I know you want us to always forgive but...ok no "buts" about it. Simply put, I am to forgive. Peter had quite the hurdle to get past the traditional teachings of the Jewish tradition of forgiving 3 times for the same "offense." I wonder, if Peter thought his original 7 times would be a sufficient number of times to forgive someone. Do I? You are telling me "no," seven times is not enough? I must not put a number on forgiveness. Peter and those who overheard this conversation must have been stunned. What were they thinking? Although the disciples had been following you, Jesus, for some time, they were thinking in terms of history, or more specifically, in terms of the law. Jesus your teachings were and are in terms of grace. That is a whole different ball of wax! Jesus please help us to understand the full measure of living with grace in one's heart. If I am grace-filled because you died on the cross to take away all the sins of the world, and mine, that grace is never-ending! The idea that our Christ died for each one of us makes my petty stubbornness seem a sin, too. Thank you Lord God, for the gift of your son, Jesus. I get it why you said, "This is my son, in whom I am well pleased." I pray for the goodness of heart that he had and his capacity to make your people think and learn from him. Patience is what I need to work on. Open my heart to be more like him and less like the "laws" of my parents and elders. Help me and others to have a more forgiving heart and to show love to those who engender negative reactions from me. Lord

God, help all of your people to be open, caring and welcoming of their neighbors. Lord God, without you and your son, I would have been lost in the family of my birth. You saved me and held my hand through some pretty tough times. Thank you God for always being with me, even when I sinned. Thank you for saving me and making me understand what it means to forgive. Be with us all and save us. I pray in your blessed son's name. Amen.

AUGUST 6

MATTHEW 19:13-15
JESUS BLESSES LITTLE CHILDREN

Then little children were being brought to him in order that he might lay his hands upon them and pray. The disciples spoke sternly to those who brought them; but Jesus said, "Let the little children come to me, and do not stop them; for it is to such as these that the kingdom of heaven belongs." And he laid his hands upon them and went on his way.

Lord, there is a song playing in my head, I can hear the sweet voices singing it even now: "Jesus loves the little children, all the children of the world. Red and yellow, black and white they are precious in his sight, Jesus loves the children of the world. May it be so. As a new day dawns, and reality sets in, I want to hold fast to those words and how precious each one is in your eyes, Lord God. Be with the family and loved ones today who lost a child, or who has a desperately ill child and is powerless to heal them. What we can do is pray, donate to medical research for the physically, mentally or emotionally needy ones wherever they might be. Help them to evolve into healthy, productive and loving children of God. Where there is hate, sow love, where there is sorrow may there be brilliant rainbows, and where there is illness, may there be healing. Be with us Lord God and help us this day to do something for someone else that might make a difference, if only for a single person. Comfort those who are in need and help us welcome the stranger who may be alone and frightened. Be with us as we struggle to find the key to joy in your world and to use our wealth for the good of humankind. Be with us and save us Lord. In your blessed and holy name I pray. Amen.

MATTHEW 22:24, 29-33
THE QUESTION ABOUT
THE RESURRECTION

"Teacher, Moses said, 'If a man dies childless, his brother shall marry the widow, and raise up children of his brother.'

Jesus answered them, "You are wrong, because you know neither the scriptures nor the power of God. For in the resurrection they neither marry nor are given in marriage, but are like angels in heaven. And as for the resurrection of the dead, have you not read what was said to you by God, 'I am the God of Abraham, the God of Isaac, and the God of Jacob'? He is God not of the dead, but of the living." And when the crowd heard it, they were astounded at his teaching.

All knowing and loving God, your patience with those who would not understand the order of life, death, and resurrection surely must have become tiring and disappointing to you. Moses was among those in the Old Testament who brought forth the message of the resurrection of the dead, and yet it was ignored, discredited. Those who choose not to believe, Lord God, put up barriers to evade your teachings and pull out preposterous suggestions for surviving wives and children. In your infinite wisdom and love you knew the only way to reveal all was through a Divine plan...Jesus would be the way, the truth and the light. Through his teachings, death and Resurrection the mystery would once again be revealed. On earth, in this world, one after another is taken away, and so ends all earthly hopes, joys, sorrows, and connexions. What hope you give to those who are left without a beloved. What a powerful and everlasting example you provided the world! I am thankful Lord, you have provided hope and assurance there is something wonderful awaiting beyond the grave! I have engraved in my very being words of comfort, "in my father's house there are many rooms...where I go to prepare a place for you, if it were not so, I would have told you." You are the "living God " and heaven is your glorious abode and it is for all who have received the grace promised by Jesus' life, death and resurrection! You are my hope and my salvation. Thank you Lord for your gift of a son, the Messiah who came to take away the sins of the world, even mine. Be with me this day and each day as I struggle with worldly realities which I am powerless to change or even to understand. Save me, in the strong name of Jesus, until one day I too shall find my place in your heavenly home, I pray. Amen.

AUGUST 8

MATTHEW 22:34-40
THE GREATEST COMMANDMENT

When the Pharisees heard that he had silenced the Sadducees, they gathered together, and one of them, a lawyer, asked him a question to test him. "Teacher, which commandment in the law is the greatest?" He said to him, 'You shall love the Lord your God with all your heart, and either all your soul, and with all your mind.' This is the greatest and the first commandment. And a second is like it: 'You shall love your neighbor as yourself.' On these two commandments hang all the law and the prophets."

Holy God, your son did not fall into the traps set up by those who would not accept him. Jesus' response to the Sadducees was to silence the ones who would try to trap him. Quite simply, love God, love all the people just as the prophets declared. Concise, clear, no equivocation. Who could argue with that? Then, why now does it seem many have turned away from you and the teachings of your son? What is happening in our world to cause such a decline in worshiping the Lord? People seem to have turned away, churches are in financial and spiritual trouble. No one seems to hold the key to stopping the trend. Today I pray for your congregations and houses of worship. May they find ways to turn the tide of the exodus of congregants. May we find ways to reach the children of parents who decided to "stay home" on Sunday mornings. May those who say things like "we are letting our children decide about religion when they grow up." What seems incredible is how could they possibly find God when they have no basis to realize what they are missing? I pray for enlightenment and leadership to bring people together to learn of your love and care for people. When the moral compass you have set for us is understood, the avarice of humankind will hopefully be softened by people helping people. Let us follow the lead of special programs that specifically seek those who have a great need and are helping our youth and those who seem lost. May programs designed to help the poor, like the programs to end Human Trafficking, various church led Youth Initiatives, and the work to get food to those in need. Helping those who need it the most while at the same time bringing blessings and your love, is what Jesus would do. Hunger initiatives throughout the world are vibrant ways we can show our love and care for our brothers and sisters. Help us Lord God, to bring the "good news" of Jesus to all who are hungry and in need of sustenance, not just in nutrition, but also in spiritual ways. Let your people stand up to those who have lost their way by feeding their souls as well as their growling bellies. Be with us Lord, and save us this day, in your blessed name, I pray. Amen.

AUGUST 9
LUKE 4:9-13
THE TEMPTATION OF JESUS

Then the devil took him to Jerusalem, and placed him on the pinnacle of the temple, saying to him, "If you are the Son of God, throw yourself down from here, for it is written,

> *"He will command his angels concerning you, to protect you,' and 'On their hands they will bear you you up, so that you will not dash your foot against a stone.'"*

And Jesus answered him, "It is said, 'Do not put the Lord your God to the test." When the devil had finished every test, he departed from him until an opportune time.

Loving God, you gave us your son, to take away the sins of the world! So, of course, you would be the architect of leading your people through the pitfalls of life. You gave us the gift and the tools to face painful realities with courage and faith, just as Jesus did. Jesus told the devil, "Do not put the Lord your God to the test." We must also stand up and reject evil in our lives, in our country, in our world.

This post was from "In Search of A New Eden," it is helping me.

May God bless you with discomfort
At easy answers, half truths, and superficial relationships
So that you may live deep within your heart.

May God bless you with anger
At injustice, oppression, and exploitation of people,
So that you may work for justice, freedom and peace.

May God bless you with tears
To shed for those who suffer pain, rejection, hunger and war,
So that you may reach out your hand to comfort them and
To turn their pain into joy.

And may God bless you with enough foolishness
To believe that you can make a difference in the world,
So that you can do what others claim cannot be done

To bring justice and kindness to all our children and the poor.

May it be so Lord, Amen.

AUGUST 10

LUKE 4:14-15
THE BEGINNING OF THE
GALILEAN MINISTRY

Then Jesus, filled with the power of the Spirit, returned to Galilee, and a report about him spread through all the surrounding country. He began to teach in their synagogues and was praised by everyone.

———————————

Lord, thank you for the teachings of Jesus who returned to his hometown with a solid reputation. The prophets foretold what was going to happen and the Christ child, now man, walked boldly into the synagogues and read the word and preach to adoring and believing congregants. They loved the miracles he performed and praised his work! He went there following the trials of the devil, because he felt called by the Holy Spirit to do so. What is the Holy Spirit calling us to do? My life's journey as a Christian and as an educator, Lord called me to work with teens in a way that would help them know good and have an advocate when, if they needed one. We are all called by you, some search and search for what that calling is. Thank you God for helping me see a way to disengage from a challenging childhood, and to march boldly into a plan to help those who needed me the most. I pray today for those who perhaps still search for what it is they are 'supposed' to do. May you lead them into a life that fulfills them and helps others. Be with the sick, the lonely and the lost. Help them through positive relationships with family, friends and colleagues who can guide them and shield them from harm. Be with us this day and save us, I pray in your holy name, Amen.

AUGUST 11

LUKE 6:1-5
THE QUESTION ABOUT THE SABBATH

One sabbath while Jesus was going through the grainfields, his disciples plucked some heads of grain, rubbed them in their hands, and ate them. But some of the Pharisees said, "Why are you doing what is not lawful on the sabbath?" Jesus answered, "Have you not read what David did when he and his companions were hungry? He entered the house of God and took and ate the bread of the Presence, which it is not lawful for any but the priests to eat, and gave some to his companions. Then he said to them, "The Son of Man is lord of the sabbath."

Lord God, how your patience must have been tried, listening to the Pharisees and their comments judging others. I know the guilt I have for comments I have made in judgement of others. The truth is, we do not know what motivates others nor how they think. The disciples were hungry, they ate. Thank you for the enlightenment of Jesus who used the teachable moment to hope for a deeper understanding from the Pharisees. God's plan, your play Holy God, has no beginning nor end. Sometimes I am guilty of the same reckless judgement on others. Help me, Lord God, to know how to place my priorities in the context of your patient love. May I ask for clarity, first and keep listening for your guidance. Jesus tells us to look to God, seeking not merely the "letter of the law," but to seek what is liked in your heart. Your, Lord hold the key to our lives and you do not give up when we disappoint you. Help me to always remember to not give up. Be with me this day and each moment of my being. I pray for the forgiveness of my sins and especially for judging others. I pray you will save me and that one day, I shall dwell in the house of the Lord, forever. Amen.

AUGUST 12

LUKE 6:27-31 LOVE FOR ENEMIES

"But I say to you that listen, Love your enemies, do good to those who hate you, bless those who curse you, pray for those who abuse you. If anyone strikes you on the cheek, offer the other also, and from anyone who takes away your coat do not withhold even your shirt. Give to everyone who begs from you; and if anyone takes away your goods, do not ask for them again. Do to others as you would have them do to you.

L ord God, how your patience must have been tried, listening to the Pharisees and their comments judging others. I know the guilt I have for comments I have made in judgement of others, too. The truth is, we do not know what motivates others nor do we know how they think. Jesus had a message about hate, cursing and abuse, he was speaking then and to us now, Lord. He said "do good to those who hate you, bless those who curse you, pray for those who abuse you." Again, Lord, when I need Jesus' message the most, it is there for me. I have struggled and have been having a difficult time with issues relating to how our government is treating those who have fled their countries in search of asylum and those who are working illegally in the United States. Children are involved and I am "soft" on the emotional stability they are losing. The "buts" have to go and I have to focus on the things that I can change...starting with me. Help me Lord, to follow the way you would have me go and grant me peace as I move into each new day a bit uncertain of what is next. I pray that the prayers I offer make sense to all who receive them and that together we can follow the golden rule, "do unto others...". Keep me grounded Lord, I pray for the forgiveness of sins, the courage to pray your truths. Be with me and save me, I pray in the name of the Risen Son. Amen.

AUGUST 13

LUKE 6:37-38 JUDGING OTHERS

"Do not judge, and you will not be judged; do not condemn, and you will not be condemned. Forgive and you will be forgiven; give, and it will be given to you. A good measure, pressed down, shaken together, running over, will be put into your lap; for the measure you give will be the measure you get back."

Lord God of all, thank you for the blueprint you provided via Luke. The list of "do nots' ' is not all that long. I think it is doable! Let us work really hard this day to hang on to the not judging and not condemning. That opens the door to the greatest gift of all, forgiveness. I know I really need to work on that one. How much better I feel, Lord, when I am doing something for someone! Making time to connect in good ways with family, friends and even strangers, gives me a joyful heart. I cannot tell you how many have held doors for me recently as I have needed to use assistance when walking. My heart skips a beat knowing that what I've been thinking, is not true. I am not invisible. I know the words I have spoken to those who help me, bring joy. I began trying to find a way to just say "thank you" to people who help me. I can tell you, those who check me out at establishments always smile and interact in positive ways when I look them in the eye and say, "thank you for your help today, I really appreciate it." For it is in the giving that we see and feel you at work through us. What a most powerful and loving gift and when we return the favor, we make someone feel they are loved and appreciated. Thank you Lord, you know what is in my heart and in my head and help me reset. Be with me this day and each day as I try to avoid judging others. May we all take a deep breath and resist unsolicited advice. Help us to advocate in positive ways for the ideals and goals you have taught us are important. Be with us Lord God, and save us, I pray. Amen.

AUGUST 14

LUKE 6:43-45 A TREE AND ITS FRUIT

"No good tree bears bad fruit, no again does a bad tree bear good fruit; for each tree is known by its own fruit. Figs are not gathered from thorns, nor are grapes picked from a bramble bush. The good person out of the good treasure of the heart produces good, and the evil person out of evil treasure produces evil; for it is out of the abundance of the heart that the mouth speaks."

Savior God, praise and glory to you for all you have done and continue to do for your people, for us. You know introspective reality is not necessarily a character trait people undertake regularly. We humans turn a bind eye to our own faults and yet those various sins are glaringly obvious to others. Jesus teaches us to get real with our own sin instead of trying to hide it under the cover of complacency or a desire to hurt someone else. We are a vain people who would not stand for an imperfection in our outward appearance to go unchecked. You, Lord God want us not to look at the surface but to look into our hearts to see what sin is living there. Help us to overlook our actions and behaviors and go straight to what is living and causing our hearts to beat. Help us loving God, to be like figs produced from trees or grapes from vines. Help us harvest our deeds free from thorns or bramble bushes. The harvest from them is worthless, undesirable, painful and irritating. We do not want to be defined by those words or deeds. Lord, help us to change. May the abundance living within, be what shines forth from the love shown in our eyes, in our smiles and especially in our deeds. Lord, help us to recognize the weeding we need to do to purify what dwells within our hearts so that what we say and what we do will glorify you and be a welcome contribution to society. Continue to inspire and help us to regularly cut the rhetoric that causes us to throw thorns when you intend for us to harvest sweet fruit. Be with us this day as we spend time examining what is in our hearts and weeding out what is not pleasing to you. Be with us, and save us, I pray in your glorious name. Amen.

LUKE 6:46-49

"Why do you call me 'Lord, Lord,' and do not do what I tell you? I will show you what someone is like who comes to me, hears my words, and acts on them. That one is like a man building a house, who dug deeply and laid the foundation on rock; when a flood arose, the river burst against that house but could not shake it, because it had been well built. But the one who hears and does not act is like a man who built a house on the ground without a foundation. When the river burst against it, immediately it fell, and great was the ruin of that house.

Wise and wonderful Lord, the stories Jesus told invite us into his heart and soul and yours. His conversations, recounted by Luke, have succinctly articulated the way to salvation. Where Jesus said "practice what you preach" today we might say, "be your authentic self." Where Jesus said "I will protect you if you obey me," we might say "It is my way or the highway." And finally Jesus teaches destruction to those who do not obey. The hip new phraseology vs the historical rhetoric, which one will I choose? Does it matter? No it does not matter. Lord your will be done is what matters and how one chooses to follow the teachings should not be greatly altered by vernacular. Luke was a master at restating and interpretation for the times. Thank you Lord, for the voices of wise ministers of the word who bring vibrant life to tales of old. Help me to always seek your will and follow it. Help me lead in ways that are pleasing to you. I pray to live a life built on the foundation laid out by Jesus and you. The Ten Commandments set forth the basic roadmap for each of us. Help us to embrace the teachings and to live our lives honoring you. And Lord, finally when our time on earth is over, may we hear the words "well done, good and faithful servant." Thank you for each day and the blessings you have given us. Help us to put you first and to build our life's foundation according to your plan. Be with us and save us, I pray in your blessed name. Amen.

AUGUST 16

LUKE 8:9-10
THE PURPOSE OF PARABLES

Then his disciples asked him what this parable meant. He said, "To you it has been given to know the secrets of the kingdom of God; but to others I speak in parables so that 'looking they may not perceive, and listening they may not understand.'

Teacher, blessed are we who have spent a lot of our lives learning about you, Jesus and how we are to be in this world. As a child, I received a tiny mustard seed (inside some sort of orb) necklace. It was a tangible connection to the parable and more importantly to the power of a tiny grain and how your love is like that seed. Jesus knew the news he was bringing was not news all people wanted to hear. Thank you Lord God, for the gift of Jesus and for his innate ability to perceive and to connect. The goal of the parables was to bring the story of salvation to the attention. Knowing there are those who would not be receptive to his message, Jesus made his comments in parables the disinterested would not understand. Lord, we understand and we have learned the lessons that non-believers cannot embrace. Be with those who resist your power and more importantly your love. Show them the way to salvation and eternal life. For, Savior God, it is in the living that we shall find life eternal. May it be so. Bless us this day, as you continue to be with us. Help those who are seeking answers, to find them in your truth, save them and us, even as we draw our very last breath. Amen.

AUGUST 17

LUKE 8:16-18 A LAMP UNDER A JAR

"No one after lighting a lamp hides it under a jar, or puts it under a bed, but puts it on a lamp stand, so that those who enter may see the light. For nothing is hidden that will not be disclosed, nor is anything secret that will not become known and come to light. Then pay attention to how you listen; for to those who have, more will be given; and from those who do not have, even what they seem to have will be taken away.

Holy God, your beauty and your heart jump out at us in so many different ways. Sometimes I marvel at the beauty you provide in sunrises and sunsets. The majesty displayed takes my breath away, as does the harmony of two voices like Bocceli and Sherran. Thank you for the gift of song and making people and things that appear incongruous take me to tears in the joy and beauty of the sound. May those who have more use their wealth and talents to enrich all the earth and her people. Help us to live authentic lives dedicated to following the example of your son and ways to feed the hungry, care for those who are ill, bring comfort to those who are facing the end of their days, and those who will mourn their passing. We are a compassionate people Lord, and sometimes we need to stop the busyness in our lives, taking time to know that where we go, you are there with us, too. Thank you for your constant and abiding love, especially when our attention has been temporarily blinded by the glossy and sexy things all around us. May we live our lives helping those less fortunate and teaching our children about you. Help us to always marvel at the "perfect symphony" you have provided and to always praise your name. Be with us and save us from our sinful ways as each day reveals another treasure you have provided. In your name I pray. Amen.

AUGUST 18

THE APOSTLE'S CREED

I believe in God, the Father almighty,
creator of heaven and earth.
I believe in Jesus Christ, his only Son, our Lord,
who was conceived by the Holy Spirit
and born of the virgin Mary.
He suffered under Pontius Pilate,
was crucified, died, and was buried;
he descended to hell.
The third day he rose again from the dead.
He ascended to heaven
and is seated at the right hand of God the Father almighty.
From there he will come to judge the living and the dead.
I believe in the Holy Spirit,
the holy catholic church,
the communion of saints,
the forgiveness of sins,
the resurrection of the body,
and the life everlasting. Amen.

LUKE 8:25 JESUS CALMS A STORM

He said to them, "Where is your faith?" They were afraid and amazed, and said to one another, "Who then is this, that he commands even the winds and the water, and they obey him?"

L ord, you are a patient Lord. Jesus led by your example and when he was questioned, Jesus said to them, "Where is your faith?" And still, they did not get it. Jesus, whose days were numbered once again had to find another way to bring clarity to each one. Do we carelessly repeat our belief in the Lord? I believe that we do not. Where is our faith? Our faith is in you and your son, Lord. Jesus challenged the disciples to have faith. Faith in you, loving God, is essential in our lives. Without faith, one is powerless to do good works for humankind. These acts are done in part to show what being a Christian means and of course to share, in small and large ways, our faith and love in you, Lord God. We profess our faith saying what we believe, when we say The Apostle's Creed. That is it, Holy God, This is what Christians say and this is what they believe. This belief is essential and the way we know God's promises will be kept. The promise kept is the promise Jesus reminded us of, saving those who give their lives to Christ. We must be confident, have faith that you, Lord God, will see us through the difficulties life presents us. When we know you are with us, all will turn out, according to your wisdom Lord. Lord help us to re-commit our love of you and to live our lives in ways that are pleasing to you. Be with us each day in our waking and in our sleeping, in our coming in and in our going out. Help us to allow our faith in you, Lord God when our way is difficult and our hearts are broken. Make us whole and keep us on the path you would have us go. Be with us and save us, we pray. Amen.

LUKE 9:1-2 THE MISSION OF THE TWELVE

Then Jesus called the twelve together and gave them power and authority over all demons and to cure diseases, and he sent them out to proclaim the kingdom of God and to heal.

———————————

T hank you Lord, for giving Jesus to the world for our salvation. Jesus realized he alone would need help in order bring your will into reality. Traveling throughout many places and among throngs of people he preached and healed the mentally and physically ill. Thank you for giving your son powerful tools to show your people what he was proclaiming and advocating was real. And so, Lord, Jesus empowered his disciples to go out and rid those afflicted by demons and to cure those with diseases. Each of their actions were linked to proclaiming your kingdom, Lord. Jesus knew, just as disciples had questions, others doubts would be just as great. Shifting to today, we know if a person were to walk among us preaching and healing our reactions might be skeptical to that message. There are unexplained miracles proclaimed by some and there are doubters. Are we looking for proof, quick fixes? Yes! In times of great stress some are and some are even bargaining with you. Lord, we pray for many things and make promises we cannot keep and you, loving God, know that. In desperation, we pray for a miracle, hoping you will save a loved one. The truth is, the miracle we pray for may not be the one you provide. The curing of demons and diseases was granted to the chosen twelve and of course their time on earth would be finite. While that hope has long been gone, you alone Lord show power as mankind tackles the great mysteries and problems in life. As we evolve to be a people who are environmentally responsible and educationally advanced, we sometimes forget to praise and teach of your love and your son's ultimate gift of salvation. Help us to be people who share your message and live as Jesus and you instructed. Lord, today I pray you will be with the sick, the physically or mentally challenged and those who care for them. Help your young people as they begin another school year today, or soon. Be with the children as they are bombarded by bullies and overloaded with school work and social pressures. Keep them safe Lord, from evil people who seek to hurt them and perhaps steal their youth. Help each one of us to know we can come to you in prayer, and you will help us manage our stress or anxiety. Help us Lord to calm the anxious hearts of our children and our friends as they connect with you seeking your loving guidance throughout new circumstances. May they know they can come to you in prayer any time and in any place about anything in their hearts and minds. Be with us this day and each day, holy God and save us from our sinful ways. Be with all of your children and comfort them as they face new challenges. I pray in your blessed name. Amen.

AUGUST 20

LUKE 9:18-20
PETER'S DECLARATION ABOUT JESUS

Once when Jesus was praying alone, with only the disciples near him, he asked them, "Who do the crowds say that I am?" They answered, "John the Baptist; but others, Elijah; and still others, that one of the ancient prophets has arisen." He said to them, "But who do you say that I am?" Peter answered, "The Messiah of God."

Wise and wonderful God, your son and in your wisdom his actions, bring to light our uniqueness in the world. When we are in community with you, our world seems large. In fact, the community of believers is relatively speaking, small. And yet, you have given us a vital tool...to recognize you and to recognize Jesus Christ as the Messiah you sent into the world! Help us Lord, to take that knowledge, your love of us and the understanding that Jesus was, is and forever shall be our Savior. And so, armed with that tool, how can we as 21st century disciples serve you in the world in which we live today? Lord, the evolution of the world is astounding and yet, the evolution of Christians living their faith in a complex world has faltered. We are told to separate church and state, and yet, the moral compass of Christians cannot obliterate basic tenants of life: the thou shalts and thou shalt nots. How in our world in particular in the United States now, can we accept the way the country has treated others? Help us Lord to accept the challenge of Jesus to make imperatives of ways to treat one another. I am confused about the outrage or lack thereof of the way African Americans were imported to the United States to serve white masters and yet, why Native Americans were pushed out of desired areas? Both oppressed, yes. The people have mistreated both groups and generally, women as well. How can we fix the holes in the sweaters of life? How will we welcome the stranger, feed the hungry, heal the sick, educate our children and love our brothers and sisters? We have dropped so many stitches, Lord, and our sweater shall surely fall apart without going back, picking up the dropped stitches and mending the garment that is the country I live in? Help your people Lord God, to fix the injustices, to lean into Jesus' teachings and love for humankind. When we wear the garment of the Bible, make us proud leaders of women, children and men. Empower us to do what we know is just, carefully and continually. "The Messiah of God" is watching us and waiting for us. Be with us this day, Lord, give us new tools to fix the messed up sweater of our lives, forgive our sinful ways and save us, I pray. Amen.

AUGUST 21

LUKE 9:46-48 TRUE GREATNESS

An argument arose among them as to which one of them was the greatest. But Jesus, aware of their inner thoughts, took a little child and put it by his side, and said to them, "Whoever welcomes this child in my name welcomes me, and whoever welcomes me welcomes the one who sent me; for the least among all of you is the greatest."

Wise and wonderful Teacher, how petty we are! So and so got a beautiful new .... and I want a better one. My car is the best, my house is bigger than yours, my friend cannot be your friend...Your beloved son took time to talk about senseless comparisons that only serve to divide and hurt. True greatness as defined by Jesus is not petty, not a competition. And yet, the vulnerable disciples were doing just that: competing for Jesus' favor. Simply, the persons who welcome Jesus into their hearts and minds are the ones Jesus calls "the greatest." The poorest person who loves Jesus but who has nothing else gets it. Do we get it? Are we trying to be the "greatest" by constantly competing to outperform others? Help us Lord to pivot to what matters. Jesus' teaching shows just how petty the chosen ones could be. Jesus teaches us to resist coveting what others have and rejoice in their good fortunes, remaining true to you. Help us Lord to always think of others before ourselves and to put you and your son first! Let us set aside the needless attempt to compete and begin to focus on what really matters. Help us to be generous in our love of your people and to help those in need. Lord, forgive our greed, soften our hearts and minds to do your will. Be with us this day, and save us, in your holy name I pray. Amen

LUKE 10:21-22 JESUS REJOICES

At that same hour Jesus rejoiced in the Holy Spirit and said, "I thank you, Father, Lord of heaven and earth, because you have hidden these things from the wise and the intelligent and have revealed them to infants; yes, Father, for such was your gracious will. All things have been handed over to me by my Father; and no one knows who the Son is except the Father, or who the Father is except the Son and anyone to whom the Son chooses to reveal him."

T hank you loving God, for the wisdom and trust you had in sending Jesus into the world. Jesus learned his lessons well and was the Savior Messiah you intended him to be. While it is hard to fathom the suffering and the trials Jesus faced, what is understandable is the wisdom and understanding he exuded. Jesus' pleasure was connected to his love and understanding of the Holy Spirit. The joy in his heart was linked to the successes his ministry was having and especially because he knew the Holy Spirit was with him during the trials and victories over Satan. How blessed we are today when we feel your love and know you are with us, always, Lord. Jesus' comments are a blessing to us and give us hope for a glimpse of you, Lord. What joy there is in our hearts, knowing the Holy Spirit dwells within us, too. Holy God, what a loving parent you were, allowing Jesus to discern human nature and intelligence. Help us to grow in faith and love of you, Lord God as we continue our life with you. We know the path is not always easy, and yet you have provided us. We pray daily "thy will be done, on earth as it is in heaven." We are studying the Bible, what the prophets wrote and especially all that Jesus said and did. We know Jesus died to take away our sin and because he died for us, we live for him and for you. Be with us and save us Lord, in the name of you son, Jesus, I pray. Amen.

AUGUST 23
LUKE 10:23-24

Then turning to the disciples, Jesus said to them privately, "Blessed are the eyes that see what you see! For I tell you that many prophets and kings desired to see what you see, but did not see it, and to hear what you hear, but did not hear it."

Loving God, how proud you and your son were at the moment Jesus realized in that moment the disciples were fully convinced of the majesty and power being the savior has. Having the faith to believe without seeing or hearing, what a gift! Thank you God for helping us to carry that faith in our hearts and minds. Your love and light throughout the world has been our saving grace. No matter the path, no matter the pain, we know you are with us, always. We are truly a blessed people, for we have hindsight and wisdom that allows us to boldly step into all of our tomorrows with you and because of your son, salvation is ours! Thank you for the wisdom and love of Jesus who frees us from sin and saves a place for us in your eternal home. Be with us today and each day, and save us from our sins, in the name of Jesus. Amen.

AUGUST 24
LUKE 10:25-28

Just then a lawyer stood up to test Jesus. "Teacher," he said, "what must I do to inherit eternal life?" He said to him, "What is written in the law? What do you read there?" He answered, "You shall love the Lord your God with all your heart, and with all your soul, and with all your strength, and with all your mind; and your neighbor as yourself." And he said to him, "You have given the right answer; do this, and you will live."

God of Heaven and Earth, thank you for the blessings you gave us, a Savior who walked among mortals, teaching, preaching and showing the world a new way to live. We are blessed to have an historical record of Jesus' birth, life's teachings, and the sure knowledge that he came to take away the sins of the world. What happens to us, between birth and death is what also happened to your son, the cross. Not a dash not an emoji, a cross. Quite simply, Christians live their lives celebrating, learning and living out their faith. Jesus' walk on earth was a beautiful gift and for that and the promise of forgiveness of our sins we can walk boldly through each day. We read the stories from both the Old and New Testament and see the proof of the prophets. We acknowledge your beloved son, Jesus and rejoice that you loved us, he loved us so much, he takes away our sin. Thank you, is a small word, may we back up that thank you by following your Commandments and by giving you the glory for all we are, all we have and all we do. Help us to honor you and your son by feeding the poor, helping the sick, and loving our neighbor as ourselves. We acknowledge our shortcomings and impulsive actions that hurt others and pray for your forgiveness. Help us to prayerfully remember your love and generosity and be more loving and giving. Be with those who are suffering and struggling in life, in place of anxiety, give them peace. Lord, be with us and save us, in the name of Jesus Christ, we pray. Amen.

AUGUST 25

LUKE 11:28

But he said, "Blessed rather are those who hear the word of God and obey it!"

Heavenly God, your earthly family is diverse, head strong and prayerful. The seeds of Christianity and other religions with different names, but still know you. We are struggling in the world, Lord God, to live in harmony or at least respect for one another. It is so difficult at times for we are a stubborn people. The faithful communities I know of, strive more to follow your example and show we are Christians by our love and faithful work on behalf of those in need. We pray for the work World Vision, the Human Trafficking Initiative, UNICEF, The Red Cross, and a myriad of other charitable organizations, helping our earthly neighbors. Be with each group who works to end hunger, discrimination and war. Love us Lord as we continue our walk with you while trying to make this world a better place. Help us to act with kindness, generosity and love. Show us the way. We are listening and acting in ways we hope will be pleasing in your sight and which will glorify your holy name. Be with us this day and each of our tomorrows as we love our neighbors throughout the world as ourselves. May your saving grace forgive our sins and lift up our world in love and peace. In your name I pray. Amen.

AUGUST 26

LUKE 12:1-3
A WARNING AGAINST HYPOCRISY

Meanwhile, the crowd gathered by the thousands, so that they trampled on one another, he began to speak first to his disciples, "Beware of the yeast of the Pharisees, that is, their hypocrisy. Nothing is covered up that will not be uncovered, and nothing secret that will not become known. Therefore, whatever you have said in the dark will be heard in the light, and what you have whispered behind closed doors will be proclaimed from the housetops.

Holy God, your people are hungry to hear your words and understand the mysteries of Christianity. We need to learn more about the grace of salvation received because you sent Jesus to walk among humans teaching and preaching. Help those who are ignorant and perhaps yearning for answers find you in a church community. Some are drawn to glitzy buildings and mega churches and are absorbed with the pageantry. May they realize that only the pageantry on Sunday mornings is not what Jesus' message is all about. It is about loving you, serving you, and loving our neighbor as ourselves. The hypocrisy of doing nothing to help our fellow humankind, especially those in need is not what you have taught us. Help us to be a welcoming community of believers who yes, sin, but also sincerely repent for our sins. Help us continue the discipleship Jesus modeled in ways that show love for your children and give aid to those in need. May our churches resound in the glory of your love and may our children learn early in life the stories of your glory and plan for each one. Be with us this day and every day and save us, I pray in your blessed name. Amen.

LUKE 12:8-10, 12

"And I tell you, everyone who acknowledges me before the angels of God; but whoever denies me before others will be denied before the angels of God. And everyone who speaks a word against the Son of Man will be forgiven; but whoever blasphemes against the Holy Spirit will not be forgiven.

For the Holy Spirit will teach you at that very hour what you ought to say,

---

H oly God, sometimes being "out in the open" about one's faith is not appropriate. We worry about what others might think of us or how to live out our faith when perhaps that faith compromises our working environment. I pray we will have integrity and love for you to let our faith's light shine in a world where it is not always welcomed. Sometimes our moral compass is incongruous with our chosen profession. The strain is palpable. Help us Lord, to be able to serve in our occupations without having our faith clash with them and when they do, may our differences be resolved without loss of our moral convictions. Lord God, help us to be open to the calling from the Holy Spirit. Soften our hearts and minds in order that we may receive your forgiveness. Lord, grant us the grace necessary to keep an open heart that prompts us to listen and trust in you. It is not always easy to profess our love of Jesus before others. It is especially difficult if we are uncertain how our message will be received. There is a quiet, uncomfortable feeling that keeps us silent until a more comfortable feeling with those around us softens our anxious feelings and encourages us to speak our truths. So today, I pray for courage to live our lives and speak our truths about our faith and love for you. When words fail, may our actions represent the lessons learned and glorify you. May we live out our faith and love for you. May our ways be kind and above reproach and quietly turn around practices which are not pleasing to you. Be with us and save us I pray. Amen.

AUGUST 28

Today is the anniversary of Dr. Martin Luther King's famous "I have a dream" speech on the steps of the Lincoln Memorial (August 28, 1963)

LUKE 12:22-25 DO NOT WORRY

He said to his disciples, "Therefore I tell you, do not worry about your life, what you will eat or about your body, what you will wear. For life is more than food, and the body more than clothing. Consider the ravens; they neither sow nor reap, yet they have neither storehouse nor barn and yet, God feeds them. Of how much more value are you than the birds! And can any of you by worrying add a single hour to your span of life?"

Lord of All, thank you for your wisdom and that of your son. We live in a fast paced and demanding world. Meeting higher and higher expectations for job performance, school performance, etc. places such stress on each of us. We just keep adding to our pile of "have to do" and sometimes, we just snap! Help us to remain calm and to be methodical about the constraints or expectations others have put on us. Jesus wanted us to "chill" and not worry so much. Make that happen Lord. As a new school year begins and the last quarter of another year is entered, help us to set realistic goals and to remember to put you first! We want to honor you and to do that, we have to model how your son's walk through life projected assurance and confidence. Even when he knew his time on earth was drawing near, Jesus was not filled with paralyzing anxiety. He did the mundane: washed the disciples' feet, fed them a banquet and then offered the first communion. He modeled how to go through life's ups and downs with honor and confidence. Jesus didn't act as a man in panic mode or filled with anxiety. He methodically went about fulfilling the plan while remaining steadfast to the end. Jesus did all he could to project confidence and to refocus the disciples in ways to honor their fellow Christians. May we learn by example and realize worrying is a needless mental activity that demeans the human spirit. Thank you for the example of your son, who knew how to calm the storms and the people. Help us to slow down as we embrace our days and tomorrows with the confidence of one who knows we are already saved which is the most important knowledge we need to have. Be with us Lord, and save us from ourselves and our needless anxiety. In your dear son's name I pray. Amen.

AUGUST 29
LUKE 12:27-28, 30-31

Consider the lilies, how they grow: they neither toil nor spin, yet I tell you even Solomon in all his glory was not clothed like one of these.

For it is the nations of the world that strive after all these things and your Father knows that you need them. Instead, strive for his kingdom, and these things will be given to you as well.

———————————

Gracious and loving God, you have helped your flock learn ways to live in harmony with one another by following a plan. When we get wound up about something we have to do for work, family, school, etc ...help us remember how to plan and how to execute the task at hand. Worrying about what to do is a detriment to task completion. We must remember, loving God to do your will and to honor you by what we say and what we do. Help us to put you first and to look to your words and the words of Jesus to gain insight into our problem solving, even what might seem the most difficult of tasks. Show us the way to network with Christian brothers and sisters, taking into consideration advice or suggestions as we tackle the task at hand. Help us to put you and your glory first in our thoughts and plans so that on that day when we shall join you we will hear you say "well done." Be with us Lord and save us from our worrisome ways and the sin that creeps in when we go astray. Thank you God for all that you have provided for us. Amen.

AUGUST 30

LUKE 12:32-34

"Do not be afraid, little flock, for it is your Father's good pleasure to give you the kingdom. ... Sell your possessions, and give alms.

For where your treasure is, there your heart will be also."

———————————

Caring Lord God, thank you for reassuring and blessing us each day. Help us to learn from the words of your disciples. We live in a society filled with glitter and glitz and most of it, at the end of the day, is just waste. Help us to be generous with our possessions and to share our wealth with those less fortunate. Lord, I pray especially today for ways to help those who struggle to feed, clothe, house their family members or to provide medical care. Help those that can, share their abundance with those in need. For those who are struggling to find affordable places to live, proper clothing for school or work, and ample food to put on the table may our generosity be abundant and freely given. Lord, continue to be a beacon of hope to those who are without the necessities of life. A country with pockets of poverty and illness are in desperate need of basic necessities that many simply take for granted. May those that have the ability continue to help those without. Help us find ways to be less wasteful and more ecologically conscious. I pray the businesses will share their food with the homeless and use acceptable food supplies that cannot be served or sold, but are still fit for human consumption. I pray school cafeterias will join in this process as many hungry students need more sustenance. Thank you Lord, for doctors, dentists, and other professionals who lovingly give their time and talent to those in need. Jesus wanted his disciples to come into his community without possessions and the distractions of their daily lives. Giving time, talent and money shaped his ministry. May Jesus' example inspire us to help those who are less fortunate. We pray today for the conviction to help end poverty and health crisis that are ignored due to financial constraints. Lord, your leadership and example sustains us. May our hearts be with you always as we ask you to be with us in our efforts to help those less fortunate, and save us, I pray. Amen.

AUGUST 31

LUKE 12:49-53
JESUS THE CAUSE OF DIVISION

"I came to bring fire to the earth, and how I wish it were already kindled! I have a baptism with which to be baptized, and what stress I am under until it is completed! Do you think that I have come to bring peace to the earth? No, I tell you, but rather division! From now on five in one household will be divided, three against and two against three; they will be divided: father against son and son against father, mother against daughter and daughter against mother, mother-in-law against her daughter-in-law and daughter-in-law against mother-in-law."

Merciful and loving God, you have provided for us in every way. Jesus also addressed the need for strife in our world. His perception of complacency was to snap out of it! We are encouraged to challenge, test, and to re-think the paths we take as the day of judgement approaches. Jesus wanted this day to be over. Do we think about that? Consider Lord, the mercy you have provided to those who are at or near death. Haven't we prayed for mercy for the one who would not recover? Don't we thank you for your mercy in ending pain and suffering? I believe we do. Your care for your people is merciful. Jesus yearned for the end as he hung on that cross and to take his seat next to you, Lord God. Your love and confidence in Jesus, and welcome into the kingdom gives us hope as we face our own mortality. We are a blessed and saved people! Thank you Lord for the gift of Jesus who was born, lived and died to take away the sins of the world. Your love and grace have provided for all believers. Thanks be to you, our God. Be with us this day and all the days of our lives and save us, I pray in your blessed name. Amen.

SEPTEMBER 1
LUKE 12:54-56

He also said to crowds, "When you see a cloud rising in the west, you immediately say, 'It is going to rain'; and so it happens. And when you see the south wind blowing, you say, 'There will be scorching heat'; and it happens. You hypocrites! You know how to interpret the appearance of the earth and sky, but why do you not know how to interpret the present time?

———————————

L oving God, how tedious it must be for you to see how the world is spinning out of control. Your people are intelligent about many matters, when it comes to predicting the weather, the phases of the moon and its impact on tides, how to cure many diseases, etc. However, the non-believer is ignorant and excluded. You are a patient Lord, and yet even you have limits! Each day is filled with challenges which is a way to test, to reassure a pathway of action. It's not a bad thing...we should find ways to reassure and to adjust our plans, thoughts and actions. Of course you are impatient. We are impatient, too. How is it, we are so ignorant at times? We know through history false imprisonment and inhumane treatment of others is sinful, and yet we continue. Nelson Mandela, a great man who spent years imprisoned for his stance on apartheid, went on to lead his nation past the notion of dividing people on the basis of race. The day he was released from prison brought great celebration throughout the world. I remember the sermon that Sunday morning and the sound of church bells ringing in my town, later we witnessed them ringing throughout the world. What rejoicing there was! And yet, today the non-believers are building fences, incarcerating innocent people and attempting to return to a despicable time in history. Help us Lord, free the world of the radical, unfounded and cruel treatment of humans against humans. We do know how to interpret the present time," may we fix the messiness of our country, our world. Help us find peaceful ways to reset our path and show love and acceptance of the humans who just want to live in a safe world with basic necessities available to all. Be with us and save us from our sins and ourselves, I pray in the name of Jesus Christ. Amen.

SEPTEMBER 2

LUKE 12:57-59

"And why do you not judge yourselves what is right? Thus, when you go with your accuser before a magistrate, on the way make an effort to settle the case, or you may be dragged before the judge, and the judge will hand you over to the officer, and the officer will throw you in prison. I tell you, you will never get out until you have paid the very last penny."

———————————

Holy God, leaning in toward our inner soul informs us. Jesus wanted the people to look inward to analyze the appropriateness of their convictions. We are taught to look into our own consciousness before running to someone else to arbitrate a matter. We know that electing to go to court with a dispute no matter how small nor how large should not be our first step. Jesus tells us to "make an effort to settle the case." And so Lord, thank you for the earliest teaching of compromise to settle differences. Help us to use our intellect to the end of needlessly spending money on frivolity when two or more can reasonably settle differences. Help us Lord to settle differences great and small in humane ways which, while giving up a bit on each side seems uncomfortable, in the end is a more just way. Lord, we have many humane and governmental issues facing us today. Please help our elected officials sit down and act in responsible ways to begin to resolve issues of great importance in our nation, indeed, in our world today. We must address the issues of controlling semi and automatic weapons of war, how our country will deal with people seeking asylum from their home countries, climate change, uncontrolled spending, and leaders whose irrational actions are hurting your people and making the world more unstable. We pray for cooler heads and brilliant, workable solutions to our problems. May we debate them honestly and in ways that enhance life. These things, I pray in the name of Jesus, the one who died to take away the sins of the world. Amen.

SEPTEMBER 3
LUKE 13:1-5

At that very time there were some Galilean whose blood Pilate had mingled with their sacrifices. He asked them, "Do you think that because these Galilean suffered in this way they were worse sinners than all other Galileans? No, I tell you; but unless you repent, you will all perish as they did. Or those eighteen who were killed when the tower of Siloam fell on them—do you think that they were worse offenders than all the others living in Jerusalem. No, I tell you, but unless you repent, you will all perish just as they did."

D ear Savior of the world, we remember your teachings and those of your son. Those memories are horrifying. When we learn of hateful actions that harm others we wonder why the lessons of history are senselessly repeated. The actions of Pilate, mingling the sacrifices of the Galileans with their very blood harken back to pagan, unchristian times. Pilate slaughtered people carelessly, needlessly. Pilot used brutal instincts ordering assassinations which were a preamble to presiding over Jesus' trial and ultimate crucifixion. Can we equate murderous decrees to natural disasters? Lord, you do not work that way. Plotting the demise of another human being is not an accident, it is murder. Murder is a sin. Thank you for sending your son to "take away the sins of the world" by the sincere act of repentance. Help us Lord to see the light Jesus brought to the world and to acknowledge our inner conscience and sincere repentance of sin. Be with those who make decisions on behalf of a country, municipality, other people. May they do so wisely and appropriately, considering all of the important ramifications of such action. Be with the leaders of the world, watch over them and help them to be wise and compassionate of the lives of others. Lord, help the tyrants of the world to reform their murderous and mean spirited ways. Their actions sicken us and especially because we have little power to cease their murderous ways. Shine the light on their dark hearts and minds, ending their oppression of innocent people. Holy God, be with us each day as large and small decisions have consequences. We pray the consequences will have positive improvements and not place an undue burden on anyone. Be with us and save us, I pray in your holy name. Amen.

SEPTEMBER 4

LUKE 13:6-9 THE PARABLE OF THE BARREN FIG TREE

Then he told this parable: "A man had a fig tree planted in his vineyard; and he came looking for fruit on it and found none. So he said to the gardener, "See here! For three years I have come looking for fruit on this fig tree, and still I find none. Cut it down! Why should it be wasting the soil?" He replied, "Sir, let it alone for once more year, until I dig around it and put manure on it. If it bears fruit next year, well and good; but if not, you can cut it down."

———————————

Merciful Lord, Jesus taught patience when he spoke in parables. The metaphors used made sense to his audience, sometimes we have to work to understand what he meant. Jesus' words offer hope and encourage us to try to resolve issues without making radical decisions initially. In Jesus' day, cutting down a fruit tree would be radical. Thank you Jesus for planting seeds of hope and love where you went and when you spoke. We are encouraged to try to improve a situation, peacefully and only after sincere efforts have been made to take action that will be more radical. Patience is a virtue which one must exercise in order to avoid making unwise and devastating decisions. Lord, right about here is where I beg for patience and understanding. Were Jesus alive today he would speak in parables that have a more direct association to our world today. How would Jesus react to a notion of using an atomic bomb to dissipate a hurricane? It would be far worse than bringing a fire hose out to extinguish a match! Lord, help us discern when it is appropriate to take extreme measures, and help our leaders understand the full import of their words and deeds. May we use our breath of God to extinguish hatred and gluttony. " Breathe on us breath of God, fill us with life anew. That I may live as thou did live, and do what thou would do." God, be with us and save us, I pray. Amen.

SEPTEMBER 5

LUKE 13:10-17
JESUS HEALS A CRIPPLED WOMAN

Now he was teaching in one of the synagogues on the sabbath. And just then there appeared a woman with a spirit that had crippled her for eighteen years. She was bent over and was quite unable to stand up straight. When Jesus saw her, he called her over and said, "Woman, you are set free from your ailment." When he laid his hands on her, immediately she stood up straight and began praising God. But the leader of the synagogue, indignant because Jesus had cured on the sabbath, kept saying to the crowd, "There are six days on which work ought to be done; come on those days and be cured, and not on the sabbath day." But the Lord answered him and said, "You hypocrites! Does not each of you on the sabbath untie his ox or his donkey from the manger, and lead it away to give it water? And ought not this woman, a daughter of Abraham whom Satan bound for eighteen long years be set free from her bondage on the sabbath day?" When he said this, all his opponents were put to shame; and the entire crowd was rejoicing at all the wonderful things that he was doing.

All-knowing God, your son who was wise beyond his years, was ever the teacher. On a day reserved for teaching, Jesus saw a woman in need and tended to her. It made a difference to the leader of the synagogue who probably did not appreciate Jesus' "shining star" taking the spotlight. The leader's crutch, a "law" forbidding work on the sabbath. Jesus' reply to this leader was to call him a "hypocrite." That woman went to great effort to get to the temple that day. She did not just get up and stroll there. For her, bent over, using crutches and trying to weave her way through the streets to the temple was an herculean effort. Jesus sensed her need and set her free from the prison in which her body had placed her. Help us Lord to refrain from making "artificial" rules to regulate our behavior and imposing them on others. May we live our lives following in the example of Jesus: feeding the hungry, caring for the sick and ever praising you. Keep our egos in check and our love for our neighbors and those in need ever on display. Let us pray for those less fortunate in physical, mental or emotional health and give them all of the assistance possible. Use our brilliant minds, Lord God to find cures for diseases and affirmations that make life difficult for many. Help our hospitals and universities teach and discover ways to make those with such infirmities or conditions whole again. God of love and light, shine on those that need our help, be with those who are alone, reassure them Lord God, you hear their prayers and indeed they are not alone. Let those who are able speak up and speak out advocating for their brothers and sisters. Lord, I pray your will be done and I know it is for all to reach their full, God given potential. Be with us and save us, I pray in your holy name. Amen.

SEPTEMBER 6

LUKE 13:31-35

At that very house, some Pharisees came and said to him, "Get away from here, for Herod wants to kill you." He said to them, "Go and tell that fox for me, 'Listen, I am casting out demons and performing cures today and tomorrow, and on the third day I finish my work. Yet today, tomorrow and the next day I must be on my way because it is impossible for a prophet to be killed outside of Jerusalem.' Jerusalem, Jerusalem, the city that kills the prophets and stones those who are sent to it! How often have I desired to gather your children together as a hen gathers her brood under her wings, and you were not willing! See, your house is left to you. And I tell you, you will not see me until the time comes when you say, "Blessed is the one who comes in the name of the Lord."'

Holy Lord God, your son brought such light into the world. He boldly called Herod a "fox," which was Herod's true self. Jesus knew all people are accountable to you, God. How many like Herod are there in our world today? One thing we know is, allegiance to anyone other than you, Holy Father of Jesus is misaligned. I pray for those who are oppressed by mean spirited rulers. Help all people learn to live together with love and respect, following the examples set forth by you. No one knows how long their lives will last, but all of your children Lord, are to act in ways that are pleasing to you. They are to be decent and kind, using their unique talents and skills for good. Being greedy is not one of those ways Lord. Help us learn to use our abundance for good and not gluttony. Jesus tells us when the day of judgement comes, those who have not been saved and who do not believe in you, will lack an invitation into your kingdom. We do not know when our time on earth will end, I pray Lord, on those days you will welcome your saved children, freeing all from the ravages of pain and suffering. Be with us this day and each day Lord and save us, I pray. Amen.

LUKE 14:7-11

When he noticed how the guests chose the places of honor, he told them a parable. "When you are invited by someone to a wedding banquet, do not sit down at the place of honor, in case someone more distinguished than you has been invited by your host; and the host who invited both of you may compare and say to you, 'Give this person your place,' and then in disgrace you will start to take the lowest place. But when you are invited, go and sit down at the lowest place, so that when your host comes, he may say to you, 'Friend, move up higher; then you will be honored in the presence of all who sit at the table with you. For all who exalt themselves will be humbled, and those who humble themselves will be exalted."

Wise and magnificent Lord, your words hit at the core of young adults and their drive to be "the best" or "number 1". Our young people, embarking on career paths have been encouraged to have large egos. As one matures, I see a more compassionate attitude in many. Help those growing into themselves and lives outside of the family home to remain steadfast to you. May they remember their training in the family home, school and church. Even the great Presbyterian Mr.Rogers spent his career teaching children how to be different from the "me first" attitude children sometimes develop. Encourage each of us, loving God to remain humble, not seeking recognition nor glory, rather to do our jobs the best we can and when others acknowledge or to recognize one's accomplishments, that is when we will feel humbled. Jesus wants all to remain humble and giving. Let us follow the example and as one grows, leave a path for others to follow by the example of deeds. Be with the young adults as they learn and grow and perhaps even make mistakes along the way, it is ok, its part of the process of maturation.

When we stumble, help us to ask those we offended to forgive us and to take our misdeeds to you in prayer, know that by your grace we will be saved. Be with us this day and know how deeply we love you, Lord, and in the name of Jesus Christ, save us. Amen.

SEPTEMBER 8

LUKE 14:13-14

But when you give a banquet, invite the poor, the crippled, the lame, and the blind. And you will be blessed, because they cannot repay you, for you will be repaid at the resurrection of the righteous."

———————————

Lord of Hosts, you want those who follow your teachings to be sociable, in a God-like way. There are many who are lonely and searching for a way to be in conversation with someone. When I think about people I know, who perhaps live alone or have recently lost a loved one, I know how helpful sharing a meal with that one is. When one opens the heart to speak about faith and you, Lord God, the guest is reminded in a gentle way how special he or she is to you and to the host. Jesus in his travels more often than not ate with strangers who were anxious to learn more about him and his faith and healing journey. Jesus was welcomed into home after home. Jesus' journey shows us how to lift the spirits of a sad or lonely one and how to share lessons in Christianity in an intimate setting. The generosity of food and conversation is truly a gift that benefits the giver as well as the receiver. "It is more blessed to give than to receive." In that vein, when we give, we are following your plan, Holy God, when we pay attention to the lonely. Genuine hospitality and a welcoming spirit makes everyone feel better. Lord, please bless the hosts in our lives: the welcoming host on Sunday mornings, the hosts who greet their students every day, and the host who holds a door for someone or helps another by carrying packages from the store to the car for a person in need. Be with all of us and especially the hosts, dear Lord, and save us, I pray. Amen.

SEPTEMBER 9
LUKE 14:15-24

One of the dinner guests...said to him, "Blessed is anyone who will eat bread in the kingdom of God!" Then Jesus said to him, "Someone gave a great dinner party and invited many. ...but they all alike began to make excuses....So the slave returned and reported this to his master. Then the owner of the house became angry and said to his slave, "Go out at once into the poor, the crippled, the blind,, and the lame. And the slave said, "Sir, what you ordered has been done, and there is still room." Then the master said to the slave, "compel people to come in, so that my house may be filled. For I tell you, none of those who were invited will taste my dinner."

Lord of Hosts, words of your teaching come to us in many ways, and for that we are most thankful. Luke's story about the invitation to a feast reminds me of the song children's choirs sing, "I cannot come to the banquet, don't bother me now....". The song is silly and yet carries a magical punch. Help us Lord to be generous with our hospitality. Serve those who need our help in kind and loving ways. Help us to cook and serve the hungry. May we joyfully give loving and kind gestures to those in need and may we welcome sincere kindness and assistance. Help us to volunteer to serve meals at soup kitchens or homeless shelters. The recipients love interacting and learning about the kindness given to them by strangers. The part of the interaction that is not "strange" is the recognition of Christian love for a brother or a sister or a child. Help us Lord, to be generous in sharing our faith and our food. Be with us and save us, I pray in your son's blessed name, Amen.

SEPTEMBER 10
LUKE 14:25-33

Now large crowds were traveling with him; and he turned and said to them, "Whoever comes to me and does not hate father and mother, wife and children, brothers and sisters, yes, and even life itself cannot be my disciple. Whoever does not carry the cross and follow me cannot be my disciple. For which of you intending to build a tower, does not first sit down and estimate the cost, to see whether he has enough to complete it. … So therefore, none of you can become my disciple if you do not give up all you possessions.

Heavenly Father of Jesus, your son was what we would call "purposeful." He was becoming popular and had a following of "believers" following him. He wanted his chosen disciples to understand completely what they had to do to become one of the twelve. They were chosen, Jesus expected he would come first, in their hearts and minds. First above all, above father, mother, wife, children, brothers, sisters, and yes, life itself. Jesus wanted the disciples to love him and to give up everything to go on the amazing journey he was undertaking. I wonder, Lord God, would I have felt the "call" and readily given up everything to follow your blessed son? What is it we are willing to do in the name of Jesus Christ? Jesus had a clear understanding of what he was undertaking and in order to please you, Lord. He also knew his disciples must put him first and focus on the tasks as the clock was ticking on the timeline of life. Giver of life, thank you for making my life what it is today. I do know that if my time should end tomorrow, I shall welcome entrance into such a magnificent kingdom. None of us is perfect, but all of us can ask God to forgive us our sins. The sincere petition to ask for forgiveness of sins is the one requirement to being granted salvation.

You are a kind and loving God. Comfort those who struggle with the question of salvation and those who have great suffering during life. May we all be together in heaven with you one day. Be with us and save us, I pray. Amen.

SEPTEMBER 11

LUKE 14:34-35

"Salt is good; but if salt has lost its taste, how can its saltiness be restored? It is fit neither for the soil nor for manure piles, they throw it away. Let anyone with ears to hear listen!"

Savior, how dangerous was the choice of the twelve to be followers of Jesus.

Disciples were instructed to abandon all other personal relationships in order to follow him. Jesus is the teacher to the students, in this case the disciples. The charge to the disciples was to follow Jesus, no one else. The disciples followed Jesus' path, even to the cross and his death. Are we all not students of Christ? Where our faith in Christianity causes division with those we love, grant patience, a willingness to listen and open minds to ponder the majesty of you and Jesus Christ. Help us teach our children to learn of your glory, to learn to pray, and to bring them to church regularly. Be with us in this world of diversity, and save us, Lord God as we humbly prepare the next generation to know you and to love you. Save us from our sins and be with us today. Amen.

SEPTEMBER 12
LUKE 15:1-7

Now all the tax collectors and sinners were coming near to listen to him. And the Pharisees and the scribes were grumbling and saying, "This fellow welcomes sinners and eats with them." So he told them this parable: Which one of you, having a hundred sheep and losing one of them, does not leave the ninety-nine in the wilderness and go after the one that is lost until he finds it? When he has found it, he lays it on his shoulders and rejoices. And when he comes home, he calls together his friends and neighbors, saying to them, 'Rejoice with me, for I have found my sheep that was lost. Just so, I tell you there will be more joy in heaven over one sinner who repents than over ninety-nine righteous persons who need no repentance.

Lord, we have heard of your love and your patience in teaching and re-teaching members of the flock. Grumbling about compassion and exhibiting jealousy towards others continues to haunt our thoughts and prayers. We pray for patience and understanding as we work with your children, attempting in kind and gentle ways to warm cold hearts. Jesus wanted us to get the parallel between lost and found. "Amazing grace, how sweet the sound, that saved a wretch like me! I once was lost, but now, I am found, was blind but now I see." Lord, how we fret over losing something we need, like perhaps our cell phone! I feel such panic when I cannot locate mine, and I've witnessed others who feel the same way. And then... suddenly we find it! What joy we have, and I suppose great relief, too! Lord Jesus' example of the lost sheep gives us understanding of the tension that exists when we lose something while pointing out how vital it is for those who sin to discover and repent of their sins in order to be saved. To experience your blessing, we must listen. Give us ears to hear, and hearts open to your love and grace. Help us to follow the example of Jesus in ways we do not even think about today. May our lives gently guide those who are lost. Open the eyes of those blind to you and your love for us. Be with us this day, may we see your glory in the sunrise and sunset, and Lord, save us, I pray. Amen.

LUKE 15:8-10

"Or what woman having ten silver coins, if she loses one of them, does not light a lamp, sweep the house, and search carefully until she finds it? When she has found it, she calls together her friends and neighbors, saying, "Rejoice with me, for I have found the coin that I had lost. Just so, I tell you, there is joy in the presence of the angels of God over one sinner who repents."

Lord God, your son came to earth to show the way sinners can be found, saved. Each one is important to you. In fact, we are all of utmost importance to you. Great rejoicing in heaven follows our sincere acts of repenting. Your unique plan for salvation was to bring Jesus Christ into the world. In the Parable of the Lost Coin, we learn of great rejoicing by the woman upon finding her precious coin. She calls her friends and neighbors in order to share her good news. The metaphor of finding something (or someone) is not lost on us, God. When a sinner is enfolded into fellowship with you, it is an opportunity to rejoice. Your plan of salvation is amazing, it was why Christ came. We are encouraged to rejoice with sinners who have repented for not only are they found, but also forgiven. Help us Lord, to encourage parents with children to teach them and lead them to you through the churches who relate how Jesus came to take away the sins of the world, and their sins, too. May parents continue to lead their children in ways that introduce and celebrate the Christian church. I pray for Christian educators and programs teaching and reassuring children about the goodness in the world and how to be forgiven when one sins. Bless those who have repented and whose lives are now forever changed. Praise and glory to you, for those who not only have obliterated their sinful ways, in sincere repentance, moreover, who have become like the shining beacon on a hill. Thank you God, for their public testimonies which impact the listeners to turn from sin toward a life with you. Help these testimonials to be the words those who have fallen from grace need to hear. May hearing them impel the change that needs to happen in order to begin the process of healing and salvation. May we all rejoice in that good news. Be with us Lord God and save us, I pray. Amen.

SEPTEMBER 14

LUKE 16:1-3

Then Jesus said to the disciples, "There was a rich man who had a manager, and charges were brought to him that this man was squandering his property. So he summoned him, "What is this that I hear about you? Give me an accounting of your management, because you cannot be my manager any longer."

Holy Lord, the disciples of your son had much to learn, and they had to learn it quickly. Jesus felt the urgency of time to save and educate humankind. The disciples had to be honest and make friends for their purpose of spreading Christianity throughout the territory to which Jesus had entrusted them. Jesus wanted the disciples to have gratitude which would make their task of spreading the word a positive and welcoming experience. Help us follow Jesus' example and remarkable plan. We pray for the 'managers' of the world. May their actions be honest, kind and render positive results. May we love our neighbors, invite them into the loving arena of church settings that prepare our spirits for a life that is pleasing to you, God. We know Lord, closing doors and refusing to listen creates a barrier of distrust. Keep us open to new ideas and to your teachings as we make choices for our children and loved ones. May your home be a place for us to grow our faith among a community of believers so that on that day when we join you in heaven you will be pleased with our walk and that it glorifies you. Be with us Lord, help us when we falter and save us from our sinful ways, I pray in the blessed name of the one who came to take away the sins of the world, Jesus Christ. Amen.

LUKE 16:14-15

The Pharisees, who were lovers of money, heard all this and they ridiculed him. So he said to them, "You are those who justify yourself in the sight of others; but God knows your hearts; for what is prized by human beings is an abomination in the sight of God."

Holy Lord, clearly the Pharisees placed value on money. As the poet Geoffrey Chaucer, in The Canterbury Tales, once declared "avarice is the root of all evil." Your holy word also declares the same. What is it Lord that makes humans care more about the glitz and glamor and less about the substance of one's soul? How is it that the love of money and what it can buy to impress is so sexy? We realize it is not the new "toy" or the fancy clothes, rather what is written on our hearts and minds. Help us Lord, to use our riches to help elevate your kingdom here on earth with loving gestures to your people and to the environment, may they glorify your name. May we set aside our yearning for the newest and the best, and help those in need. Help us follow the example of Jesus, enjoying what we have a little less by helping those who need our generosity and making the world a better place. May we give freely to support the sick, feed those that hunger, and work for your glory in what we say, do and the ways we choose to use our money. Help us find a way to be more freely giving of our time, talents and financial resources. Be with us Lord, and may we never cause you to question what is in our hearts. Be with us when we pull out our wallets to use our resources for your people, keep us ever mindful that money is the root of all evil. In the name of your son, Jesus Christ, we pray for wisdom in our actions and salvation that forgives our sinful ways. Amen.

LUKE 17:7-10

"Who among you would say to your slave who has just come in from plowing or tending sheep in the field, 'Come here at once and take your place at the table'? Would you not rather say to him, 'Prepare supper for me, put on your apron and serve me while I eat and drink, later you may eat and drink'? Do you thank the slave for doing what was commanded? So you also, when you have done all that you were ordered to do, say, "We are worthless slaves; we have done only what we ought to have done!"

Dear Lord, your people have lived their lives more or less goal oriented. Therefore Lord, we sometimes become impatient, just as the disciples did. We know there is a "proper time" for rewards and we know it is not our time, but yours. Your servants sometimes become haughty in their expectations of rewards. We struggle to tamp down those feelings because we are truly unworthy. Your disciples were urged not to be impatient when the reward they sought was not immediately provided. Help us to realize that when we do what is expected, what we are supposed to do, there is no need for a reward, after all we have merely done what was expected. To receive a reward, we have to do more. To do "more" implies one has to ascertain something beyond the goal. Be with us Lord when we strive to do your will so that we will exceed your expectations and thereby please you. Lord, help us to find loving and giving ways to minister in our communities. May we be generous with love and praise of your children and let the goal of service to our earth and earthly inhabitants without regard to anything in return. Be with us each day, for give us our sins and strengthen our resolve to be the people you want us to be. In your holy name, I pray. Amen.

LUKE 17:11-19

On the way to Jerusalem Jesus was going through the region between Samaria and Galilee. As he entered a village, ten lepers approached him....they called out, saying, "Jesus, Master, have mercy on us!" ... Jesus said to them, "Go and show yourselves to the priests." And as they went, they were made clean. Then one of them, when he saw that he was healed, turned back, praising God with a loud voice. ... He prostrated himself at Jesus' feet and thanked him. ... Then Jesus asked, "Were not ten made clean? But the other nine, where are they? Was none of them found to return and give praise to God except this foreigner?" Then he said to him, "Get up and go on your way; your faith has made you well."

Healing God, your only son was so wise. Thank you for sending him to walk among humans, to live and teach and die for our salvation. Jesus did not hesitate when entering a village, ten lepers approached him. Healing all, caring about each one, and yet only one gave praise for what God had done. How ironic that in today's world, people ask for things and when they receive what they requested, go on their way. Jesus' instruction to the one who prostrated himself and praised you for healing him was what all should have done, but failed to do. Help us, your living servants, to remember to give thanks for the many blessings we receive each and every day. Our faith in you is what carries us through the day. We pray to model the teachings and to do all we can to demonstrate our appreciation and gratitude for the miracles you provide. Be with us Lord, and save us, I pray. Amen.

SEPTEMBER 18

LUKE 17:20-21

Once Jesus was asked by the Pharisees when the kingdom of God was coming and he answered, "The kingdom of God is not coming with things that can be observed...For in fact, the kingdom of God is among you."

Lord, Paul teaches in his letters about your kingdom. He tells us righteousness, peace and joy in the Holy Ghost is within each of us. Do you know God's intentions for those around us? The impression I am left with when impacted by a special soul lives on inside of my heart and consciousness. Thank you Lord God for the power of recognition of just how alive you are today! As we associate with faith filled people, we recognize the uniqueness of your amazing power and glory. May our traditions honor you Lord for all that you have poured into us, especially the tradition of participating in Holy Communion. It is one church tradition that always reminds me of your love, suffering, and hope for tomorrow. When I receive the elements I am flooded with memories of your love and kindness as well as those I have known who have gone home to be with you. It is bittersweet and heart warming to know they are with you now, that your promises are being fulfilled. May each of us feel your gentle and abiding love and may you feel our love for you. Be with us this day and each day as we walk together. Lord, save us from all evil and especially our sinful ways. Be with those who do not yet know of your saving grace, may it be one Christ-filled follower and friend away. Amen.

LUKE 17:22-26

Then he said to the disciples, "The days are coming when you will long to see one of the days of the Son of Man, and you will not see it. They will say to you, 'Look there!' Or 'Look here!' Do not go, do not set off in pursuit. For as the lightning flashes and lights up the sky from one side to the other, so will the Son of Man be in his day. But first he must endure much suffering and be rejected by this generation. Just as it was in the days of Noah, so too it will be in the days of the Son of Man."

Heavenly God, your blessed son, Jesus, the Messiah fulfilled the purpose for which he was conceived. We marvel at the wisdom and maturity with which he moved throughout his homeland. We read of his teachings and how patient he was with his disciples and those who followed him throughout his ministry. He came into the world to take away the sins of the world, which means he came to spread the message of salvation and to die. Jesus told the twelve after he died, do not seek for that which you cannot attain. In many ways, in the blink of the eye, he would be gone. The metaphor of the lightning flashes quickly disappear compared to the rapidity of his life and death are meant to instruct the disciples and those he taught by parables and healing miracles. Wise beyond his years, Jesus also told of his impending suffering and rejection. He knew history tends to repeat itself, as illustrated by Jesus' comparing his time on earth to how it would be for him. Lord, we are stubborn people! Help us learn the lessons of Noah and Jesus. May we work to bring love and kindness, faith and faithfulness into our hearts and minds. May we take those qualities into our daily lives as we strive to share the abundant love and faith you intend us to have. May we follow the golden rule, "Do unto others as you would have them do unto you."

Help us to confidently walk with you and your spirit, which is alive in the family of believers, using our faith to make our world a better place for all. Be with us and save us, I pray in the name of the Messiah, Jesus Christ. Amen.

LUKE 17:30, 33-37

... —it will be like that on the day that the Son of Man is revealed. ...Those who try to make their life secure will lose it, but those who lose their life will keep it. I tell you, on that night there will be two in one bed; one will be taken and the other left. There will be two women grinding meal together; one will be taken and the other left." Then they asked him, "Where Lord?" He said to them, "Where the corpse is, there the vultures will gather."

Father of the Messiah, in every age and time wicked people have defiled and are defiling your universe. Help us merciful Lord, to lean in to your teachings and those of your son, for it is in leaning in and learning how to have compassion for one another the sinful nature of humankind might begin to find your love and the salvation of Jesus Christ. Jesus was wise beyond his years, his observations of human nature at its worst was grim. Humanity has always had a power struggle and Jesus certainly recognized the capacity for violence during his life. He knew human nature: humans have the capacity to act like vultures picking at the bones of a dead animal. In fact, when Jesus was stripped of his clothes the vultures were in full force. Our species can be heartless at times. I pray you will help us dig out of the pit we find your people in. Help us treat people with dignity and kindness. May we be compassionate, loving and faithful Christians. Soften the hearts of those who step on and over the less fortunate. Mold them into people who make accommodations for the less fortunate with their generosity and caring ways. Be with us and save us, Lord, on this day and the next. Amen.

SEPTEMBER 21
LUKE 18:1, 6-8

Then Jesus told them a parable about their need to pray always and will not God grant justice to his chosen ones who cry to him day and night? Will he delay long in helping them? I tell you, he will quickly grant justice to them. And yet, when the Son of Man comes, will he find faith on earth?"

L oving God, the great mystery of having prayers answered continues to haunt many. They wonder, why? Ecclesiastes 3:1 gives an explanation: "For every thing there is a season and a time for every matter under heaven...". Songs have been written and sung addressing the mystery. The answer, only you know, Lord. We must wait patiently praying. It is not our time, but your's. We wait for the time to come while praying it will be soon. Meanwhile, our world is suffering the ravages of man and of nature. Help us to be better caretakers of Mother Earth, all of her people and things living on her land. Lord, help us to stop asking "Why do bad things happen to good people?" Let us ask, "What would you have me do, Lord God?" May we use our time and talents for good as we strive to save the planet and your people. We can make impure water clean throughout our land, not just in Flint, Michigan and Trenton, New Jersey, but throughout the earth. Help us to make drinking water potable throughout the earth for all peoples and creatures. Help us to improve deplorable living conditions of the poor and those seeking help from persecution. Be with us in our waking and in our sleeping, comfort the sick and the dying. Help turn angry and hateful hearts and minds from violence and death to peaceful coexistence. Be with those who care for the critically ill, who know there is little hope for healing, but who lovingly continue to pray and provide the best care possible. Lord, we pray "your time" will give us time to do better, to be better and await your wisdom and discernment. Stay with us as we try to live lives that are pleasing to you, and save us, I pray in your blessed name. Amen.

SEPTEMBER 22
LUKE 18:11-14

The Pharisee, standing by himself, was praying thus, 'God, I thank you that I am not like other people: thieves, rogues, adulterers, or even like this tax collector. I fast twice a week; I give a tenth of all my income.' But the tax collectors, standing far off, would not even look up to heaven, but was beating his breast and saying 'God, be merciful to me, a sinner!' I tell you, this man went down to his home justified rather than the other; for all who exalt themselves will be humbled, but all who humble themselves will be exalted."

Precious Savior, how tired you must be when your people judge others, insisting they are better than other sinners. Turn our intentions to discover ways we can be better people. Help us to love our neighbors as ourselves, to feed the hungry, take care of the sick. We know you are "the way, the truth and the light" always encouraging those who will learn from your words and those of your son and others who love you. Turn our minds to possibilities for improving how we live. Help us stop abusing one another and our lands. Let us be hopeful seeking ways to make change possible throughout our lives. Help us do all we can to follow your example as well as the teachings of your son and his disciples. May the disciples of today, spread the news of your love and hope for all people. Let us turn our attention to helping people live harmoniously with one another, celebrating our differences in peaceful and loving ways. May we be more than survivors, let us be leaders in our families, neighborhoods and nations. Help us, Lord and show us the way to resolve difficult issues peacefully and to lovingly listen to one another in search of solutions for all. I pray for all these requests and those on our hearts and minds by humbly asking you to be with us and save us. Amen.

SEPTEMBER 23

LUKE 18:18-25

A certain ruler asked him, "Good Teacher, what must I do to inherit eternal life?" Jesus said to him, "Why do you call me good? No one is good but God alone. You know the commandments: 'You shall not commit adultery; You shall not murder; You shall not steal; You shall not bear false witness; Honor your father and mother.'" He replied, "I have kept all these since my youth." When Jesus heard this he said to him, "There is still one thing lacking. Sell all that you own and distribute the money to the poor, and you will have treasure in heaven; then come, follow me." But when he heard this, he became sad; and said, "How hard it is for those who have wealth to enter the kingdom of God! Indeed, it is easier for a camel to go through the eye of a needle than for someone who is rich to enter the kingdom of God."

Lord, doubters continue to place roadblocks in their paths to you. Jesus' ministry was specific and purposeful. Asking people to turn their lives upside down, going in an opposite direction is a nagging temptation. He said, "if you love me...", those with much to lose, hesitated. We see the paradox between conviction and corruption. Walking away from "things' ' and what money can provide is difficult. Lord, we pray to courageously share what we have in ways that help those who desperately need our help. May our convictions be acted upon in unselfish ways, in order to demonstrate acts of kindness, letting our good intentions inform our choices. May we follow the examples of great leaders throughout the world: Mother Teresa, President Jimmy Carter, Malala Yousafzai, Bill Gates, and many others. These servants dedicate their time, talent and capital to venture into places where the most needy may be found. They minister in thoughts, words and deeds to help the needy, sharing the bounty of their love and loving ways to help those who live in desperate times and places. May we find unique opportunities to give back, Lord, in great and small ways. Help us to find unique ways to uplift others, perhaps by being a mentor, driving one who needs transportation, preparing hygiene kits for a homeless person, volunteering to help out at a homeless shelter, donating unused or unwanted clothing, eyeglasses, hearing aids, no longer needed hospital equipment, or to just speak or smile at one whose eyes lock with ours. Let us show we are Christians by our love and generosity. Lord, please be with others whose random acts of kindness help their sisters and brothers throughout the world. Help us to learn to follow our convictions in ways that help others instead of hesitating and doing nothing. Lord, we can always try to be better, do better. We may not be able to pass a camel through the eye of a needle, but what we can do is stretch open the hole! Be with us as we continue to try to elevate the poor living conditions of others less fortunate. Lord, please save us from our sinful ways, and continue to be in our hearts and heads, I pray. Amen.

SEPTEMBER 24
LUKE:18:26-30

Those who heard it said, "Then who can be saved?" Jesus replied, "What is impossible for mortals is possible for God." Then Peter said, "Look, we have left our homes and followed you." And he said to them, 'Truly I tell you, there is no one who has left house or wife or brothers or parents or children, for the sake of the Kingdom of God, who will not get back very much more in this age, and in the age to come eternal life."

Teacher, you answered the question, "Then who can be saved?" You remind us and instruct us, through God everything is possible. Humans cannot compete nor defeat God, for God is omnipotent. What we all can do is to love you, Lord in very human ways. Jesus pointed out the desire of everyone is to have enough to be able to afford whatever is desired. Desiring to be rich is not confined just to those who have abundant wealth, but to everyone. Giving up everything as Jesus asked, was a boulder-sized stumbling block. We are all guilty in some way to having a devotion of wealth. Help us Lord, to help those who need our help and to devote our abundant resources, using them for your people, our people. We know the answer to the question, who can be saved? Jesus' response to the greedy and wealthy was purposely rhetorical. We can all be saved! Your son and our Messiah, died that we might all be saved. What we do with our abundance is to help our neighbors. Jesus wants us to be unselfish with our wealth and he especially wants us to share what we have with those in need. Help us be cheerful in sharing and caring. Encourage those with great means to lead the way for all in areas of your word, Lord. Loosen the greedy grip on abusing our planet and wasteful ways by stubbornly holding onto environmentally tone deaf practices and failing to share with those in need. Lord, be with us as we try to do the right things for all people and this world. We know it is going to be difficult, we also know we can change the world for the better. Forgive our sins of gluttony and waste. We give thanks and praise for Jesus' gift of our salvation, In his name I pray. Amen.

LUKE 18:31-35

Then he took the twelve aside and said to them, "See, we are going up to Jerusalem, and everything that is written about the Son of Man by the prophets will be accomplished. For he will be handed over to the Gentiles; and he will be mocked and insulted and spat upon. After they have flogged him, they will kill him, and on the third day he will rise again." But they understood nothing about all these things; in fact, what he said was hidden from them, and they did not grasp what was said.

Heavenly Teacher, how you must have suffered by unselfishly and intentionally sending your son, the Messiah, that we might be saved. We say there is almost nothing we would not do for our child, but we do not really mean it literally. You did! Thank you Lord for sending Jesus to take away the sins of the world, our sins, too! You modeled how to be loving, giving, and unselfish. Knowing the pain and agony Jesus would endure for all, was the most horrifying and loving gift ever. It is little wonder that the disciples were unable to comprehend the horror Jesus would suffer. It is heartbreaking to learn there are those today who cannot believe in You. Help us to spread the word through peaceful and loving ways, that you are the Lord of all and that you love us. Your love is incomprehensible, just as knowing the number of hairs on our heads is baffling. Thank you for not giving up on us and our sinful ways. We pray to you for courage and strength to face each day and each challenge. Help us to always do the right thing and to love your gift to us of Jesus. Lord, empower us to have the courage needed to face adversity even when we do not know what shall happen, for we know no matter what happens, you are with us. Guide our thoughts and deeds even when we do not know exactly what is next for us. Sometimes it is hard to grasp the full power you have, may we just accept that your ways are just and your intentions for Christians are pure. Be with us this day and save us, I pray in the name of Jesus. Amen.

LUKE 18:35-43

As he approached Jericho, a blind man was sitting by the roadside begging. When he heard a crowd going by, he asked what was happening. They told him "Jesus of Nazareth is passing by." Then he shouted, "Jesus, Son of David, have mercy on me!" Those who were in front sternly ordered him to be quiet; but he shouted even more loudly, "Son of David, have mercy on me!" Jesus stood still and ordered the man to be brought to him; and when he came near, he asked him, "What do you want me to do for you?" He said, "Lord, let me see again." Jesus said to him, "Receive your sight; your faith has saved you." Immediately he regained his sight and followed him glorifying God; and all the people when they saw it, praised God.

———————————

Healing Lord, you are merciful and kind, and your son was, too. Thank you for the miracles great and small that you provide. They teach us in ways allowing us to bridge the gap of time. When we think about the blind man Jesus healed, we marvel. We also marvel at the awe inspiring story of Helen Keller. Although she did not recover her vision, in a way she saw more than many with the sense of sight. Thank you Lord for the brilliant, intelligence of people who have challenges that in today's world allow them to far exceed expectations in their lives. We realize the miracles you provide save so many, too. There is no other explanation for why a person awakens from a comatose state after years. There is also no explanation for a comatose person living a decade before dying. In your mercy Lord, we acknowledge the miracle we pray for is not always the miracle we receive, but it is still, a miracle nonetheless. We rejoice knowing you are with us always in the tiny and grand miracles that happen around us. Your wisdom and love are patient and kind. As painful as that reality is, Lord God, we know your decisions are for the best. Thank you for helping those in need and for reminding us your son died on the cross for our salvation. Your saving grace, is all we need. Be with us each day, and save us, I pray in the name of Jesus. Amen.

SEPTEMBER 27

LUKE 19:5-10

When Jesus came to the place, he looked up and said to him, "Zacchaeus, hurry and come down; for I must stay at your house today." So he hurried down and was to happy to welcome him. All who saw it began to grumble and said, "He has gone to be the guest of one who is a sinner." Zacchaeus stood there and said to the Lord, "Look, half of my possession, Lord, I will give to the poor; and if I have defrauded anyone of anything, I will pay back four times as much." Then Jesus said to him, "Today salvation has come to this house, because he too is a son of Abraham. For the Son of Man came to seek out and to save the lost."

Heavenly Savior, the miracles of Jesus were many and varied. Jesus restored the sight of a blind man, cured afflictions of lepers, and healed a woman so bent over she could hardly walk. Jesus' love and power was transformative but never more on display than with Zacchaeus as he stood before Jesus. Realizing the error of his ways Zacchaeus repented and took action by making a plan to give to the poor and to repay those he had defrauded four times over the amount he stole. Jesus who came to take away the sins of the world was moved. Jesus forgave Zacchaeus. And you know what? We have learned Jesus will forgive us, too! There is nothing we can do in the sincerity of repentance Jesus will not forgive! Help us to always do what is just and right and to sincerely repent our sins. Thank you for the life and teachings of Jesus and the prophets of old. Help us Lord, to be more willing to repent and to be more willing to forgive. Making reparations to those whom we have harmed is the right thing to do. May we be quick to say "I am sorry" and to make sincere efforts to enlighten our thoughts and unfair ways. Help us learn to be better listeners and to help resolve differences and avoid talk that is mean spirited and harmful. May our words and actions be helpful in resolution of conflict. Be with us in our going out and our coming in, and save us, Lord. Through Jesus we are made whole again and forgiven. Thanks be to God. Amen.

SEPTEMBER 28

LUKE 19:26-27

"I tell you, to all those who have, more will be given; but from those who have nothing, even what they have will be taken away. But as for these enemies of mine who did not want me to be king over them—bring them here and slaughter them in my presence."

D ear Teacher, we know that the muscle we use continues to strengthen and develop. Conversely unused muscles atrophy and become useless. So too, a person who uses the brain to increase knowledge grows in intelligence. The one who does not study has an undeveloped and under used brain. Similarly, those who hear the word and grow up loving you and your son develop a rich understanding of all you want us to know. A lazy person or one who does not believe cannot be made to learn and love you. How sad that is. Christians must be intentional in their thirst to learn all they can about you and the lessons from both you and your son. We must make the effort to use our abilities to prepare ourselves to speak your truth and love. We especially want to be sensitive and deliberate in our teaching the children about you. We want the impression we give them about you and your mighty power and love to seep into their pores and hearts. Our time and our talents will continue the perpetual love of you and faith-filled life. Help us Lord, to teach our children and to keep moving and growing our faith, doing what you would have us do for all of humankind. Be with us on this journey and in the name of Jesus who died to take away the sins of the world, forgive us our trespasses. In your glorious name I pray. Amen.

LUKE 19:29-32

When he had come near Bethpage and Bethany, at the place called the Mount of Olives, he sent two of the disciples, saying, "Go into the village ahead of you, and as you enter it you will find tied there a colt that has never been ridden. Untie it and bring it here." If anyone asks you, "Why are you untying the colt?" Just say this, "The Lord needs it."' So those who were sent departed and found it as he had told them.

Holy God, we know the story, we feel the excitement of the disciples and those around who heard the excited words, "Jesus is coming!" The Christ Child, now a man is prepared and yet not quite sure how things will unfold. One thing Jesus does know is his time on earth is almost over. He marched toward it and you with a bold and confident purpose. Finding a fitting way to make a triumphant entry, setting the stage for what was to come must have been so painful for you to watch and for Jesus to endure. When your loyal servants are prepared, as Jesus was, we can arrive at a point feeling all is well, even as it is actually spinning out of control. Lord, thank you for teaching us and for having us rejoice when we know our loved one has gone to his or her reward. You knew and helped your son teach us everything will work out and our loved one will live in your house, the house of the Lord, forever. May it be so and may it be with deliberate and loving care we love and comfort those who will be joining you soon. Be with them Lord and comfort us in our sorrow. May we rejoice in the newness of life that one day, we too shall be called home. Be with us and save us. Amen.

LUKE 19:35-40

Then they brought it to Jesus; and after throwing their cloaks on the colt, then set Jesus on it. As he rode along, people kept spreading their cloaks on the road. As he was now approaching the path down from the Mount of Olives, the whole multitude of the disciples began to praise God joyfully with a loud voice for all the deeds of power that they had seen, saying "Blessed is the king who comes in the name of the Lord! Peace in heaven, and glory in the highest heaven!" Some of the Pharisees in the crowd said to him, "Teacher, order your disciples to stop." He answered, "I tell you, if these were silent, the stones would shout out."

L ord God, when evil permeates the air we breathe how are we to cope? Sometimes it is not only hard to clear our heads and move forward, but hard to figure out our next steps. And yet, as your beloved son demonstrated, the will of evil ones cannot silence what is just and good. I felt your love when I was or thought I was all alone in the world, a world that could have overcome me and left me destitute and frightened. You were there for me and for many others who love you and boldly pray that your love and care will save us. You teach your children how to be in the world and equip us with tools to be successful. Thank you Lord, for the gift of your son, Jesus and for his wisdom and abilities in transforming evil and idolatry. We celebrate the triumphant walk, Jesus' last to be celebrated before he would take a final walk in human form, carrying a cross. The great joy became great sorrow until that, too, turned to joy. Those who question you and the life, death and resurrection of your son, have only to learn of the virgin birth and the prophecies. They have only to read words of those who recount the miracle of the resurrection and Jesus' ascension. "Surely goodness and mercy shall follow me all the days of my life, and I shall live in the House of the Lord, forever." Lord be with us and save us for the day when we too shall be in your glorious home, our sins forgiven, in His name, I pray. Amen.

OCTOBER 1

LUKE 19:41-44

As he came near and saw the city, he wept over it, saying, "If you, even you, had only recognized on this day the things that made for peace! But now they are hidden from your eyes, indeed, the days will come upon you, when your enemies will set up ramparts around you and surround you, hem you in on every side. They will crush you to the ground, you and your children within you, and they will not leave within you one stone upon another; because you did not recognize the time of your visitation from God."

Holy Lord, when we read of the horrific events leading to your son's crucifixion, how sad we become. Jesus did everything he could, he understood what had to happen. Its not that it did not matter, of course it did, but what mattered was and perhaps is the sad state the city was in. It matters the sad state we are in. So of course you cried, and we cried. How was it, with all the teachings, miracles and healings they did not know? Lord, we pray for the non-believers and doubters. Show them your love and mercy and how Jesus laid down his life for each one of us. Knowing we are loved unconditionally brings tears to our eyes, for we know that although we feel unworthy, you and Jesus feel our love and through Jesus' sacrifice our sins are forgiven. Be with us all of our days and in all of our fears, show us the way to tomorrow. Help us be leaders of the faith to the faithless. May we be faithful to your teachings Lord God and may our efforts show our love for you and our determination to bring the word to those around us. Be with us each one on this journey and save us, I pray. Amen.

OCTOBER 2

LUKE 19:45-49

Then he entered the temple and began to drive out those who were selling things there; and he said, "It is written, 'My house shall be a house of prayer; but you have made it a den of robbers." Everyday he was teaching in the temple. The chief priests, the scribes, and the leaders of the people kept looking for a way to kill him; but they did not find anything they could do, for all the people were spellbound by what they heard.

Fairest Lord Jesus, you entered the world to bring salvation. It was no easy task, and you endured many hardships, rejections and a hideous ending to the glory of your life. How despondent those who loved you were as they were powerless to stem the tide of hatred and dogma. Your vision of reality clashed with the activities in the temple and angered some who were only able to "go through the motions" never realizing that the religious leaders of the day had their priorities shall we say 'out of whack." Today, we also see priorities that are far from in line with your teachings, and yet, there are cracks of goodness to be found. We see your children leading and learning lessons of love and kindness to those less fortunate. Today I remember a special person who was filled with your spirit and who was called home too soon. He loved life more than most. I give thanks for the special person he was and his love and devotion to his family, colleagues and friends. His faith-filled walk inspires me to this day. Like him, I see others who help others, unselfishly. Lord, I pray you will help the youth step up and be a force for good over evil and a force for love over hate. They are courageous leaders in conservation efforts and ending gun violence. We give thanks for those who try to do good in this complex world and move to positive action those who are fixated in place, unable to follow a vision you set for us. May our joyful salvation provide a roadmap of Christian activities that will enable your world, our world to be a better place, where war is no more, and humankind is treated justly. Help us to keep moving forward toward a world you envisioned for us all, showing we are Christians by our love and understanding of your will for us. Be with us all, Lord, and save us, we pray in the name of the Savior, Jesus Christ. Amen.

OCTOBER 3

LUKE 20:1-4

One day, as he was teaching the people in the temple and telling the good news, the chief priests and the scribes came with the elders and said to him, "Tell us by what authority are you doing these things? Who is it who gave you this authority?" He answered them, "I will also ask you a question, and you tell me: Did the Baptism of John come from heaven, or was it of human origin?"

Dear Lord, what must your son have been thinking when the chief priests, scribes and elders challenged his authority! I mean, had they learned nothing? Well yes, there's that...they wanted Jesus to admit he was the Messiah, your beloved son. They must have been salivating hoping to catch our Savior in blasphemy! Wisdom, preparation, dedication and your love prepared him well. The maneuver Jesus deftly handled was to ask them a question, thereby sidestepping the issue. The point is their answer would also be the answer to the question posed to Jesus. Genius, right? If they answered Jesus' question, there would be no need for him to answer theirs'. Their refusal to answer sent them away, frustrated and yes, a bit defeated. As Christians we are called to answer some of the mysteries of faith. Let us remember the teachings and encourage each one to seek the answer of one's faith. Your glory, teachings and yes, mysteries do not always produce "easy answers" but, it is in the searching that we look within ourselves and begin to see and to love the great mysteries upon which our faith is based. I give your thanks, Lord God, for the wisdom you have imparted and the joyful ways our Savior spread the good news throughout the land. Be with us Lord, when we question our faith and seek answers that we already know, but desperately do not want to acknowledge. Help us live out our lives to your glory and may we find the forgiveness of sin as freely given as your love for us. In your glory I pray. Amen.

OCTOBER 4

LUKE 20:5-8

They discussed it with one another, saying, "If we say 'From heaven, 'he will say, 'Why did you not believe him?' But if we say, 'Of human origin,' all the people will stone us for they are convinced that John was a prophet." So they answered that they did not know where it came from. Then Jesus told them, "Neither will I tell you by what authority I am doing these things."

Teacher, you have given us a road map to how you were able to survive until the "time was near "for you to leave the world. By refusing to answer the question the interrogators were left with a conundrum, they thought there was no solution. What a wise son! Thank you God for the gift of Jesus, his wisdom, his courage, his love, his power, and his kindness. May we seek to be more like him, showing love and compassion for those we meet, helping those in need, and learning how to be better people. Continue to prepare us, Lord, to be faithful and faith-filled disciples. May we shine our lights on those less fortunate wherever and whenever we can. Be with us Lord, forgive us our sins, and save us, I pray. Amen.

LUKE 20:9-19

He began to tell the people this parable: "A man planted a vineyard and leased it to tenants, and went to another country for a long time. When the season came, he sent a slave to the tenants in order that they might give him his share of the produce of the vineyard; but the tenants beat him and sent him away empty- handed. Next he sent another slave; that one they also beat and insulted and sent away empty-handed. And he sent still a third; this one also they wounded the threw out. Then the owner of the vineyard said, "What shall I do? I will send my beloved son; perhaps they will respect him." But when the tenants saw him, they discussed it among themselves and said, 'This is the heir; let us kill him so that the inheritance may be ours.' So they threw him out of the vineyard and killed him. What then will the owner of the vineyard do to them? He will come and destroy those tenants and give the vineyard to others." When they heard this, they said, "Heaven forbid!" But he looked at them and said, "What then does this text mean?"

"The stone that the builders rejected has become the cornerstone?"

Everyone who falls on that stone will be broken to pieces; and it will crush anyone on whom it falls." When the scribes and chief priests realized that he had told this parable against them they wanted to lay hands on him at that very hour, but they feared the people.

L ord God, today we pray that your dear son, Jesus will be the "cornerstone" of our lives. May we follow by His example, showing love and mercy to those less fortunate. Help us to cease hoarding and share our abundance. In all we do and say, may we give glory and honor to Jesus, our Lord and Savior. When we kneel in prayer, or simply close our eyes and speak to you, may our thoughts, words and deeds be pleasing to you and a beacon reflecting your light in the world. As we cling to the stories and teachings, help us to model the specific behaviors in the Bible. May we be kind and generous with our smile and words and may we measure our words and thoughts that are not in keeping with your teachings, your expectations. Help us to share our lives and love of Christ with all who would hear. Be with those who boldly travel and speak your truths throughout a world where hatred and discord seem to have obliterated the rule of law. Help those who are shining a light in ways we can help other humans, our environment and our planet. Give us strength to find ways to improve lives, air, water, and humane treatment and to honor you and the one you sent to take away the sins of the world, Jesus Christ. Be with us this day, remind us of your glorious gift to the world and save us, I pray. Amen.

OCTOBER 6

LUKE 20:20-24

So they watched him and sent spies who pretended to be honest, in order to trap him by what he said, so as to hand him over to the jurisdiction and authority of the governor. So they asked him, "Teacher, we know that you are right in what you say and teach, and you show deference to no one, but teach the way of God in accordance with truth. Is it lawful for us to pay taxes to the emperor, or not?" But he perceived their craftiness and said to them, "Show me a denarius. Whose head and whose title does it bear?" They said, "The emperor's." He said to them, "Then give to the emperor the things that are the emperor's, and to God, the things that are God's." And they were not able to trap him by what he said; and being amazed by his answer, they became silent.

Holy God, Jesus' life was one of loving and teaching. In the end of his ministry, there were those who tried to "catch" Jesus and make him pay for any foray into blasphemy, and for failure to honor the sabbath. Jesus was wise beyond reason, thankfully he did not fall for the trap. Are we also in some lesser way walking in the same footsteps? Lord, I believe we may be. Help us to hold fast to the truth, your truth, Jesus' truth. Do not let wicked people cast aside the teachings and traditions that Christ intended for us to follow. Help us love you Lord, with all our hearts, with all our minds, and yes, with all our souls. Never again allow evil and denial to punish your people, your followers because someone else does not believe. May we evade the traps put out to derail our walk with you. We know what type of loving, caring, faithful people say and do. May we continue to live our lives mirroring the life of Jesus and your expectations of us. Be with us today, as we face many challenges, filled with the Holy Spirit and the courage to do your will. Save us from sin and temptations that do not honor you, I pray, in your name. Amen.

OCTOBER 7

LUKE 20:27-28, 33-36

Some Sadducees, those who say there is no resurrection, came to him and asked him a question, "Teacher, Moses wrote for us that if a man's brother dies, leaving a wife but no children, the man shall marry the widow and raise up children for his brother.

In the resurrection, therefore, whose wife will the woman be? for the seven had married her."

Jesus said to them, "Those who belong to this age marry and are given in marriage; but those who are considered worthy of a place in that age and in the resurrection from the dead neither marry nor are given in marriage. Indeed they cannot die anymore, because they are like angels and are children of God, being children of the resurrection.

Holy God, when contemplating the end of life, many are fearful. Not so for Christians, for we know, when our time on earth is finished, we shall dwell "in the house of the Lord, forever." Thank you God, for giving strong leadership through your son, who came to take away the sins of the world. When we feel your words, in our hearts and minds and your love for us, we are generally calmer and free of worry about "what's next." Whether young or old, we teach as we were taught to ask for the forgiveness of sin and in that sense, the path to eternal life in your house is assured. We will all be 'children of the resurrection' and in a place where pain and suffering are no more. Those who doubt the resurrection and your teachings, are in many ways "lost." We pray for those who do not know you, your life's work devoted to our very salvation and how we are connected to you. The ancient ideas of men taking care of their brother's widows has been debunked by you and the Christian church. Learning of your love for us and that you died on the cross to take away our sins is a great comfort to believers. Turning our backs on pagan historical norms frees us, because we "are like angels and are children of God, being children of the resurrection." What a blessing you continue to be to those who have studied and embraced your teachings. Be with us, Savior Jesus, as we pick our way through the pitfalls of life. Help us to share the stories of your life, teachings, death, and resurrection. Be with us as we continue our walk, forgive us of our sins and save us, we pray, in the blessed name of Jesus. Amen.

OCTOBER 8

LUKE 20:37-40

And the fact that the dead are raised Moses himself showed, in the story about the bush, where he speaks of the Lord as the God of Abraham, the God of Isaac, and the God of Jacob. Now he is God not of the dead, but of the living; for to him all of them are alive." Then some of the scribes answered, "Teacher, you have spoken well." For they no longer dared to ask him another question.

L oving and wise God, thank you for being our teacher and savior. When we ponder the "what ifs' ' your words translated and analyzed by scholars and believers awaken in us to certainty that humans do not always comprehend. When we have doubts, we search our hearts and minds and the literature that speaks of your great love for us. As parents, we try to teach our children important life lessons, giving them the tools needed to navigate life. And that is exactly what you have done for all of humanity by sending your son to walk among mortals, teaching the way to eternal life and our salvation. Thank you for being a living God in our thoughts and in our hearts. Help us spread the "good news" of you and your son throughout the world. May we sow seeds of love, peace and grace throughout by reflecting your intentions for how we are to live with and treat one another. Soften hard hearts and deaf ears. Turn each one toward your intentions for how we live our lives and interact with others. Help us find ways to demonstrate how to comport ourselves in a world confused by differing intentions regarding how to be leaders, doing good for all. Be with those who are persecuted in words and deeds when they are working, in your name. Be with teachers and leaders who are following your example throughout the land. Help us lead in humane ways for the good of all. Be with us in our waking and our sleeping and save us I pray. Amen.

OCTOBER 9

LUKE 20:45-47

In the hearing of all the people he said to the disciples, "Beware of the scribes who like to walk around in long robes, and love to be greeted with respect in the marketplaces, and to have the best seats in the synagogues and places of honor at banquets. They devour widows' houses and for the sake of appearance say long prayers. They will receive greater condemnation."

———————————

Thank you Holy God, for providing clarity in the face of blinding abuse of power. When religious leaders step forward with a "kiss my ring" attitude, help us to understand their intentions have gone astray. The trappings of leadership sometimes makes humans take their eyes off the goal for the people, rich and especially needy. As it was in Jesus' day, so it is today. People who see the error of their ways are subjected to the whims of egregious words and deeds that are often unjust. We have learned that to those who have much, much is expected. Sometimes the teachers forget the last part, and forget much is expected of them. Help those refocus on what their true mission and calling is. Jesus wanted the leaders to "fit in" with the people as they walked with them. He was telling them to be one with them and to avoid the expectation of being exalted for their religious positions. How tiresome it must have been for Jesus to realize the gluttony of humankind. Jesus preached the "Golden Rule" in so many ways, hoping we would understand the best of intentions for how we are to live. Lord, remove the desire to be great, rather refocus us to do your will without regard to social standing. Be with us when our egos eclipse our work and love for you. Shine the light on humbly walking through our lives for your glory, not ours. Be with us this day, forgive our sin of feeling 'privileged' and help us to treat each one as we would desire to be treated. May our salvation be our goal in this life and the next. Amen.

OCTOBER 10
LUKE 21:1-4

He looked up and saw rich people putting their gifts into the treasury; he also saw a poor widow put in two copper coins. He said, "Truly I tell you, this poor widow has put in more than all of them; for all of them have contributed out of their abundance, but she out of her poverty has put in all she had to live on."

Loving God, teach us how to give generously to the church. The widow gave extravagantly when she gave all she had, therefore, Jesus praised her unselfish gift. It is in giving up our selfish ways that we shall feel the warmth of our generosity. Help us to plan to be generous just as we plan for our spending in other areas. May we plan our giving for the good of your people. May the grace of giving reflect how we see ourselves in Christ's world. The widow shows us everyone can participate in the act of giving to you God. Help us Lord to be cheerful givers with a plan. Jesus told us generosity is not reserved for one socio-economic group over another. We can all be generous. There is room for everyone! Generosity flows from everyone from the poorest, too. Lord, we know you appreciate a cheerful giver, help us to be cheerful and purposeful in our plan to give financial support for the church. Be with us as we prepare to tithe and to find ways to support the church and the programs that help your people, our neighbors and those who struggle with economic stability. Be with us as we plan to be generous and faithful to the church we love. Forgive us our sin of gluttony and save us, I pray. Amen.

LUKE 21:5-6

When some were speaking about the temple, how it was adorned with beautiful stones and gifts dedicated to God, he said, "As for these things that you see, the days will come when not one stone will be left upon another, all will be thrown down."

T eacher, Jesus knew before his disciples the temple would be destroyed. The foreboding nature of the things to come, Jesus' own demise lay heavy in the writings. Fast forward to today. What is happening to "organized" religion? Churches are closing, smaller churches are beginning to "share" one pastor among 2-5 congregations! Why is that, Lord? To be able to minister to a congregation takes faith and funding. It seems there is a decline in membership and financial support. Have we become, Lord God, a walk in Sunday, walk out Sunday society? Have we no time, nor interest in delving deeper into what you want for your people? Are our lives too busy for worship? What about the children? Where are the supports that help parents augment teaching their children how to be? Yes, Lord, the church is where you are. I pray we can be more deliberate with our congregational habits. For Lord, when we are in "your house" and when we have set aside a special time to honor you and to learn how your ministry has meaning today, we are a better society of believers. Help us Lord, to use our worship experience to grow, to learn, to pray and to be citizens you want us to be, and that we want to be. Help us Lord to rekindle interest in corporate worship and in doing good not just in our unique congregations, but also to share your love and teachings throughout our world. Be with us as we step out and share the "Good News" of Jesus Christ, to be kind to our neighbors and those in need. Save us from our sinful ways by your merciful love. In the name of Jesus Christ. Amen.

LUKE 21:7-8

Then they asked him, "Teacher, when will this be, and what will be the sign that this is about to take place?" And he said, "Beware that you are not led astray; for many will come in my name and say, 'I am he! and, 'The time is near!" Do not go after them.

Holy Lord Jesus, how perplexing are the times in which we live. These times, in many ways offer the same confusion found in the early days of the Christian church. We are surrounded with churches, and yet, some are struggling to survive. Help us to know what the "mega church" has that we want and to learn what is missing from each. It is powerful to worship with many, and yet, the intimacy of a smaller congregation affords so much more. I have learned that in the larger church, the drive to pay the bills to maintain the facility and pay the staff is the focus. In churches with "organized" religions, there seems to be a more balanced use of the dollars that come in. There is a reach outwardly to support important mission and evangelical endeavors. Jesus warns the people to stay focused, pay attention to what others' claim. How will we recognize the second coming? What are we seeking? Lord help us to focus on exactly what our church is and how it meets the needs of the congregants and the communities in which each church serves. Be with us as we move through troubling times and help us to be more discerning of the needs of the people, the desire to bring your word to the people and the need to achieve a balance in the hustle of lives today. Help us to remember to teach our children about you and to instill in them a desire to hear the "Good News" regularly and to participate in activities that strengthen each of us as well as your church. Be with us and save us, I pray. Amen.

OCTOBER 13

LUKE 21:9-11

"When you hear of wars and insurrections, do not be terrified; for these things must take place first, but the end will not follow immediately." Then he said to them, "Nation will rise against nation, and kingdom against kingdom; there will be great earthquakes, and in various places famines and plagues; and there will be dreadful portents and great signs from heaven.

Dear Lord, we feel the urgency in Jesus' tone. He knows what is coming and for him, it is going to be, well terrifying. At the same time, Jesus wants to prepare future generations for a deeper understanding of this new religion. The last two words in the verse, "from heaven" give us hope and that was the central theme of his ministry. Many things are going to happen to us one during life, but, hang in there heaven is the place for one to aspire. So all sorts of things will be tossed our way, the faithful servant will be rewarded in the end. I believe it, Lord God. The ones who have lives filled with realities that seem crazy, cope because they are filled with your spirit and have the faith learned throughout their life's experiences. The lucky ones, have a deep belief and abiding faith in the promises of the kingdom. When one has "God moments" one's faith is reassured. We hear stories of those dying seeing loved ones who have passed. Sometimes those desperately ill, also see signs from loved ones. Lord, you work in mysterious ways and comfort your people in loving ways. Thank you God for breathing love and comfort into our hearts and heads as we continue our walk through life. Thank you for beautiful rainbows, sunrises and sunsets, for the beauty of nature and a single moment when we feel your loving presence. Thank you for the "great signs from heaven," they comfort us. Be with us Lord as we face "dreadful portents" and know that we are looking for "great signs from heaven." We seek your presence and will in our lives. Be with us in our unsettled fears and save us, we pray in your holy name. Amen.

OCTOBER 14

LUKE 21:12-19

"But before all this occurs, they will arrest you and persecute you; they will hand you over to synagogues and prisons, and you will be brought before kings and governors because of my name. This will give you the opportunity to testify. So make up your minds not to prepare your defense in advance; for I will give you words and wisdom that none of your opponents will be able to withstand or contradict. You will be betrayed even by parents and brothers, by relatives and friends; and they will put some of you to death. But not a hair on your head will perish. By your endurance you will gain your souls.

Jesus, you prepare us for all sorts of things, as you were prepared by your Heavenly Father. The disciples must have been distraught beyond our imaginations. You told your disciples that things were going to be very difficult because of you and their association with you. The comfort, you said, would be you speaking to the disciples when they were testifying. We can imagine the panic, friends turning against them, even family members would betray them. And then the promise. "I will care for you. No matter what happens, your souls shall be reunited with me in heaven." Jesus, you told them and reassure us by sticking with you to the end, we will be saved. Thank you for the preparation and time you spent reassuring all, in the face of your unspeakable pain and suffering, you were not thinking of yourself, you were preparing to welcome us home. Thanks be to God! Be with us always, as your vow declares, and save us from our sinful ways. In your blessed name, we pray. Amen.

LUKE 21:20-24

"When you see Jerusalem surrounded by armies, then know that its desolation has come near. Then those in Judea must flee to the mountains, and those inside the city must leave it, and those out in the country must not enter it; for these are days of vengeance, as a fulfillment of all that is written. Woe to those who are pregnant and to those who are nursing infants in those days! For there will be great distress on the earth and wrath against this people; they will fall by the edge of the sword and be taken away as captives among all the nations; and Jerusalem will be trampled on by the Gentiles, until the times of the Gentiles are fulfilled."

———————————

Dear Lord, thank you for the gift of your son, Jesus. He taught us well, even when we were afraid, Jesus gave us a clear picture of what was going to happen to the people. Great distress and wrath from armies set on destroying everyone and everything would come. Thank you for the care Jesus took in preparation for the devastation that would occur. The temples, the city and the people would be obliterated by a mighty Roman Army. Your promises to save the people and the country sustain us and them. Christ's purposeful words were meant to encourage and lead a vigilant people and faith. We too, are part of the watchful throng, preserving the word of God and the teachings of Jesus. Lord, we patiently await for your will for your people to be carried out and promise to do what we can to make it so. Lord, some of what I see happening in our world today frightens me. I am fearful for this country I love. I feel unrest and under a leader who is not acting like a leader, things are changing and hurting people needlessly. It seems we have not learned from history. I fear many of the leaders are not acting on anyone's behalf, but their own. Help us to stand up for your teachings and do what is right. Save our world Lord. Be with us Lord God, help us face each day of uncertainty with the conviction of your teachings, keep those less fortunate safe. Lord forgive our sinful ways and save us I pray. Amen.

OCTOBER 16
LUKE 21:25-28

"There will be signs in the sun, the moon, and the stars, and on the earth distress among nations confused by the roaring of the sea and the waves. People will faint from fear and foreboding of what is coming upon the world, for the powers of the heavens will be shaken. They will see 'the Son of Man coming in a cloud' with power and great glory. Now when these things begin to take place, stand up and raise your heads, because your redemption is drawing near."

Lord God, what chaos at least in the minds of the disciples. Lord, we are reminded of Jesus' purpose for being. It was not to keep us from the uncomfortable, rather it was to prepare us. Cutting through the chaos Jesus tells the disciples the temple and Jerusalem itself would be destroyed. He tells disciples to "stand up" and to "raise" their heads, "your redemption is drawing near." Change of this magnitude was not understated by The Messiah! When Jesus spoke, he must have been trying to instruct and reassure his chosen ones about the future, one without him. When we pray, Lord, sometimes we are praying to be released from our fears, but certainly we do not imagine what Jesus was talking about. What are we to do, when we are afraid or anxious? Jesus tells us to raise our heads and stand up. We are to be brave Christians in the face of everything for we know that all we need to do is to confess our sins to you and salvation will be ours. Thank you God for your unselfish gift of Jesus, who has taught us well. Be with us when we are afraid, when we have failures, and when we come to you in prayers of supplication and when we sincerely request forgiveness for our sins. Be with us when our honesty doubles us over in regret and guilt. We know you hear our prayers and moreover, we know you love us. Thank you. Be with us this day and each day, and save us from our sins, may we stand up and raise up our heads to your honor and glory. Amen.

OCTOBER 17

LUKE 21:29-33

Then he told them a parable: "Look at the fig tree and all the trees; as soon as they sprout leaves you can see for yourselves and know that summer is already near. So also, when you see these things taking place, you know that the kingdom of God is near. Truly I tell you, this generation will not pass away until all things have taken place. Heaven and earth will not pass away."

Teacher, the way you reached the disciples most effectively was via the use of parables. Agriculture works because of your grand plan, moving from one season to the next. When the leaves turn green, summer will soon be upon us. We also know not long after the fruit and harvest has occurred comes e a dormant time. Dormancy of growth happens with the seasons and with humankind. What comfort your words bring to us as we contemplate our own mortality. Knowing believers albeit "saved" believers, comfort our hearts and minds. We understand there is no need to fear the passing from this life to the next because you came and brought salvation to the world, to us. Lord today I pray for the family of a great man, Elijah Cummings who entered the Kingdom on this day in 2019. Mr. Cummings was a great leader in our Congress who grew up in the south, upheld the cause of Civil Rights and helped teach Americans how people are to treat one another. He is with you now, having left a nation and especially a family with memories of a life well lived. Mr. Cummings did not fear death because he knew where he was going, to the place you have prepared for him, for us. There by your grace, each one of us goes. Thank you Lord God, for the life and example of Mr. Cummings and thank you for saving us, a sinful people. Amen.

LUKE 21:34-38

"Be on guard so that your hearts are not weighted down with dissipation and drunkenness and the worries of this life, and that day does not catch you unexpectedly, like a trap. For it will come upon all who live on the face of the whole earth. Be alert at all times, praying that you may have the strength to escape all these things that will take place, and to stand before the Son of Man."

Every day he was teaching in the temple and at night he would go out and spend the night on the Mount of Olives, as it was called. And all the people would get up early in the morning to listen to him in the temple.

———————————

Holy Lord, the teachings of Jesus were purposeful and with great focus. His ability to warn about taking mind-altering drugs, like wine, was stunning to me. I thought alcoholism was a more current social issue. The way Jesus mentions it, seems to have as great a concern in his lifetime, as it continues to have in ours today. Be alert, pay attention, have strength to act; these are all actions inhibited by drugs and alcohol. Lord, be with those who are in the grips of addiction of any kind and be with the loved ones and especially the children. Each new fad of addiction draws a younger crowd: we used to worry about "weed" and now we are legalizing it, but now we worry about the addiction and deaths of our young high school and college age who are addicted to vaping. They are dying! We pray for strength and courage to face all of our tomorrows and that those who are unable to pray and be free from the scourge of addiction may seek you and assistance to resist the temptation that informs their lives. May we come to you in our waking and our sleeping, seeking love and comfort, but most of all we seek forgiveness. Like those who yearned to hear your voice in the temple, may we yearn to feel your presence and love from the moment we awaken. Lord, awaken our hearts and minds to feel your love and to understand your teachings in such a way as we may be made whole again. Be with us, save us from our sins and help us by leading us down the paths you would have us follow. In Jesus' name, I pray. Amen.

OCTOBER 19

PSALM 103:1-5

Bless the Lord, O my soul, and all that is within me, bless his holy name.

Bless the Lord, O my soul, and do not forget all his benefits—who forgives all your inequity, who heals all your diseases, who redeems your life from the Pit, who crowns you with steadfast love and mercy, who satisfies you with good as long as you live so that your youth is renewed like the eagle's.

———————————

L oving God, the Psalm assures us of your abiding love for us. We are invited to come to you in prayer under all circumstances. Thank you for listening to our petitions. Today, I pray for all those who feel lost, anxious or depressed. Be with those Lord, who perhaps have lost their way. Help them to feel your power and your love and know that the lost ones, Lord God, are important to you. Lord, I pray especially for the most vulnerable in society, our youth, women, the homeless, and those with emotional or psychological illnesses. We know that you have demonstrated you can provide for us. Help these people who suffer from anxiety, despair, depression. May they feel there is a "way out" for them or better yet, a way into feeling your love and care. I pray for those who have given up and are hurting themselves, or contemplating their life's end. May they feel your love and seek your guidance and just how much you care about others. Lord, make them whole again. Crown those in the snare of human trafficking, redeem them from this scourge and help them to move forward in life with your love and care. May all those who seek to help them on their journey out of human bondage. Lord, thank you for listening and demonstrating the love you have for all. May they be supported by your love as they work to find their way back to healthier and safer life. Lord, we need your grace and mercy as we deal with the problems our youth and adults have today. Show us the way to shower them with unconditional love and support. Lord, help us open their minds and hearts to You. Be with those less fortunate and with each one of us, save us from our sins, I pray. Amen.

OCTOBER 20

PSALM 106:1-3

Praise the Lord!

O give thanks to the Lord, for he is good;
  for his steadfast love endures forever.
Who can utter the mighty doings of the Lord,
  or declare all his praise?
Happy are those who observe justice,
  who do righteousness at all times.

———————————————

Heavenly God, for many years, for some decades, we have devoted our lives to learning about you and your son. The psalmist's poetry is filled with your wisdom, power and grace. Help us to continue to learn and to teach our youth about your wisdom and your all-knowing love for each of us. May we seek your council when facing choices, decisions or responsibilities. May we turn to you in prayer and to your words for guidance. May we make sound decisions, informed by your words and those who have taught us. Help us Lord, to ignore the busyness of our lives instead of your words, intended to uplift and help us find our way. Open our hearts and minds to your love, your truth and your wisdom. Be with us as we move through our days and face decisions that perhaps are difficult to make. We thank you for your great gift, Jesus who was born, lived, died and was resurrected for our salvation. Be with us today and guide our ways to your will. In Jesus' name. Amen.

PSALM 108:1-4

My heart is steadfast, O God, my heart is steadfast,
I will sing and make melodies. Awake, my soul!
Awake, O harp and lyre! I will awaken the dawn.
I will give thanks to you, O Lord, among the peoples,
and I will sing praises to you among the nations.
For your steadfast love is higher than the heavens,
And your faithfulness reaches to the clouds.

Loving and generous God, thank you for the vision and wisdom you give to us. The beauty of the Psalms is a perfect place for us to visit. Finding and using the uplifting poems gives us comfort from others throughout history. None are more beautiful nor more meaningful than the Psalms. Lord, I pray for those who seek ways to worship you and I pray they find their voices and dialog with you as well. May you renew in each of us a heart filled with your love. May each of us find ways to live a faith-filled life that is pleasing to you. I pray for those who do not know you and are searching for a way to add understanding of meaning in their lives. I believe what they seek is you, Lord God. Open their minds and hearts to learn more about Christianity and your teachings. Be with them and those who help spread the "good news" for those who would hear. Be with us this day, and may we be mindful of the power of our words and may each bring you into the conversation. Lord, we humbly ask for the forgiveness of our sins and I pray your will be done. Amen.

OCTOBER 22

PSALM 113:1-9

Praise the Lord! Praise, O servants of the Lord; praise the name of the Lord.

Blessed be the name of the Lord from this time on and forevermore. From the rising of the sun to its setting the name of the Lord is to be praised. The Lord is high above all nations, and his glory above the heavens. Who is like the Lord our God, who is seated on high, who looks far down on the heavens and the earth? He raises the poor from the dust, and lifts the needy from the ash heap, to make them sit with princes, with the princes of his people. He gives the barren woman a home, making her the joyous mother of children. Praise the Lord!

Dear Lord, King over every nation, we acknowledge your power and wisdom over us. Your glory shines over all the earth and greater than anything else in the earth and sky. There is no one nor anything as great as you. We believe that your glory and dominion over all is just and true. Thank you for providing for your people, you are exalted above all and your love for us is everlasting. Your name is to be praised forever and ever. Lord, we give thanks for brilliant authors of the Psalms, other books of the Bible and the writings throughout the ages of loving Christians.

We must learn to live each day, each hour,
yes, each minute as a new beginning, as a unique
opportunity...

And then we must open our minds and our hearts
to the voice that resounds through the valleys and
hills of our life saying: "Let me show you where I live
among my people. May name is. 'God-with-you.'

I will wipe away all the tears from your eyes.

– Henri Nouwen

Thank you loving God for never giving up on us. Help us to know
you and to love you as you love us. Be with us this day, loving God,
and help us to be true servants, sharing your teachings and living the
life you want us to live. May we be generous and loving in all that we
do. Be with us as we find our way, and save us as we walk this walk
with you in our hearts and minds. Amen.

PSALM 119:9-13

How can young people keep their way pure? By guarding it according to your word. With my whole heart I seek you; do not let me stray from your commandments. I treasure your word in my heart, so that I may not sin against you. Blessed are you, O Lord; teach me your statutes.

———————————

Holy God, at an appointed time in the divine history of the world, you carved your laws on stone tablets. Today, you carve those laws in our minds and hearts. We take your word, your laws and hold them inside, that we would not sin against you. Lord, I am thankful today for the ministers of the word and sacrament in our lives: for those who baptized us, and those who first taught us about you. I give thanks to the Sunday School leaders, Bible School facilitators, leaders of youth groups, children's choir directors and all who unselfishly give of their time and talents. Their hearts are pure Lord and their devotion to you is rock solid. The lessons they teach and their personal testimonies, live with us in so many significant ways. I give thanks to the courageous ministers of the word who have bridged the gap between your teachings and our world. The imprint of your dedicated servants continues to inspire and assist those who need to hear your words the most. Be with your faithful servants and us as we move through this day, celebrating each leader. Help us to remember the lessons and how they have informed and impacted our lives. I pray new leaders and mentors will continue to bring alive the words written and the stories told about you, your beloved son and the great sacrifice Jesus made for our salvation. Be with us and save us, I pray. Amen.

GALATIANS 1:3-5

Read the words of the Apostle Paul, written to the churches of Galatia:

Grace to you and peace from God our Father and the Lord Jesus Christ, who gave himself for our sins to set us free from the present evil age, according to the will of our God and Father, to whom be the glory forever and ever. Amen

---

Heavenly Teacher your servant Paul who was one of Jesus' chosen disciples gives us insight into our future. He was ever so faithful to your son and wrote prolifically to the churches under his care. We see, through his writings to Galatia, Paul's loving words succinctly telling the church how he did receive his commission, it was not from any human source, but directly from you, Lord God. The blessings evoked came directly from you, God. You are our redeemer, just as you were and are to all the people. Paul's letter was written to set the Galatians straight and in a real sense telling them to "get their act together" for they had relapsed into the ways of the world around them, which did not comport with your teachings. Paul was frustrated, like you, Lord must sometimes be frustrated with your people today. The people disparaged his authority and moved away from the spiritual view of Christianity. They moved away from your saving grace through Jesus Christ and reverted to Jewish ceremonialism traditions. Paul emphatically reminds the Galatians about the redeeming work of Christ, and the purpose for which everything happens: freeing mankind from the evil surroundings into the grasp of which they appeared to be falling. Help us this day, Holy God, to always remember the gift you gave us, Jesus Christ and why you sent him to us. We shall forever be filled with love and awe that you loved us so much you sent your only son to take away all of our sins. WOW! I can think of no greater love than that, thank you Lord. Be with me this day and save me as I continue to walk, and breathe and, yes sin. In your honor and glory, I pray. Amen.

OCTOBER 25

GALATIANS 1:11-17; 20-24

For I want you to know, brothers and sisters, that the gospel that was proclaimed by me is not of human origin, for I did not receive it from a human source, nor was I taught it, but I received it through a revelation of Jesus Christ.

You have heard no doubt, of my earlier life in Judaism, I was violently persecuting the church of God and was trying to destroy it. I advanced in Judaism beyond many among my people of the same age, for I was far more zealous for the traditions of my ancestors. But when God, who had set me apart before through his grace, was pleased to reveal his Son to me, so that I might proclaim him among the Gentiles, I did not confer with any human being, nor did I go up to Jerusalem to those who were already apostles before me, but I went away at once into Arabia, and afterwards I went to Damascus.

In what I am writing to you, before God, I do not lie! Then I went to the regions of Syria and Cilicia, and I was still unknown by sight to the churches of Judea that are in Christ; they only heard it said, "The one who formerly was persecuting us is now proclaiming the faith he once tried to destroy." And they glorified God because of me.

Dear Lord, thank you for your servant Paul! He worked so hard and suffered greatly, all to bring to the churches entrusted to him by Jesus the story and the purpose of the new religion, Christianity. He tells of his own persecution and the attempts of his captors to eradicate Christianity. We, just like Paul, at times cling to ancestral traditions that are not a part of the Christian tradition. Can you imagine the faith in Christ your servant Paul had? He declared all who are converted are called by the grace of God; their conversion and ours is a result of your mighty power, Lord, and your grace working in each one. Hearing the reassuring words of Paul then must have been astonishing to those who perhaps doubted. I know it is for some of us this day, too. Lord, give me the confidence to make bold decisions for your good. Help me to work hard for the important challenges in life. May all that I do, be pleasing to you and helpful in our chaotic world. Be with us this day and save us. In your Holy name, I pray. Amen.

GALATIANS 2:11-14

But when Cepheus came to Antioch, I opposed him to his face, because he stood self-condemned; for until certain people came from James, he used to eat with the Gentiles. But after they came, he drew back and kept himself separate for fear of the circumcision faction. And the other Jews joined him in this hypocrisy, so that even Barnabas was led astray by their hypocrisy. But when I saw that they were not acting consistently with the truth of the gospel, I said to Cepheus before them all, "If you, though a Jew, live like a Gentile and not like a Jew, how can you compel the Gentiles to live like Jews?"

———————————

T hank you Lord for the courage of Paul. It is hard to call someone to task about their inappropriate behavior, even if the calling is deserved. When Paul saw Peter was not living up to the principles taught in the Bible, it was too much. Lord, I pray for the courage and wisdom and eloquence of this brave disciple. The bravery expressed shows his understanding of the salvation promised. By urging a life taught by the Savior Jesus made Paul on the same parallel status as the other disciples. Lord, thank you for the bravery and confidence of Paul, who did not hesitate to do the work of the new church and to do all he could to make sure the people were following Jesus' teachings. It sounds so simple, and yet, of course we know it is not really easy. We struggle today with hiding our faith from non-believers or from guarding our beliefs in a society believing in the separation of church and state. Christians cannot hide no matter what efforts they make to be "politically" correct. Help us Lord to let our light of understanding and devotion inform our days and nights. May our walk with you be a beacon for the lost and downtrodden. Lord, we know the way, let it be the guiding force for good over evil and may it be a welcome guide to those who are lost. May our faith help us to withstand societal atrocities in a peaceful way in order that change and positive results may be the outcome. Lord, forgive us our sins and save us from all evil. Be with us this day and each of our tomorrows. In your beloved son's name. Amen.

GALATIANS 2:15-21

We ourselves are Jews by birth and not Gentile sinners; yet we know that a person is justified not by the works of the law but through faith in Jesus Christ. And we have come to believe in Christ Jesus, so that we might be justified by faith in Christ, and not by doing the works of the law, because no one will be justified by the works of the law. But if, in our effort to be justified in Christ, we ourselves have been found to be sinners, is Christ then a servant of sin? Certainly not! But if I build up again the very things that I once tore down, then I demonstrate that I am a transgressors. For through the law I died to the law, so that I might live to God. I have been crucified with. Christ; and it is no longer I who live, but it is Christ who lives in me. And the live I now live in the flesh I live by faith in the Son of God, who loved me and gave himself for me. I do not nullify the grace of God; for if justification comes through the law, then Christ died for nothing.

Holy God, your faithful servant Paul was ever the "explainer." He wrote to the Galatians in clear and precise terms with the goal of making everyone understand the differences between both Jew and Gentile. Paul did not regard the Jews as sinners, but perhaps he did mean that they were not born under the disadvantages of the Gentiles regarding the knowledge of the way to salvation. They knew one could not be saved by works alone. Christians were learning that their salvation was already assured with the birth, life, death and resurrection of Jesus. Paul clearly ends this portion of his letter affirming that Christ's life and death were for the unique purpose of forgiveness of our sins and eternal life in heaven. Lord, we are sometimes mired in the minutia of the virgin birth and Christ's resurrection and assent to heaven. What have we forgotten? Oh yes, faith! Through our faith Christians know that by grace we are forgiven of our sins, we have only to ask! Thank you for saving us through Jesus our Savior. Be with us each day and know that we pray for the forgiveness of our sins. Save us as we pray always in your Holy name. Amen.

OCTOBER 28

GALATIANS 3:3-5

Are you so foolish? Having started with the Spirit, are you now ending with the flesh? Did you experience so much for nothing?—if it really was for nothing. Well then, does God supply you with the Spirit and work miracles among you by your doing the works of the law, or by your believing what you heard?

Dear Lord, we feel the exasperation of Paul. After all, the people of Galatia had learned of the gift from the Holy Spirit. Were the Galatians reverting to the flesh? Of course Paul was disheartened. He was frustrated, too. Lord, sometimes we too are frustrated and perhaps even disillusioned. We know turning toward you and your teachings is the way for us to define our lives, and yet, sometimes we lapse. Help us to remind ourselves and our children of the amazing grace given to us through the life, death and resurrection of your son, Jesus. Help us to live our lives with the full and sure knowledge that you are our Lord. May we teach our children and live lives that that will glorify you and Jesus. Help us Lord God, to use a portion of each day learning and reinforcing the nature of your gift of Jesus and the importance of his purpose, your purpose. Loving God, continue to be with us in spirit and to show us the way to help others find you. Be with us each one, and save us, I pray. Amen.

GALATIANS 3:10-14

For all who rely on the works of the law are under a curse; for it is written, "Cursed is everyone who does not observe and obey all the things written in the book of the law." Now it is evident that no one is justified before God by the law; for. "The one who is righteous will live by faith." But the law does not rest on faith; on the contrary, "Whoever does the works of the law will live by them: Christ redeemed us from the curse of the law by becoming a curse for us—it is written, "Cursed is everyone who hangs on a tree"—in order that in Christ Jesus the blessing of Abraham might come to the Gentiles, so that we might receive the promise of the Spirit through faith.

The tone of Paul's letter to the people of Galatia was one of exasperation. Once again the people were focusing on how to be "justified." They were operating under the idea that justification by faith without works of law is dead. It is clearly stated in Ephesians 2: 8-10:

> For by grace you have been saved through faith. And this is not your own doing; it is the gift of God, not a result or works, so that no one may boast. For we are his workmanship, created in Christ Jesus for good works, which God prepared beforehand, that we should walk in them.

Thank you Lord, for our grace given through faith to each one. We shall treasure the law and never forget what a beautiful gift you gave us...a savior who walked among the people for the singular purpose of giving us eternal salvation. Be with us each moment, forgive our sins, and save us all. Amen.

OCTOBER 30

GALATIANS 3:19-22

Why then the law? It was added because of transgressions, until the offsprings would come to whom the promise had been made; and it was ordained through angels by a mediator. Now a mediator involves more than one party; but God is one. Is the law then opposed to the promises of God? Certainly not! For if a law had been given that could make alive, then righteousness would indeed come through the law. But the scripture has imprisoned all things under the power of sin, so that what was promised through faith in Jesus Christ might be given to those who believe.

Creator God, you sent your son to take away the sins of the world. Jesus Christ brought his message to thousands before he was crucified, dead and buried. The third day he rose from the dead and sits on your right hand, God. The birth, life and death of your son was such a gift. What do you ask of us? Simply that we confess our sins and sincerely ask for forgiveness. Why does it seem like such a "tall order?" Help us God, to pray for forgiveness of our sins knowing that you, loving Lord will forgive each one. We are thankful for your promises and for your gift to us of Jesus. May we carry your love for us and our responsibility to come to you in prayer. Help us to be faithful and to seek a life where you will find pleasure in each of us. Be with us this day and every day, forgive our sins, saving us into eternal life when our time on earth has ended. In the name of Jesus, I pray. Amen.

OCTOBER 31

GALATIANS 3:23-26, 28

Now before faith came, we were imprisoned and guarded under the law until faith would be revealed. Therefore the law was our disciplinarian until Christ came, so that we might be justified by faith. But now that faith has come, we are no longer subject to a disciplinarian, for in Christ Jesus you are all children of God through faith.

There is no longer Jew or Greek, there is no longer slave or free, there is no longer male and female; for all of you are one in Christ Jesus.

Holy God, thank you. As the disciple Paul relates, much changed in the land after the revelation of faith. We became justified by faith...and by that we were no longer subjected to any governmental authority for the forgiveness of our sins. And, not only that, but our spiritual life was removed from governmental authority. The best part, is we are subjected to you, loving God through faith. When we come to you and our earthly days have ended we are all one in Christ Jesus. Thanks be to you, God! Be with us this day and save us from our sin. In Jesus' name, I pray. Amen.

NOVEMBER 1

GALATIANS 4:4-7

But when the fullness of time had come, God sent his Son, born of a woman, under the law, in order to redeem those who were under the law, so that we might receive adoption as children. And because you are children, God has sent the Spirit of his Son into our hearts, crying, Abba! Father! So you are no longer a slave, but a child, and if a child then also an heir, through God.

D ear God, we have learned of the story of Jesus' birth, life, death and resurrection. What was important, all was done for us! We are all children of God and through your grace and Jesus' death for our salvation, we have life and shall be welcomed into your kingdom. We have heard the words of Jesus: "Do not let your hearts be troubled, Believe in God, believe also in me. In my father's house there are many dwelling places. If it were not so, would I have told you that I go to prepare a place for you? And if I go and prepare a place for you, I will come again and will take you to myself, so that where I am, there you may also be." John 14: 1-3

Jesus you are the way, for no one comes to the Father except through you. We have learned the lessons of forgiveness of our sins and the need to bring our sins to you in prayer. Hear our prayers and forgive our sins. Be with us and save us this day. In your blessed name, I pray. Amen.

NOVEMBER 2

GALATIANS 4:16-20

Live by the Spirit, I say, and do not gratify the desires of the flesh. For what the flesh desires is opposed to the Spirit and what the Spirit desires is opposed to the flesh; for these are opposed to each other, to prevent you from doing what you want. But if you are led by the Spirit, you are not subjected to the law. Now the works of the flesh are obvious: fornication, impurity, licentiousness, idolatry, sorcery, enmities, strife, jealousy, anger, quarrels, dissections, factions, envy, drunkenness, carousing, and things like these. I am warning you, as I warned you before: those who do such things will not inherit the kingdom of God.

Holy God, your servant Paul has been quite clear about the type of life we are to live. The list of the "do not do these things" is not long, nor is it unreasonable. Paul warns the people of Galatia just as he had been taught by your son, Jesus. It is to live a life with a moral compass. The warning was also clear: do not do those things, if you do, you will not inherit the kingdom of God. The negative consequences of our actions should be expected. It is up to each of us to live lives that meet your approval, Lord. If we are led by the Holy Spirit, we would not subject ourselves or others to improper actions. Loving God, we are human and we make mistakes, but we are committed to living lives pleasing to you. Help us to be leaders in the way we conduct our personal lives. May we have integrity and teach our children the same. Be with us and guide our ways toward a life that is always pleasing to you. Save us from our sins. Lord know how much we love you and seek to follow. Amen.

GALATIANS 5:1

For freedom Christ has set us free. Stand firm, therefore, and do not submit again to a yoke of slavery.

Loving and faithful Lord, thank you for the gift your son Jesus. Jesus' life was crafted for your Divine purpose. You knew we needed to understand who you are and what your aspirations are for all people. Recognizing the cracks in Judaism, through Jesus you brought a new religion, a more perfect way of living in the faith. It is humbling and more than a bit frustrating to live in this world that seems to be spinning out of control. As a recently departed said often, "Come on now, we are better than this!" May the words of Elijah Cummings be a clarion call for us all. Help our children, all of them, not just some. We must resist the yoke of anti Semitism, elitism, prejudice, racial biases, elitism, racism. "Come on now, we ARE better than this!" Take away the yokes that are so harmful. We must love our neighbors...all of them. The only yoke we should submit to is loving our neighbor as ourselves. Lord, I pray for those who need more to survive and for those who hoard their abundance with no regard for those in need. May our loving touches be inclusive of others. Help me to share your love and guidance through prayer and actions. May the message of love and faith and truth and kindness inform the people and drive them to do your will. May your churches be filled with Christians who make the time and take the time to learn more about you and yearn more to step up. Be with us Lord, shower us with your saving grace and empower us to be better. In the name of the Messiah, Jesus Christ. Amen.

NOVEMBER 4

GALATIANS 5:6, 13-15

For in Christ Jesus neither circumcision nor uncircumcision counts for anything; the only thing that counts is faith working through love.

For you were called to freedom, brothers and sisters; only do not use your freedom as an opportunity for self-indulgence, but through love become slaves to one another. For the whole law is summed up in a single commandment, "You shall love your neighbor as yourself." If however, you bite and devour one another, take care that you are not consumed by one another.

All-knowing Lord, you have taught us rituals, icons, idols, and the like have no place in our lives. What is important is using our faith, works freely and lovingly given to your honor and glory. We are warned about gluttony and meanness, and yet continue to amass both. Help us learn to love our neighbors. Is that so hard? What is it that becomes the roadblock? Is it the evil envy and coveting of those who have more? Lord, help us find the balance and turn to your instructions and aspirations for the faithful people. May today be a day when we share with someone in need. May we work hard to raise children who want to do good for others and to stop worrying about what someone else has that they do not. Our abundance in this country is well documented: massive homes, gold toilets, personal excesses, etc. Let us hope to use our blessings to help others in need and to live lives that show our love for humankind. May we find ways to be generous and purposeful and kind as we honor you and one another. Be with me Lord, as I seek ways to serve and teach others about your love and goodness. Forgive my sinful ways, especially my critical comments that are not helpful and failure to share more with others in need. Jesus died to take away the sins of the world, and my sins, too. Knowing that fact is comforting and gives me hope. May it be so. In the name of Jesus, I pray. Amen.

GALATIANS 5:22-26

By contrast, the fruit of the Spirit is love, joy, peace, patience, kindness, generosity, and self control. There is no law against such things. And those who belong to Christ Jesus have crucified the flesh with its passions and desires. If we live by the Spirit, let us also be guided by the Spirit. Let us not become conceited, competing against one another, envying one another.

———————————

L ord, Paul's letter to Galatia gives a list of aspirations that are a result of the "Spirit." He encourages me to be guided by the very spirit I claim guides me. The admonition to avoid becoming conceited flew out the open door of Jesus' invitation. How is it I have become so competitive and envious of others? Why is it practically impossible to be happy for one another? Or have I? Lord, continue to guide and help me to show love, joy, peace, patience, kindness, generosity, and self control to humankind. I pray that self control will guide my way to all the thoughts and deeds in my life. Let me learn to hold my tongue and harmful actions as I ponder the consequences and potential harm they cause. To this day, Lord, I regret sending an essay of dissent for an incident in my life decades ago. I have learned I am better than what my anger engendered. I spend more time, Lord, praying for understanding and hoping the words I use will be helpful in my community. May my ways be your ways, Lord. Be with me this day, and save me from further sinful remarks that do not help anyone and diminish my genuine intentions. In Your name, I pray. Amen.

GALATIANS 6:6-8

Those who are taught the word must share in all good things with their teacher. Do not be deceived; God is not mocked, for you reap whatever you sow. If you sow to your own flesh; but if you sow to the Spirit, you will reap eternal life from the Spirit. For let us not grow weary in doing what is right, for we will reap at harvest time, if we do not give up. So then, whenever we have an opportunity let us work for the good of all, and especially for those of the family of faith.

———————————————

Holy and loving God, I am learning and praying for myself and for your people. I feel your loving spirit washing over my heart and soul. You have given me so many gifts, the greatest has been the gift, your son. His life and teachings comforted and instructed me. I remember when I sat in church feeling alone and afraid. You comforted me and helped me face each new day. You were there when I had to stand up and be the adult in the room with my parents. You gave me courage to do the right thing in spite of my fears. You gave me a sense of purpose and showed me the way. I am blessed to have had opportunities to work for you and for the good of others. The lessons I learned from you inform most of my choices: working with children including my own son, working in a family business, and now, finding a way to share your love with others through prayer and daily examples. I pray others will find perhaps a more gentle way of living a life that is filled with your love and grace. Thank you for loving me, in spite of…no that's not right. Thank you for always loving me and for the ways you showed that love to a frightened me. I carry your love and words in my mind, my body and my soul. The times I prayed for your help, you came to me in very real ways. You saved me again and again and again. I know you do the same for all who seek you. May they seek you each and every day. Lord, be with me and save me. In your blessed name I pray. Amen.

NOVEMBER 7

GALATIANS 6:9-10

Those who are taught the word must share in all good things with their teacher. Do not be deceived; God is not mocked, for your reap whatever you sow. If you sow to your own flesh, you will reap corruption from the flesh; but if you sow to the Spirit, you will reap eternal life from the Spirit. So let us not grow weary in doing what is right, for we will reap at harvest time, if we do not give up. So then, whenever we have an opportunity, let us work for the good of all, and especially for those of the family of faith.

Gracious and loving God, you have taught us true grace is for everyone and is given freely by you and nothing will separate us from your love. Your grace is unrelenting. Be with us Lord as we move through each day. Give us courage and stamina to face each challenge and each blessing. May our example be pleasing to you and may those who receive our kind words and sincere desire to be a beacon of hope for those who are less fortunate. Help us in our homes, our schools, and communities to show we are Christians by our love and care for one another. Lord, we are in concerning times throughout the world. Today I pray for the leaders and those whose power has been delivered without care and concern for the people who are hurting and need help. There are many in the world who are hungry and yet, the food supply is squandered and often thrown out, may we use our resources of food and clothing to the best purposes possible. Lord, be with those who persecute others, especially the poor and those seeking safety from violence or despots. Help all peoples seeking safety to find a place where they can be safe and their families can have basic necessities exceeded. May we "work for the good of all" and help spread the word of Jesus Christ who died for our salvation. Be with us as we journey forward and save us, I pray. Amen.

NOVEMBER 8
GALATIANS 6:17-18

From now on, let no one make trouble for me; for I carry the marks of Jesus branded on my body. May the grace of our Lord Jesus Christ, be with your spirit, brothers and sisters. Amen.

Fairest Lord Jesus, you gave yourself for us, for our salvation. That "purchase" insinuates that we are to submit to your will. Christians devote much time trying to figure out exactly what that means. How to carry the mark of a Christian is the question. What does that look like, Lord? What would you have us do? How may we serve you? We love you Lord and are committed to finding ways to serve you. There are many clues about how Christians are to act, and with each, there is a kindness towards others, helping the downtrodden, feeding the hungry are but two ways to march in your army. Lord, we shall serve you with all of our hearts. We know it is not our will, but Yours. We will devote ourselves to love one another as ourselves as we take positive actions to be solid Christians in an enigmatic world. As we learn, we give our control to You. When we do, we feel your love and pray you shall feel our love for you. The demonstration of our love is manifested in the freedom we have to make choices for good. Surrendering to your will, loving God, means giving self control to you and your will. And that Lord, is the ultimate freedom. May the victory of our submission render good for your flock. Be with us Lord and save us from our sinful ways. In the name of our salvation and saving grace, Jesus Christ. Amen.

NOVEMBER 9

HEBREWS 11:1-3

Now faith is the assurance of things hoped for, the conviction of things not seen. Indeed, by faith our ancestors received approval. By faith we understand that the worlds were prepared by the word of God, so that what is seen was made from things that are not visible.

Wise and wonderful Lord God, the faithful from time forward have learned of your glory! Oral tradition evolved into the written word. Throughout the Old Testament there are stories of the very beginnings of earth. It was a bit difficult to traverse all the "be gats" but the bottom line was not difficult for the hopeful. That is what you provide the world, hope. And your provision is not all that difficult to attain. You showed us the way, the clues were obvious and easy to embrace. I mean, who doesn't want to be saved by the grace of You, God? Books have been written by young and old authors, there were series, like, Are You There God, It's Me... Others simply acknowledge you and the greatest gift ever, your beloved son who was sent by you to be The Messiah. There, by your grace, he lived and died to take away the sins of the world. Our faith embraces the glory of your works and rejoices in the love you shower upon us. Help us Lord to embrace the unselfish generosity your son teaches us. Help us to be cheerful givers to those in need and to be inclusive as his life informed us to be. What is seen was made from things unseen, and Lord, we get it. Thank you for teaching us about grace and faith as you prepared a world for your flock. My our faith be on display in the way we live our lives, teach the children of the world, and embrace a faith you created for us. Thank you, Lord! Be with us this day and every day, saving us from our sins and evil in the world, I pray. Amen.

NOVEMBER 10

GENESIS 4:3-5; 8

In the course of time Cain brought to the Lord an offering of the the fruit of the ground, and Abel for his part brought of the first lints of his flock, their fat portions. And the Lord had regard for Abel and his offering, but for Cain and his offering he had no regard. So Cain was very angry, and his countenance fell.

Cain said to his brother Abel, "Let us go out to the field." And when they were in the field, Cain rose up against his brother Abel, and killed him. Then the Lord said to Cain, "Where is your brother Abel?" He said, "I do not know; am I my brother's keeper?"

———————————

L oving God, humans have demonstrated an almost unimaginable capacity for violence and for blaming the violence on others. In the instance of the brothers Cain and Abel, Cain was laden with jealousy and lacked a true capacity to think about others first. Vying for attention and thwarted from receiving it has caused many to commit despicable deeds. The Lord knew, without asking what had happened to Abel, and in lying to the Lord, Cain had committed yet another sinful act. Scholars suggest the bounty of the earth, offered by Cain, was in recognition of the earthly life which perhaps Cain felt was due to him. In once sense, it expressed a lack of faith as opposed to the living faith of his brother, Abel. Abel's offering was a deeper, more meaningful gift. The question is Lord God, how is it Cain's faith was so obtuse? Could he not see all things come from you? Clearly we must begin to arrange our priorities so that when our days on earth have passed, we will have acquitted ourselves in your service and with your love in our hearts. Be with us Lord, help us to be generous and pure in thought, word, and deed. Save us from our sinful ways as we seek to do your will throughout our lives. Amen.

NOVEMBER 11

HEBREWS 11:4-7

By faith Abel offered to God a more acceptable sacrifice than Cain's. Through this he received approval as righteous, God himself giving approval to his gifts; he died, but through his faith he still speaks.

Loving Lord, it is clear, Abel was a man of acceptable character and in possession of a pure heart. Through living a life pleasing to God and in his dying, Abel's faith was visible to most and especially to you, Lord God. Many loving, spiritual people have passed on to eternal life we know of some of them, but there are many. We know their names, their life stories, and we know of their worldly contributions. Elijah Cummings was such a man, Saint Teresa was such a woman. Mr. Cummings devoted his life to public service through his deeds to help his hometown, Baltimore, MD escape the tyranny of segregation and poverty. Saint Teresa of Calcutta worked tirelessly to help the indigent in India have a better life. She worked tirelessly to make a better life for orphans. They are but two, each demonstrated by mighty and heroic examples their love for you and their capacity to do good. Through their faith, their voices have not been silenced. What a legacy and what an example for the world to follow! May it be so, God. Be with each of us and help us to speak the truth, love mercy and grow our faith and belief in you by our gentle and sure example. Lord we ask for the forgiveness of sin and the hope for a better tomorrow. Amen.

NOVEMBER 12

I PETER 1:1-2

Peter, an apostle of Jesus Christ, to the exiles of the Dispersion in Pontus, Galatia, Cappadocia, Asia and Bithynia, who have been chosen and destined by God the Father and sanctified by the Spirit to be obedient to Jesus Christ and to be sprinkled with his blood. May grace and peace be yours in abundance.

Lord of Heaven and Earth, what a blessing your servant Peter is to us! Peter's salutation is filled with love and praise for you, offering hope to those who believe. Your grace and mercy are gifts to the struggling Christians of that time, and frankly, to us now. They were both Jew and Gentile, and they were scattered both physically and spiritually throughout the land which is now the continent of Asia. The same kindness, protection, love and understanding you gave to them, you freely offer to all who put their trust and faith in you, Lord. Thank you Lord, for the ultimate gift, salvation to all who believe in you, who put their trust in you. What a blessing and comfort to know where our souls shall dwell when this life has passed. Be with us Lord, and save us from our sin. In your holy name I pray. Amen.

NOVEMBER 13

1 PETER 1:3-7

Blessed be the God and Father of our Lord Jesus Christ! By his great mercy he has given us a new birth into a living hope through the resurrection of Jesus Christ from the dead, and into an inheritance that is imperishable, undefined, and unfading, kept in heaven for you, who are being protected by the power of God through faith for a salvation ready to be revealed in the last time. In this you rejoice, even if now for a little while you have had to suffer various trials, so that the genuineness of your faith—being more precious than gold, that though perishable, is tested by fire—may be found to result in praise and glorify and honor when Jesus Christ is revealed.

Holy God, thank you for giving your son, Jesus to the world. What a merciful and loving gift! We have learned much about you and yet, understanding of your gift is perplexing. How? Why? How could you offer Jesus to us, knowing how he would be mistreated and die? Why would you go to such extreme? It is said "extreme times require extreme measures." That is the answer! You knew in order to save the world you had to perform the miracle of all miracles. Thank you God! The question then becomes, How could anyone deny you, knowing what you did for us? We have the hindsight and see much of the picture painted for our understanding and love. Lord God, help us to lift the veil of uncertainty and shine your light on those who seek to follow Jesus' example. May songs of praise glorify and honor your son and you. I pray we work hard to spread the word of your good news and seek to live lives that shall find our final resting place in heaven. Be with us loving God, each day and with each breath we take. Save us from our sins and temptations. In your holy name, I pray. Amen.

NOVEMBER 14

1 PETER 1:8-9

Although you have not seen him, you love him; and even though you do not see him now, you believe in him and rejoice with an indescribable and glorious joy, for you are receiving the outcome of your faith, the salvation of your souls.

Wise and wonderful Lord, you have made our lives spiritually rich. We have learned the stories of your wondrous works, especially through the birth, life, death and resurrection of your son, Jesus. Some have encountered you, through what I've heard called "God Winks." At a time when I needed your help, I saw you and I felt your loving arms and heard your voice tell me "it's not your time, you will be ok." A friend told me she was given a "God Wink" when she had a flat tire. A couple came to her rescue, repaired the tire and saved her from being stranded and in need of mechanical assistance. Lord, we feel your presence and pray for the ability to enunciate our faithful encounters with you for others. May our testimonies encourage others to share their stories, too. To receive the outcome of faith through salvation is a glorious gift and the most treasured gift of all. Be with those who are learning about you and with those who already know you. Save us from all evil and forgive our sins, I pray. Amen.

NOVEMBER 15

1 PETER 1:10-16

Concerning this salvation, the prophets who prophesied of the grace that was to be yours made careful search and inquiry, inquiring about the person or time that the Spirit of Christ within them indicated when it testified in advance to the sufferings destined for Christ and the subsequent glory. It was revealed to them that they were serving not themselves but you, in regard to the things that have now been announced to you through those who brought you good news by the Holy Spirit sent from heaven—things into which angels long to look!

Therefore, prepare your minds for action, discipline yourselves; set all your hope on the grace that Jesus Christ will bring you when he is revealed. Like obedient children, do not be conformed to the desires that you formerly had in ignorance. Instead, as he who called you is holy, be holy yourselves in all your conduct; for it is written, "You shall be holy, for I am holy."

Holy and wise Lord, thank you for showing us the way. I set my hope on the grace of Jesus Christ. Further, I join a coalition of believers who pray for guidance and endurance from all forms of evil. We weep for the treatment of Jesus and rejoice that he is with you in heaven and no longer suffering from the evils foisted upon him during his final days. When I think of the pain and hideous treatment, I am sad, although I realize the plan was set and it was your Devine plan which made it possible for our salvation. Nothing we endure even compares to the treatment given to your son. His life and death give us hope for tomorrow and a plan to endure the challenges and our own very unique pathways through life. The comfort is we are not alone, and we know the ultimate outcome.

Loving and caring God, thank you for giving us the religious tools to make our way to you clear. Be with us each day and forgive our sin as we move through life, however awkward our path might be. Be with us and save us from all sin. In the name of Jesus, I pray. Amen.

1 PETER 1:18-21

You know that you were ransomed from the futile ways inherited from your ancestors, not with perishable things like silver or gold, but with the precious blood of Christ, like that of a lamb without defect or blemish. He was destined before the foundation of the world but was revealed at the end of the ages for your sake. Through him, you have come to trust in God, who raised him from the dead and gave him glory, so that your faith and hope are set on God.

Lord, in times when we reflect on our lives, I mark my years by how your have held me in your heart. I cannot remember a time in my early youth, when I did not know you. I do remember when I knew in my heart you, Lord God were my hope and my salvation. That salvation comes to me through the blood shed by Jesus for my sake. He saved me from a life that was not easy. It made me brave and you showered me with love and most of all hope. How awesome it is to know the promise and feel your love for me. Through Jesus I too, have come to trust in you even when I don't know exactly why. You promised to always be with me and I know that you are. What a blessing my life has been with you guiding my ways. Through your glory I have lived a life capable of helping many young teens and hopefully guiding them to know they are not alone when they carry you in their hearts. We are all sinners who come to you with our deeds already revealed and we humbly ask for your forgiveness and guidance as we continue our life's journey. Thank you Lord, for always being there. You raised your son from the dead, and you have kept so many innocent ones safe. Be with each one and know that your love and promise helps us meet each day with hope, secure in the knowledge of your love for us. Forgive us our sins, loving God and be with us on our journey, I pray. Amen.

1 PETER 1:22-26

Now that you have purified your souls by your obedience to the truth so that you have genuine mutual love, love one another deeply from the heart. You have been born anew, not of perishable but of imperishable seed, through the living and enduring word of God. For

"All flesh is like grass and all its glory like the flower of grass.
The grass withers, and the flower falls,
But the word of the Lord endures forever."

That word is the good news that was announced to you.

———————————

Holy God, it is true, "the word of the Lord endures forever." Thank you for the beauty of your words, interpreted throughout the Bible in moving and loving ways. Sometimes, your words seem harsh...like when you are reacting to the evil in the world. Sometimes, you must become impatient with humans and their thoughtless and greedy ways. Thank you God for never giving up on us. We know you want us to love one another as you love us. That seems like a tall order, but we know it is possible. Long after we have left this world, stories of your goodness and mighty power will resonate on the lips of those who survive. May each one take your words to heart and may we all learn to live our lives to your honor and glory. May our imprint on the world be etched with kindness and our love for you. Be with us Heavenly Father and may your ways guide our ways each and every day of our lives. Save us Lord, from the sins we commit and know we sincerely wish to be better Christians. In your name we pray. Amen.

1 PETER 2:1-5

Rid yourselves, therefore, of all malice, and all guile, insincerity, envy, and all slander. Like newborn infants, long for the pure spiritual milk, so that by it you may grow into salvation—if indeed you have tasted that the Lord is good.

Come to him, a living stone, though rejected by mortals yet chosen and precious in God's sight, and like living stones, let yourselves be built into a spiritual house, to be a holy priesthood, to offer spiritual sacrifices acceptable to God through Jesus Christ.

Precious Savior, we have learned so much about you and yet sometimes we are so obtuse. You told us about building a house on a solid foundation. Sometimes we revisit following your teachings and pray to always remember we are precious in your sight. We are the solid foundation for Christians. We are "living stones" upholding your teachings and the faith you created for us. We pray that all that we do and all that we say may be a living testimony to our faith in You and the church. Lord, be with us this day and each day, forgive our sins and help us to re-energize our faith and Your teachings. We love You and pray to always stay focused on your love for us and ours for you and our sisters and brothers in Christ. In your name I pray. Amen.

NOVEMBER 19
1 PETER 2:6-8

For it stands in scripture: "See, I am laying in Zion a stone, a cornerstone chosen and precious; And whoever believes in him will not be put to shame." To you then who believe, he is precious; but for those who do not believe, "The stone that the builders rejected has become the very head of the corner," and "A stone that makes them stumble, and a rock that makes them fall." They stumble because they disobey the word, as they were destined to do.

Loving God, your servant Peter recognized humans may falter in their faith. We stumble as a reminder of faith and the paths we are to follow. Our faith evolves and grows, and yes, sometimes becomes complacent. Let that little pebble in our shoe remind us of our faith. We have to get the pebble out in order to march to the drumbeat of abiding love and faith in our Lord and Savior. Help us to shine a light on the goodness of humankind and how that goodness is evident in the faith-filled lives we live. May we strengthen the faint-hearted, care for the sick, and love our neighbors as ourselves. As we give thanks for our God, let us demonstrate it by showing love for one another and by helping those less fortunate. May we strive to obey your commandments, Lord and may we be compassionate to everyone. Be with us each day and forgive our sins, I pray in your blessed name. Amen.

NOVEMBER 20
1 PETER 2:9-10

But you are a chosen race, a royal priesthood, a holy nation, God's own people, in order that you may proclaim the mighty acts of him who called you out of darkness into his marvelous light.

"Once you were not a people, but now you are God's people; once you had not received mercy, but now you have received mercy."

L oving God, thank you for choosing us to be your "own people." As soldiers in Christ's army, I pray our lives will be a reflection of all that you have taught us. May we be a kind and compassionate people, helping those less fortunate. And Lord, may we seek to be more giving and caring. May those who have the means to be more generous and kind-hearted use their resources for those in need. May we enter the season of giving thanks with a generous spirit and help those less fortunate. Lord, thank you for those men and women who have devoted great portions of their lives in the service of others who are less fortunate. As a chosen race, we have the ability to help our sisters and brothers. May we follow the examples of many: like the actor, Gary Sinise, may we help the brave soldiers who gave their lives to serve in our military, like President Carter who works tirelessly to build homes for Habitat For Humanity, like Dr. George Poehlman who goes to places that need medical help in times of crisis, like Jose Andres who cooks food for hungry people affected by natural disasters. We can all do something to help those in need. May each of us in some small or grand way seek to move out of silence and darkness into your light by shining a light where we can to improve the lot of someone in need. Be with us Lord as we take action for our brothers and sisters in positive ways and save us from our sins. In your blessed name, I pray. Amen.

NOVEMBER 21

1 PETER 2:12-17

Conduct yourselves honorably among the Gentiles, so that, though they malign you as evildoers, they may see your honorable deeds and glorify God when he comes to judge.

For the Lord's sake accept the authority of every human institution, whether of the emperor as supreme, or of governors, as sent by him to punish those who do wrong and to praise those who do right. For it is God's will that by doing right you should silence the ignorance of the foolish. As servants of God, live as free people, yet do not use your freedom as a pretext for evil: Honor everyone. Love the family of believers. Fear God. Honor the Emperor.

Dear Lord, our country has entered a time of turmoil. Our world is in turmoil, too. Help us to remember to "love our neighbor as ourselves," and to begin a dialog that is respectful and helpful to all. May our tone and words tamp down the flames of hatred, distrust and arrogance. May we speak our truth without disparaging others. Help us Lord to be gentle with our words and deeds and refrain from being evil. I pray each day to honor you and humankind by being faithful and gentle with loving words and kind deeds. Be with us Lord when we are tested and our paths are frustrating. Save us this day and each day. In your name I pray. Amen.

NOVEMBER 22

On this day in 1963 John F. Kennedy, the 35th President of the United States was assassinated. It was a moment those living at that time shall never forget. Why it happened, perhaps we shall never know. What we should remember was President Kennedy's passion for this country and his encouraging words, "Ask not what your country can do for you, ask what you can do for your country."

1 PETER 2:18-22

Slaves, accept the authority of your masters with all deference, not only those who are kind and gentle but also those who are harsh. For it is a credit to you if, being aware of God, you endure pain while suffering unjustly. If you endure when you are beaten for doing wrong, what credit is that? But if you endure when you do right and suffer for it, you have God's approval. For to this you have been called, because Christ also suffered for you, leaving you an example, so that you should follow in his steps. "He committed no sin, and no deceit was found in his mouth."

Holy God, thank you for the life of President Kennedy and for his words which continue to inspire a free nation. His accomplishments were many in the three short years of his presidency. He kept the United States from a war with Russia and he served his country with intelligence and imagination. May we remember kind and gentle leaders, like John Kennedy, who was a person of faith and a "profile in courage." May each of us seek to contribute to our country in ways that help her people and may we learn to be tolerant of one another. Help us learn to serve our country in creative and positive ways, seeking your approval for the blessings we may share with others. Help us to be kind and gentle, and when we need to be harsh. Give us courage to stand up and speak out for injustice always following your example. May we love one another and help the downtrodden. Help us Lord to uplift those in need and the oppressed. Lord, help us to be leaders and to make wise choices in our personal and professional lives. Following a calling and example from Christ, may we boldly live our lives dedicated to following the paths you are leading us to follow. Be with us this day and all of our days. Forgive us our sins and help us to lead lives that make you proud and follow your directions as laid out in the Bible. Save us from sin and help us find ways to help those who live in poverty. Amen.

NOVEMBER 23

1 PETER 2:23-25

When he was abused, he did not return abuse; when he suffered, he did not threaten; but he entrusted himself to the one who judges justly. He himself bore our sins in his body on the cross, so that, free from sins, we might live for righteousness; by his wounds you have been healed. For you were going astray like sheep, but now you have returned to the shepherd and guardian of your souls.

Lord, your servant Peter knew Jesus well. His words tell us how we are to live and more particularly, how Jesus wants us to live. The "Golden Rule" is to be our guide, "do unto others as you would have them do unto you." Peter and others tell us what a giving, kind and faithful son Jesus was. Not only that, but Jesus "bore our sins" in order that we might live for "righteousness." What an awesome son! Thank you Lord for sending Jesus to take away the sins of the world, my sins. We are healed because Jesus lived. May we follow the example of the "good shepherd" and honor Jesus and you. Help us to navigate the ups and downs of our daily lives in ways that honor you and proclaim our righteousness. Be with us each day, forgive our sin and know that we honor you always. Amen.

1 PETER 3:8-12

Finally, all of you, have unity of spirit, sympathy, love for one another, a tender heart, and a humble mind. Do not repay evil for evil or abuse for abuse; but, on the contrary, repay with a blessing. It is for this that you were called—that you might inherit a blessing. For

> *"those who desire life*
> *and desire to see good days,*
> *let them keep their tongues from evil*
> *And their lips from speaking deceit;*
> *let them turn away from evil and do good;*
> *let them seek peace and pursue it.*
> *For the eyes of the Lord are on the righteous,*
> *and his ears are open to their prayer.*
> *But the face of the Lord is against*
> *those who do evil."*

Lord, we are your servants, loving and holy God. It is our responsibility to work towards uniting one another. Often it is difficult to find a "common goal" but it should never be a struggle to act towards what is good, what is just and what is seeking peace. May we emote sincere sympathy and love for one another, comforting those who mourn, those who are suffering mentally or physically. Help us to be humble and to spread blessings even in the face of evil or abuse. The song, "They'll Know We Are Christians By Our Love" is how we endeavor to be seen in this world. Lord, Jesus, help us turn from evil thoughts, words and deeds. May our goal and sincere efforts be to be peaceful people, loving our neighbor, help raise children who will first love you and secondly be righteous in thought, words, and deed. Lord, please help those who need you to save them. Save their souls and save them from others who would do them harm. May we all inherit the blessing of your love and a seat in heaven. Be with us, save us and know we love you! Amen

1 PETER 3:13-17

Now who will harm you if you are eager to do what is good? But even if you do suffer for doing what is right, you are blessed. Do not fear what they fear, and do not be intimidated, but in your hearts sanctify Christ as Lord. Always be ready to make your defense to anyone who demands from you an accounting for the hope that is in you; yet do it with gentleness and reverence. Keep your conscience clear, so that, when you are maligned, those who abuse you for your good conduct in Christ may be put to shame. For it is better to suffer for doing good, if suffering should be God's will, than to suffer for doing evil.

Dear Lord, we are blessed people. Who indeed will harm me if I am eager to do what is good? I confess there have been times when I wonder about that one. There are things happening around me that make me very anxious and even angry for my fellow human beings. You place such value on being gentle and filled with reverence, you never said our paths would be easy and indeed it is not. I do understand, however, the more consistently one practices kindness, the easier it becomes. And yes, I wish to suffer more for doing good, if that be Your will, than to suffer for doing evil. I thank you for this reminder from Peter...it helps with perspective and with a desire to "take the high road." May I remember that each day, especially when I am tempted to stray into the weeds of political atrocities. My feelings have not changed, but by speaking out loudly changes nothing and I have demeaned myself. Help me Lord to remember what I learned as a child, "If you can't say something nice, don't say anything at all." May we learn to speak our truths with kindness and love, and may I lean into positive change. Lord, be with me this day and forgive my sins, I pray. Amen.

NOVEMBER 26
1 PETER 3:18-19

For Christ also suffered for sins once for all, the righteous for the unrighteous, in order to bring you to God. He was put to death in the flesh, but made alive in the spirit, in which he also went and made a proclamation to the spirits in prison, who in former times did not obey, when God waited patiently in the days of Noah, during the building of the ark, in which a few, that is, eight persons, were saved through water.

Holy and precious God, thank you for the ultimate gift, that of your son, Christ Jesus! When I think about what you gave the world, and why, I am humbled. You made it possible for all things, by creating Jesus and allowing his death. The killing was vicious and failed to accomplish the goal set forth. Instead, Jesus died to take away the sins of the world. Jesus prayed, "forgive them, Father, for they know not what they are doing." He prayed for the murderers! I want to hit the "are you kidding me" button, but I know the answer. No, you are not kidding me! You are teaching me and all who would learn how to treat others. May we learn the lessons, absorb Jesus' teachings and stop being cruel to others. Lord, let us "kill them with kindness" and a with reverence to Jesus' purpose. May we adopt the purpose of being kind to those in need, helping those who need food, clothing, and a place to live. Be with those who have lost their homes. Especially I pray today for the people of Puerto Rico, who are still trying to recover from a hurricane that decimated the island over a year ago, and with the people in Bermuda, who literally lost all of their possessions, homes, and many of their inhabitants. Lord, be with the people in California who are fleeing their homes as the fires approach and overtake their homes. Give us courage to face the changing times we live in, Holy God. May we hang on to our faith and our resolution to speak with love and understanding as we disagree with others. We want our actions to calm the boiling attitudes that do not help resolve the differences we have. Be with us Lord, save us from our sins and know that we know Jesus is the "way, the truth and the light." Amen.

1 PETER 3:21-22

And baptism, which is prefigured, now saves you—not as the removal of dirt from the body, but as an appeal to God for a good conscience, through the resurrection of Jesus Christ, who has gone into heaven and is at the right hand of God, with angels, authorities, and powers made subject to him.

Lord, I thank you for the parents who present their children for the sacrament of baptism. They have made an important promise to teach the children they present to the church about you and your son, Jesus. The symbolism is also important to congregations who promise to help the child learn about you and the teachings of Jesus. It is a holy sacrament and usually is a family celebration. May the promises made for the children be upheld and may the children grow in their love for you and Jesus. Help us as congregants, to keep up with the children, encouraging, loving and supporting them and their parents. Renew the vows parents took for their children or ones we made for ourselves at baptism with each baptism we witness. May we teach loving ways about your love for us and Jesus' life, death and resurrection. May we remain ever faithful to the very end of our days, when we too shall find our place in heaven and our lives be celebrated for our faithful lives. Be with us on this journey and save us in your son's name. Amen.

NOVEMBER 28
1 PETER 4:1-2, 6

Since therefore Christ suffered in the flesh, arm yourselves also with the same intention (for whoever has suffered in the flesh has finished with sin), so as to live for the rest of your earthly life no longer by human desires but by the will of God.

For this is the reason the gospel was proclaimed even to the dead, so that, though they had been judged in the flesh as everyone is judged, they might live in the spirit as God does.

———————————————

Holy Lord, may each of us be "finished with sin." What a tall order that cannot be accomplished until we take full responsibility for the lives we live and the mistakes we make along the way. Living a life no longer by fulfilling human desires will not be easy, but with your help and by following the example of your son, we can be successful. Lord, you want us to "live in the spirit." It is through living a spiritual life that we shall dwell in your house, forever. Thank you for Peter, who put so succinctly what Christians have to work toward. When we "live in the spirit as God does" means we shall never become extinct, for we shall live in "the house of the Lord, forever." May it be so, loving God. Thank you for the plan to have us join the holy family and for making our way certain. We know it will not always be easy, but we also know with you in our hearts and minds, it is possible. Be with us and save us, Lord. Amen.

NOVEMBER 29

1 PETER 4:7-11

The end of all things is near; therefore be serious and discipline yourselves for the sake of your prayers. Above all, maintain constant love for one another, for love covers a multitude of sins. Be hospitable to be another without complaining. Like good stewards of the manifold grace of God, serve one another with whatever gift each of you has received. Whoever speaks must do so as one speaking the very words of God; whoever serves must do so with the strength that God supplies, so that God may be glorified in all things through Jesus Christ. To him belong the glory and the power for ever and ever. Amen.

Dear God, to you be the glory! The things you have done for humanity, for me, is beyond profound. I know to be worthy of your love, I must become more disciplined and show my love for you by loving humankind. Help me to be more loving to those with whom I do not always agree. May I remember when I speak to one in unkind ways, I am also speaking to you. I glorify and honor all the gifts you have provided and especially the gift of your son, Christ Jesus. Thank you for your Divine plan. I pray my part in that plan will be acceptable in your sight. Lord during this last part of the year, may our lives be reminded just who is in charge. I pray the leaders will remember when they speak and I pray the world will move forward in harmony and peace. To you, Lord God belongs the glory and the power for ever and ever. Be with me and save me, in Jesus' name I pray. Amen.

1 PETER 4:12-14

Beloved, do not be surprised at the firefly ordeal that is taking place among you to test you, as though something strange were happening to you. But rejoice insofar as you are sharing Christ's sufferings, so that you may also be glad and shout for joy when His glory is revealed. If you are reviled for the name of Christ, you are blessed, because the spirit of glory, which is the Spirit of God, is resting on you.

———————————————

Lord, thank you again for the wisdom and the life of Peter. Reading Peter's words and feeling your love for us is humbling and inspiring. I rejoice in Christ's love and His life, acknowledging I do not fully understand all the mysteries, but through faith, I accept His teachings and love for me. Yes, even I deserve your love and that of and Christ Jesus. Help me, Lord, to rejoice in the events of my life, even when some were happening I did not feel like rejoicing. Those who question my love for you, just do not know ... I shall pray for them and hope one day they too will feel your love and the grace and peace of your beloved son. Lord, I am praying today for two dear ones slipping toward a day when they shall dwell in your house. Keep them safe as their journey progresses and help all who love and care for them do so with love and dignity. Be with me and everyone one this day as we worry about our loved ones. Lord, forgive our sin and know we love your and shall be together with you one day. In Jesus' name I pray. Amen.

DECEMBER 1
1 PETER 4:15-17

But let one of you suffer as a murderer, a thief, a criminal, or even as a mischief maker. Yet if any of you suffers as a Christian, do not consider it a disgrace, but glorify God because you bear his name. For the time has come for judgement to begin with us, what will be the end for those who do not obey the gospel of God?

Holy God, how is it that you always hear our prayers? It is a mystery and the greatest blessing ever. I am praying today for all who find this day sad because of the loss of a special person in their lives. For me and so many others, we are sad to have lost our dear friend, mentor and spiritual leader. He is in your house now. When I once prayed about this loss, I felt as if a part of me was gone, too. The tincture of time has brought us closer in thoughts about our love for you Lord God and just how the memory of certain people bring us closer to you is comforting. It is so hard to go on when a loss happens, you have taught us to continue our faith filled journey and to obey the gospel teachings. Thank you for bringing all the people in our lives who make us who we are and who live their lives in the sunshine of your expectations for us. Thank you for taking care of your faithful flock. I pray that we shall rejoice in the faith-filled lives of those who have gone before us and when one day, we too shall join them. Thank you for your loving grace and I pray for the forgiveness of sin and courage to make each day pleasing to you. In your blessed name I pray. Amen.

DECEMBER 2

As we ponder the "whys" perhaps the great hymn, How Great Thou Art, will help as we move forward. Perhaps it will ease the pain of loved ones caring for a person on a path to life's end. Perhaps it will bring peace to those who suffer and to those who care for loved ones. Listen to Carrie Underwood and Vince Gill singing this on You Tube.

O Lord my God, when I in awesome wonder
Consider all the worlds Thy Hands have made
I see the stars, I hear the roaring thunder
Thy power throughout the universe displayed

Then sings my soul, my Savior God to thee
How great Thou art, how great Thou art
Then Sings my soul, my Savior God to thee,
How great Thou art, how great thou art.

And when I think of God, His love not sparing
Sent Him to die, I scarce can take it in
That on the Cross, my burden gladly bearing
He bled and died to take away my sin.

Then sings my soul, my Savior God to thee
How great Thou art, how great thou art.

When Christ shall come with shout of acclamation,
And take me home, what joy would fill my heart
Then I shall bow, in humble adoration,
And then proclaim: "My God, how great thou art."

Holy Lord, the words of this momentous hymn bring tears of joy and hope to your people. We know our friend or family member, a dear loved one is beginning to move toward the end of life here on earth. Help us to rejoice that our brother or sister are on a path to you. May we bring love and support to all who offer care and compassion. Help us gain a joyful posture toward the end of life as we know it. You, Lord God, set the example. Help us have glorious "Easter moments" knowing a beloved is on the path to you, where pain and suffering are no more. Lord, soften the angst and fears of those who tend to the sick and critically ill. Help us Lord to find joy in the release of a weary body or mind to your care. For we know in our father's house there is room for each believer and repentant, and for each one of us. Be with us Lord, as we go about our daily lives and save us from our sins. Lord please know that we worship and adore you from the very core of our beings. In the name of our risen Lord, I pray. Amen.

DECEMBER 3
LUKE 2:8-11

In that region there were shepherds living in the fields, keeping watch over their flock by night. Then an angel of the Lord stood before them, and the glory of the Lord shone around them, and they were terrified. But the angel said to them, "Do not be afraid; for I am bringing you good news of great joy for all the people; to you is born this day in the city of David, a Savior, who is the Messiah, the Lord.

———————————

Heavenly Father of Jesus, thank you for the greatest gift, the Christ child! His title Christ means messiah or anointed one. His arrival signals the fulfillment spoken about in the Old Testament. And yet, Jesus was far greater than any prophecy. He showed us, Lord God, how to preach to all the people, how to perform miracles that helped the least of the population, the ill and the outcasts. Jesus' ministry showed compassion and love for a population that are often overlooked. And so Lord, I give thanks and praise for the wisdom, love and saving grace. Thank you Father God, for the gift of your son, who came to transform people who had been mired in the dogma of Judaism, selfishness and gluttony.

Beautiful and inspirational words of Joy To The World

Joy to the world! The Lord is come:
Let Earth receive her king;
Let every heart prepare Him room.
And heaven and nature sing,
and heaven and nature sing,
and heaven and nature sing.

He rules the world with truth and grace,
And makes the nations prove
The glories of his righteousness,

And wonders of His love,
And wonders of His love,
And wonders, wonders of his love.

When I think of your beloved son, Lord, I am filled with joy intermingled with the pain of his final days. It must have been so painful to see what Jesus endured in order to change the world and prepare a way for all sinners to be forgiven and for Christians to receive the same forgiveness for our sins today. Thank you Lord, for the most precious gift of all, Christ! What hope He gives to each of us. As we enter the "season" and give thanks to you for the "reason" may we remember the precious gift we are given. A gift we did not anticipate, nor deserve, and yet, through your love and wisdom you knew it would be perfect for each one of us. May we treasure the gift for all the days of our lives. Be with us Lord, and help us to make better choices as we interact with others and as we prepare to share in honest ways part of what we have that might help someone in need. May we prove the "wonders of his love." Save us from our sinful ways this holiday season, Lord. I pray in the name of Jesus, the Messiah. Amen.

DECEMBER 4
MATTHEW 1:18-24

Now the birth of Jesus the Messiah took place in this way. When his mother, Mary had been engaged to Joseph, but before they had lived together, she was found to be with child from the Holy Spirit. Her husband Joseph, being a righteous man and unwilling to expose her to public disgrace planned to dismiss her quietly. But just when he had resolved to do this, an angel of the Lord appeared to him in a dream and said, "Joseph, son of David, do not be afraid to take Mary as your wife, for the child conceived in her is from the Holy Spirit. She will bear a son, and you are to name him Jesus, for he will save his people from their sins." All this took place to fulfill what had been spoken by the Lord through the prophet: "Look, the virgin shall conceive and bear a son, and they shall name him Emmanuel," which means, "God is with us." When Joseph awoke from sleep, he did as the angel of the Lord commanded him; he took her as his wife.

———————————

Thank you Lord for the gift of your precious son. The prophet Isaiah proclaimed His name, Emmanuel which means "God with us." How utterly perfect! Following Jesus' birth, some seven hundred years after Isaiah's prophecy, was fulfilled. Jesus Christ, the Emmanuel, in every sense of the word had arrived. And with his arrival so to arrived God's gift through Jesus of eternal salvation of His chosen ones from sin and also from death. The hymn O Come O Come Emmanuel renews our hope at Christmas time.

> O come, O come Emmanuel, and ransom captive Israel,
> That mourns in lonely exile here
> Until the Son of God appears.
> Rejoice, rejoice. Emmanuel shall come to thee, O Israel.

Thanks be to you, Lord God. Be with us this day and forgive us our sins. In the name of Jesus, I pray. Amen.

DECEMBER 5

LUKE 24:27

Then beginning with Moses and all the prophets, he (Jesus) interpreted to them the things about himself in all the scriptures.

Holy God, what must the disciples have thought when Jesus told the stories of Moses and all the prophets. Jesus, (hundreds of years later,) explained to the disciples what the Scriptures had to say about him! How perplexing that must have been at the outset, however, when they remembered all of their travels in the last years, they knew. The prophecies concerning Jesus out-number all the other prophecies, after all Christ is the fulfillment of law and the prophets!

As it is written in Isaiah 9:6 :

> For a child has been born for us, a son given to us;
> Authority rests upon his shoulders; and he is named
> Wonderful Counselor, Mighty God, Everlasting
> Father, Prince of Peace.

We continue to be awed by the fulfillment of the prophecies, by you and by your son, our Savior. Thank you, Lord, for giving us the wonderful gift of your son, Jesus, and his mission, to take away the sins of the world. We are so very humble knowing what He did for us and what You do for us, each and every day. Be with us and save us, I pray in the name of Jesus. Amen.

Come, Thou Long-Expected Jesus

> Come, Thou long-expected Jesus,
> Born to set Thy people free;
> From our fears and sins release us,
> Let us find our rest in Thee.
> Israel's strength and consolation,
> Hope of all the earth, Thou art;
> Dear desire of every nation,
> Joy of every longing heart.

DECEMBER 6

COLOSSIANS 2:16-17

Therefore do not let anyone condemn you in matters of food and drink or of observing festivals, new moons, or sabbaths. These are only a shadow of what is to come, but the substance belongs to Christ.

L oving God, when we gather with friends and loved ones to celebrate the birth of your beloved son, Christ Jesus, we establish a time to rejoice and take in the great gift you gave to us. For, of course we know the story and that you sent Jesus into the world to take away the sins of the world. Thank you Lord God! We rejoice in the stories of Jesus' birth. Knowing his purpose and your beautiful plan for us helps us to face the living of each day. Be with us and in the name of Jesus, save us, I pray. Amen.

DECEMBER 7

GALATIANS 4:4-5

But when the fullness of time had come, God sent his Son, born of a woman, born under the law, in order to redeem those who were under the law, so that we might receive adoption as children.

Wise Lord God, celebrating the birth of your son, Jesus, joins us with history. We are, after all, people who look to history for clarity, for meaning and for our very grounding. Jesus' birth fulfills the prophecy of the Old Testament and was born by Mary under the law of the land. We believe the Bible, written in parts by many and essentially regardless of language, the translation has been in tact once each book was written. The Bible records prophecy which has been supported. Thank you for the mysteries of Christ and the prophecies of His coming. Through the birth of your beloved son, his life and the fulfillment of the prophets, we, too, have become heirs. You, merciful and generous provider have adopted us, each one. We come to you humbly asking for the forgiveness of our sins and that you accept us into Your kingdom when our time on earth is complete. Thank you, God! Be with us as we move from this life to the next, and save us, I pray in the blessed Savior's name. Amen.

I HEARD THE BELLS ON CHRISTMAS DAY

Henry Wadsworth Longfellow

I heard the bells of Christmas Day
Their old familiar carols play.

And wild and sweet the words repeat.
Of peace of earth, good will to men.

I thought how, as the day had come,
The bell fries of a Christendom.

Had rolled along the unbroken son
Of peace on earth, good will to men.

They peeled the bells more loud and deep
"God is not dead, nor doth He sleep;

The wrong shall fail, the right prevail
With peace on earth, good will to men."

Till, ringing, singing on its way
The world revolved from night to day

A voice, a chime, a chant sublime,
Of peace on earth, good will to men.

And in despair I bowed my head:
"There is no peace on earth," I said.
"For hate is strong, and mocks the song
Of peace on earth, good will to men."

DECEMBER 8

Two books in the New Testament describe the birth of Jesus, with a focus on lineage:

Matthew writes of Jesus legal lineage from Solomon through Joseph. Luke, on the other hand, provides the natural lineage from Nathan through Mary. Perhaps both disciples traced the genealogy of Jesus—Matthew provides the "legal" line, and Luke the "natural" line. As we journey toward Christmas Day, we remember that the baby in the manger was real. The baby was a miracle, conceived in the womb of the Virgin Mary and subsequently lived a life as a carpenter, a teacher and leader, and then our Savior who was crucified, dead and buried. He was raised from the dead in order that we might receive rebirth and resurrection, too.

Thank you Lord, for the gift of your son, Jesus. What a loving gift! You helped the world learn of you and through Jesus, we also learned the words of the Old Testament prophets were true. Jesus came to offer salvation to the world. Hallelujah! Amen.

WHILE SHEPHERDS WATCHED
Nahum Tate

While shepherds watched their flocks by night
　　　All seated on the ground.
The angel of the Lord came down,
　　　And glory shone around.
　　　And glory shone around.

"Fear not," said he, for mighty dread
Had seized their troubled mind,
"Glad tidings of great joy I bring,
        To you and all mankind.
        To you and all mankind.

"To you, in David's town, this day
        Is born of David's line.
The Savior, who is Christ the Lord,
        And this shall be the sign.
        And this shall be the sign.

"The heavenly Babe you there shall find
        To human view displayed
All meanly wrapped in swathing bands,
        And in a manger laid.
        And in a manger laid."

Thus spake the seraph and forthwith
        Appeared a shining throng,
Of angels praising God on high.
        Addressed their joyful song.
        Addressed their joyful song:

        "All glory be to God on high,
        And to the earth be peace:
Good will henceforth from heaven to men
        Begin and never cease,
        Begin and never cease!"

DECEMBER 9

LUKE 2:1-3

In those days a decree went out from Emperor Augustus that all the world should be registered. This was the first registration and was taken while Quirinius was governor of Syria. All went to their own towns to be registered.

———————————

Heavenly Father of Jesus, though there are "doubters" regarding Jesus' birth and the census, history tells us this "registration" was ordered and explains why Mary and Joseph traveled to Jerusalem. Thank you for the baby, the promise and the miracle of Jesus' birth, life, and resurrection. You give hope to the hopeless and instruction to all for our very salvation. Be with us and save us in Jesus' name. Amen.

O LITTLE TOWN OF BETHLEHEM
Phillips Brooks

O little town of Bethlehem, how still we see thee lie!
Above thy deep and dreamless sleep the silent starts go by.
Yet in they dark streets shine the everlasting Light;
The hopes and fears of all the years are met in thee tonight.

For Christ is born of Mary, and gathered all above,
While Mortals sleep, the angels keep their watch of wondering love.
O morning stars together proclaim the holy birth,
And praises sing to God the King, and peace to men on earth!

How silently, how silently, the wondrous gift is given:
So God imparts to human hearts the blessings of His heav'n.
No ear may hear his coming, but in this world of sin,
Where meek souls will receive Him still, the dear Christ enters in.

O holy Child of Bethlehem descend to us, we pray;
Cast out our sin, and enter in; be born in us today.
We hear the Christmas angels the great glad tidings tell:
O come to us, abide with us, our Lord Emmanuel!

DECEMBER 10
1 CORINTHIANS 15:3-8

For I handed on to you as of first importance what I in turn had received: that Christ died for our sins in accordance with the scriptures, and that he was buried, and that he was raised on the third day in accordance with the scriptures, and that he appeared to Cephas, then to the twelve. Then he appeared to more than five hundred brothers and sisters at one time, most of whom are still alive, though some have died. Then he appeared to James, then to all the apostles. Last of all, as to one untimely born, he appeared also to me.

Holy Lord, the story of your son's life would be superfluous without the resurrection. A beautiful birth, a virgin birth and a gruesome ending all to leave a legacy for all of humankind. Jesus came to take away the sins of the world, my sins, too! Thank you for such an unselfish gift. What power you gave Jesus; birth, life, death, and resurrection. Jesus had the power to lay down His life and the power to take it up again. What did that mean? It meant Jesus is God in human flesh! In this season of Advent, may we never lose sight of all the miracles you provide. Your guidance and Jesus' witness ground us and help us when we are facing difficulty in our lives. Lord, be with us and help us to lean into your love and care, especially when we do not find answers to our questions. Be with those less fortunate, the sick, the grieving, the hungry, the lonely, those suffering all the ravages of poverty. Comfort each one's unique worries and help them find peace through your love and your great gifts to us. Thanks be to God. Amen.

GOD REST YE MERRY GENTLEMEN

Traditional English Carol

God rest ye merry, gentlemen, let nothing you dismay,
Remember Christ our Savior was born on Christmas Day;
To save us all from Satan's power when we were gone astray.
>   O tidings of comfort and joy, comfort and joy;
>   O tidings of comfort and joy.

In Bethlehem, in Jewry, this blessed Babe was born,
And laid within a manger upon this blessed morn;
To which His mother Mary did nothing take in scorn,
>   O tidings of comfort and joy, comfort and joy;
>   O tidings of comfort and joy.

From God our Heavenly Father a blessed angel came;
And unto certain shepherds brought tidings of the same;
How that in Bethlehem was born the Son of God by name.
>   O tidings of comfort and joy, comfort and joy.
>   O tidings of comfort and joy.

DECEMBER 11

COLOSSIANS 2:9

For him, the whole fullness of Deity dwells bodily

———————————

Lord, we get it. The scriptures are clear. Jesus Christ was fully God and fully man. Which is to say, Jesus existed as the 'perfect unity' in one person of a divine father and human mother. Paul expressed this profound truth of the incarnation in his letter to the people of Philippi:

PHILIPPIANS 2:5-8

Let each of you look not to your own interests, but to the interests of others. Left the same mind be in you that was in Christ Jesus,
who, though he was born in the form of God,
did not regard equality with God as something to be exploited,
but emptied himself, taking the form of a slave,
being born in human form, he humbled himself
and became obedient to the point of death—
even death on a cross.

We remain awestruck, Lord! You loved us so much, you gave us Jesus who came to take away all of our sin. Praise and thanks to you O Lord, our God. Amen.

O COME, O COME EMMANUEL

Translation by John Mason Neale

O come, O come, Emmanuel, and ransom captive Israel,
That mourns in lonely exile here until the Son of God appear.
Rejoice! Rejoice! Emmanuel shall come to thee, o Israel.

O come, Thou Rod of Jesse, free Thine
   own from Satan's tyranny;
From depths of hell They people save, and give
   them victory over the grave.
Rejoice! Rejoice! Emmanuel shall come to thee, O Israel.

O Come, Thou Day-Spring come and cheer,
   our spirits by Thine advent here;
Disperse the gloomy clouds of night, and death's
   dark shadows put to flight.
Rejoice! Rejoice! Emmanuel shall come to these, O Israel.

O come, Thou Key of David, come, and open
   wide our heavenly home;
Make safe the way that leads on high, and close
   the path to misery.
Rejoice! Rejoice! Emmanuel shall come to thee O Israel.

O come, O come, great Lord of might, who to
   thy tribes onSinai's height,
In ancient times once gave the law in cloud and majesty and awe.
Rejoice! Rejoice! Emmanuel shall come to thee, O Israel.

DECEMBER 12

JOHN 1:1, 14

In the beginning was the Word, and the Word was with God, and the Word was God. . . . And the Word became flesh and lived among us, and we have seen his glory, the glory as of a father's only son, full of grace and truth.

Holy and heavenly God, the mysteries of life begin with you! The birth of Jesus is a joining of God and human incarnation. When I ponder Jesus, It is difficult to think of him as Divine and human. In other words, Jesus is the incarnation of the Divine and mankind and that is precisely where faith enters into our understanding. We are told that God created humankind in his own image (Genesis 1:27) so it stands to reason Jesus would be human. Lord God, your expectations of humans is to be responsible or rational, to have a moral compass and of course to have a spiritual life...just like you. While we are fully-human, Christ Jesus, was ever the teacher with his gentle way of instructing through parables. One of the most overt behaviors was standing up to the money changers in the temple. Jesus' teachings were consistent with biblical teachings, linking him to you, Lord and to humanity. Thank you for helping us to comprehend the two worlds combined in your Son. In this holy season, may we focus on the amazing grace with which your beloved son became our Savior. Be with us this season, Lord and help us to share the story of your son and his miraculous life. Amen.

ONCE IN ROYAL DAVID'S CITY

Cecil Frances Humphreys Alexander

Once in royal David's city stood a lowly cattle shed,
Where a mother laid her Baby in a manger for His bed;
Mary was that mother mild, Jesus Christ, her little Child.

He came down to earth from heaven, who is God and Lord of all,
And His shelter was a stable, and His cradle was a stall.
With the poor, and mean, and lowly, lived on earth our. Savior holy.

And, through all His wondrous childhood,
He would honor and obey,
Love and watch the lowly maiden, in whose gentle arms He lay:
Christian children all must be bold, obedient, good as He.

And our eyes at last shall see Him, through His own redeeming love,
For that Child so dear and gentle is our Lord in heav'n above,
And He leads His children on to the place where He is gone.

Not in that poor lowly stable, with the oxen standing by,
We shall see Him; but in heaven, set at God's right hand on high:
When like starts His children crowned all in white shall wait around.

DECEMBER 13

REVELATION 1:17-18

When I saw him, I fell at this feet as though dead. But he placed his right hand on me saying, "Do not be afraid; I am the first and the last, and the living one. I was dead, and see, I am alive forever and ever; and I have the keys of Death and of Hades.

Holy Lord, your beloved son once asked his disciples "Who do you say that I am?" (Matthew 8: 28). During Jesus' short life in the ministry he claimed to be the "Son of God." We know the story, we have followed Jesus from the manger to the temple, to the cross. Your were constantly with Him and He with You. Lord, the words of comfort spoken continuously encourage your faithful servants, even today! Thank you for your wisdom and guidance and for making your authority as the beginning and end of all. Lord your omnipotence and revelation of just who you are is warming and chilling at the same time. Oh to be in your presence, Lord, to see you with my own eyes. I have felt your presence and love and feel so blessed to have your love and comfort at extreme expectations times in my life. You truly are the alpha and the omega. Thank you for your love and loving ways. Be with me this day and all the days of my life, forgive my sin and know how much I love you. Amen.

CROWN HIM

Matthew Bridges and Godfrey Thring

Crown Him with many crowns, the Lamb upon His throne.
Hark! How the heavenly anthem drowns all music but its own.
Awake, my soul, and sing of Him who died for thee,
And hail Him as thy matchless King through all eternity.

Crown Him the virgin's Son, the God incarnate born.
Whose arm those crimson trophies won which now His brow adorn;
Fruit of the mystic rose, as of that rose the stem;
The root whence mercy ever flows, the Babe of Bethlehem.

Crown Him the Lord of life, who triumphed o'er the grave,
And rose victorious in the strife for those He came to save.
HIs glories now we sing, who died, and rose on high,
Who died eternal life to bring, and lives that death may die.

Crown Him the Lord of love, behold His hands and side,
Those wounds, yet visible above, in beauty glorified.
No angel in the sky can fully bear that sight,
But downward bends his burning eye at mysteries so bright.

Crown Him the Lord of Heaven, enthroned in the worlds above,
Crown Him the King to whom is given the wondrous name of Love.
Crown Him with many crowns, as thrones before Him fall;
Crown Him, ye kings, with many crowns, for He is King of all.

DECEMBER 14

MATTHEW 11:2-6

When John heard in prison what the Messiah was doing, he sent word by his disciples and said to him, "Are you the one who is to come, or are we to wait for another?" Jesus answered them, "Go and tell John what you hear and see: the lepers are cleansed, the deaf hear, the dead are raised, and the poor have good news brought to them. And blessed is anyone who takes no offense at me."

Lord, when John the Baptist sent word to Jesus from prison, asking for clarification. He wanted to know if Jesus was the Messiah. Jesus answers the questions by reminding him of the wonders that can only be answered by faith. They had heard and seen the miracles and healings, Lord. Christ Jesus' loving and helping compassion to the sick and the poor demonstrate Your tender mercies, God. When we see and hear and touch, reality comes alive. Today, we do see and hear and touch your wondrous world. We see the miracles happening still pointing us to the way to our salvation. Sometimes, Lord, it all seems too much, overwhelming, and yet we see you God in the beauty of the earth and in miracles that can only be attributed to you. Thank you! Be with us this day and each day. Seeing and feeling your love gives hope for all of our tomorrows. Save us from our sins and know how much I love you. Amen.

WHAT CHILD IS THIS?

William Chatterton Dix

What child is this who, laid to rest,
On Mary's lap is sleeping?
Whom angels greet with anthems sweet,
While shepherds watch are keeping?
This, this is Christ the King,
Whom shepherds guard and angels sing:
Haste, haste to bring Him laud,
The Babe, the Son of Mary.

Why lies He in such mean estate
Where ox and ass are feeding?
Good Christian, fear: for sinners here
The silent Word is pleading:
Nails, spear, shall pierce Him through,
The cross be borne for me, for you.
Hail, hail the Word made flesh
The babe, the Son of Mary.

So bring Him incense, gold, and myrrh,
Come peasant, king to own Him;
The King of kings salvation brings,
Let loving hearts enthrone Him.
Raise, raise the song on high,
The Virgin sings her lullaby.
Joy, joy for Christ is born.
The Babe, the Son of Mary.

DECEMBER 15

COLOSSIANS 1:15-16

He is the image of the invisible God, the firstborn of all creation; for in him all things in heaven and on earth were created, things visible and invisible, whether thrones or dominions or rulers or powers—all things have been created through him and for him.

Hear my prayer O Lord. Creation wonders never cease to amaze us, we look at the beauty of the earth from the beautiful mountains, to the peaceful and sometimes taunting oceans. Then we turn to all that is good and cherished: our children, your children. The days when I struggle Lord, I think of you and how you gave us such a wonderful gift ... your son. His example of how to live a life devoted to goodness and mercy was repaid by a cross. And yet, His purpose was fulfilled for us! It is in this context I pray this morning, remembering the words of the hymn All Hail The Power Of Jesus' Name. We love the words and the power that courses through us when we sing those words. You are the reason, Jesus is the reason and in this Christmas season, may we rejoice in the glorious gift you gave us. Your message Lord God is clear for those who would hear it. Christ Jesus came to take away the sins of the world. What a gift! What faith! Thank you Lord God. We treasure the gift and your love. Salvation awaits all of us. Forgive our sinful ways and be with us each moment of our walk with you. In your blessed name I pray. Amen.

ALL HAIL THE POWER
OF JESUS' NAME

Edward Perronet

All hail the power of Jesus' name! Let angels prostrate fall.
Bring forth the royal diadem, and crown Him Lord of all.
Bring forth the royal diadem, and crown Him Lord of all.

Let highborn seraphs Tuen the lyre, and as they tune it, fall
Before HIs face who tunes their choir, and crown Him Lord of all.
Before His face who tunes their choir, and crown Him Lord of all.

Crown Him, ye morning stars of light,
of your God, who fixed this floating ball;
Now hail the strength of Israel's might, and crown Him Lord of all.
Now hail the strength of Israel's might, and crown Him Lord of all.

Crown Him, ye martyrs of your God, who from HIs altar call;
Extol the Stem of Jesse's Rod, and crown Him Lord of all.
Extol the Stem of Jesse's Rod, and crown Him Lord of all.

Ye seed of Israel's chosen race, ye ransomed from the fall,
Hail Him who saves you by His grace, and crown Him Lord of all.
Hail him who saves you by His grace, and crown Him Lord of all.

Hail Him, ye heirs of David's line, whom David Lord did call,
The God incarnate. Man divine, and crown Him Lord of all.
The God incarnate. Man divine, and crown Him Lord of all.

Sinners whose love can ne'er forget the wormwood and the gall.
Go spread your trophies at His feet, and crown Him Lord of all.
Go spread your trophies at His feet, and crown Him Lord of all.

Let every tribe and every tongue before Him prostrate fall
And shout in universal song the crowned Lord of all.
And shout in universal song the crowned Lord of all.

DECEMBER 16

MATTHEW 2:1-2

In the time of King Herod, after Jesus was born in Bethlehem of Judea, wise men from the East came to Jerusalem, asking, "Where is the child who has been born king of the Jews?

Long-awaited Savior, you are the promise of the prophets, and we are witness to your work - vision, movement, healing, music, healing, new life, good news. Enlighten and enliven us, send us out to spread the word so that may see and hear and know and believe that you are the coming of God, the Messiah. Amen.

(Author unknown)

Gracious and loving Lord, giving praise and thanks to You is so natural and feels so good, and yet at the same time, it seems too little. Your great plan for humanity remains one of the great wonders. We are nine days from celebrating the birth of your beloved son and our Savior. This season of Advent seems to be speeding by, and yet we have been celebrating and preparing. We get an inkling of the anticipation Mary and Joseph must have been feeling as they prepared for the birth of Jesus. No doubt they were a bit anxious and overwhelmed. I know I feel the same sense of anxiety and some feelings of angst that everything may not be as 'ready' as I would like.

The word advent means "coming." Literally we await the birth of Christ. Imagine all the preparations Christians make to celebrate this birth with family and friends. Churches light candles on the Advent wreath while celebrating the uniting of the Old Testament prophecies with the New Testament realities and the birth of Christianity. Be with us and give us wisdom and courage for the facing of the days yet to come. Calm our anxious feelings and help us rejoice in the fulfillment of the promise, Abraham was promised a royal seed—and that seed is Christ Jesus! Thank you for the affirmations from the apostle Paul, for he avowed all who are Gentiles are part of the body of Christ. The inheritance left to us is as sure and as strong today as it ever was. Thanks be to you, Lord. Be with us each day of Advent and help us to live our lives seeking forgiveness for our sins, compassion for others less fortunate and hope for all of our tomorrows. In the name of Jesus, I pray. Amen.

DECEMBER 17
ISAIAH 9:6

For a child has been born for us, a son given to us; authority rests upon his shoulders; and he is named Wonderful Counselor, Mighty God, Everlasting Father, Prince of Peace.

Thank you Holy and loving God for artists who praise your Holy name. During this Advent Season we remember to use our God given gifts to praise you. We lift up our time and talents to your glory.

Place your loving arms around those who are in pain, those who ache to find "the way", "the truth", and "the light." Be with us this day and save us as we boldly march forward to the glorious day we celebrate, the birth of our Savior, your beloved son, Christ Jesus. Amen.

O HOLY NIGHT

John S. Dwight, based upon a French poem by
Placide Cappeau de Roquemaure

O Holy Night! the stars are brightly shining,
It is the night of the dear Savior's birth!
Long lay the world in sin and error pining,
Til He appeared and the soul felt its worth.
A thrill of hope the weary world rejoices,
For yonder breaks a new and glorious morn.
Fall on your knees! O hear the angel voices!
O night divine, O night when Christ was born!
O night, O holy night. O night divine!

Led by the light of faith serenely beaming,
With glowing hearts by His cradle we stand;
So led by the light of a star sweetly gleaming,
Here came the wise men from Orient land.
The king of kings lay thus in lowly manger,
In all our trials born to be our Friend.

He knows our needs, to our weakness is no stranger.
Behold your King! Before Him lowly bend!
Behold your King! Before Him lowly bend!

Truly he taught us to love one another;
His law is love and His gospel is peace.
Chains shall He break, for the slave is our brother,
And in His name all oppression shall cease.
Sweet hymns of joy in grateful chorus raise we,
Let all within us praise His holy name;
Christ is the Lord, O, praise His name forever!
His power and glory evermore proclaim!
His power and glory evermore proclaim!

DECEMBER 18

ACTS 2:46-47

Day by day, as they spent much time together in the temple, they broke bread at home and ate their food with glad and generous hearts, praising God and having the goodwill of all the people. And day by day the Lord added to their number those who were being saved.

Father God, as we move closer to that moment when the little children are so excited in anticipation of the celebration of Jesus' birth, we know the "end story." Lord, we understand your word and deed and that what happened some thirty years later was the darkest period for our blessed Savior. You have helped us to understand both. I pray for those who are hurting due to a profound loss, you will comfort them and wrap your arms around them, giving them peace. Breaking bread and sharing a meal with glad and generous hearts soothes me. Lord, thank you for the gift of salvation paid by your son. May we remember those who, like you, give generously to those without. May each of us find ways to express "good will" to our fellow citizens. I pray the message of salvation will seep into the hearts and minds of each one. Be with us this day, forgive us our sins and save us, I pray. Amen.

HOLY, HOLY, HOLY!
Reginald Heber

Holy, holy, holy! Lord God, Almighty!
Early in the morning our song shall rise to Thee;
Holy, holy, holy! all the saints adore Thee,
Casting down they golden crowns around the crystal sea;
Cherubim and seraphim falling down before Thee,
Who wast, and art, and evermore shalt be.

Holy, holy, holy! though the darkness hide Thee,
Though the eye of sinful man Thy glory may not see;
Only Thou art holy! There is none beside Thee,
Perfect in power, in love, and purity.

Holy, holy, holy! Lord God Almighty!
All Thy works shall praise Thy name, in earth, and sky, and sea;
Holy, holy holy! merciful and mighty!
God in three Persons, blessed Trinity!

JOHN 1:6-8, 19-28

There was a man sent from God, whose name was John. He came as a witness to testify to the light, so that all might believe through him. He himself was not the light, but he came to testify to the light.

This is the testimony given by John when Jews sent priests and Levites from Jerusalem asked him, "Who are you?" He confessed and did not deny it, but confessed, "I am not the Messiah." And they asked him, "What then? Are you Elijah?" He said, "I am not." "Are you the prophet?" He answered, "No." Then they said to him, "Who are you? Let us have an answer for those who sent us. What do you say about yourself?" He said,

"I am the voice of one crying out in the wilderness,
'Make straight the way of the Lord,'" as the prophet Isaiah said.

Now when they had been sent from the Pharisees. They asked him, "Why then are you baptizing, if you are neither the Messiah, nor Elijah, nor the prophet?" John answered them, "I baptize with water. Among you stands one whom you do not know, the one who is coming after me; I am not worthy to until the thong of his sandal." This took place in Bethany across the Jordan, where John was baptizing.

Holy One, you have come among us to lead us in the paths of righteousness. Guide our feet through the wilderness toward the living water of your grace, following in the steps of our Savior: Jesus Christ, the light of the world. When we partake of the sacrament of Baptism, or Marriage, or Holy Communion, Lord we feel closer to you and we remember the solemnity of each sacrament. I pray we feel renewed with each one, each time we witness or participate. It brings me closer to you and reminds me you are always with me. Lord, may your faithful servants give everlasting peace, hope and love imparted by you to those they meet. While we will never be you, we get it Lord, and we want others to love you and worship you as we do. Be with us and save us I pray. Amen.

THIS IS MY FATHER'S WORLD
Franklin I. Sheppard

This is my Father's world, And to my listening ears All nature sings and round me rings The music of the spheres.
This is my Father's world: I rest me in the thought Of rocks and trees, of skies and seas; His hand the wonders wrought.
This is my Father's world: Oh, let me ne'er forget. That Though the wrong seems oft so strong, God is the Ruler yet.
This is my Father's world: The battle is not done; Jesus who died shall be satisfied, And earth and heaven be one.

DECEMBER 20
LUKE 1:68-80

Then his father Zechariah was filled with the Holy Spirit and spoke this prophecy:

"Blessed be the Lord God of Israel, for he has looked favorably on his people and redeemed them. He has raised up a mighty savior for us in the house of his servant David, as he spoke through the mouth of his holy prophets from of old, that we would be saved from our enemies and from the hand of all who hate us. Thus he has shown the mercy promised to our ancestors, and has remembered his holy covenant, the oath that he swore to our ancestor Abraham, to grant us that we, being rescued from the hands of our enemies, might serve him without fear, in holiness and righteousness before him all our days. And you, child will be called the prophet of the Most High; for you will go before the Lord to prepare his ways, to give knowledge of salvation to his people by the forgiveness of their sins, By the tender mercy of our God, the dawn from on high will break upon us, to give light to those who sit in darkness until the day he appeared publicly to Israel.

Wise Father God, the prophet Zechariah, told of birth to come, Jesus' birth. By your love and mercy, Lord, your son came to enlighten the world. To tell all who would hear of a new religion, that would grant to believers a seat with you in heaven. Salvation would be ours and we would earn through our belief in You, an everlasting life under your auspices. It seems simple, believe, act thusly, earn your reward. The doubters might say, "Ok, but what's the catch?" No catch, no tricks, just believe and ask for forgiveness when you sin. Sometimes, even in private moments of prayer, asking God to forgive our sin is stressful, almost impossible. But our God is a loving God and He assures us through the death of

His son, Jesus, that salvation is ours for the asking. So today, Lord, I pray for courage for each believer. Have the courage and faith to take that first step toward salvation. Lord, be with us and save us, I pray. Amen.

COME, THOU ALMIGHTY KING
Felipe de Giardini

Come Thou Almighty King, Help us Thy name to sing,
Help us to Praise: Father, all glorious, O'er all victorious,
Come and reign over us, Ancient of Days.

Come Thou Incarnate Word, Gird on Thy mighty sword,
Our Prayers attend". Come and Thy people bless, And give Thy
Word success; Spirit of holiness, On us descend.

Come Holy Comforter, Thy sacred witness bear
In this glad hour: Thou who almighty art, Now rule in every
heart, And ne'er from us depart, Spirit of power.

To thee, great One in Three, The highest praises be,
Hence ever more! They sovereign majesty May we in glory see,
And to eternity Love and adore.

DECEMBER 21

MATTHEW 1:18-25

Now the birth of Jesus, the Messiah took place in this way. When his mother Mary had been engaged to Joseph, but before they lived together, she was found to be with child from the Holy Spirit. Her husband, Joseph being a righteous man and unwilling to expose her to public disgrace, planned to dismiss her quietly. But just when he had resolved to do this, an angel of the Lord appeared to him in a dream and said, "Joseph, son of David, do not be afraid to take Mary as your wife, for the child conceived in her is from the Holy Spirit. She will bear a son, and you are to name him Jesus, for he will save his people from their sins." All this took place to fulfill what had been spoken by the Lord through the profit:

> *"Look, the virgin shall conceive and*
> *Bear a son,*
> *And they shall name him*
> *Emmanuel,"*

Which means, "God is with us." When Joseph awoke from sleep, he did as the angel of the Lord commanded him: he took her as his wife, but had no marital relations with her until she had borne a son; and he named him Jesus.

Holy and merciful God, your power is beyond our comprehension. I pray that during our slumber, we too may feel your grace and power. Come into our lives and help us to understand a powerful reality: although some things we cannot understand, by faith we shall know what Joseph and Mary knew, that you are omniscient. Be with us this holy season and give us the boldness to affirm You in our lives. I pray all shall live with your love and grace. Save us and help us to proclaim your holy name. Amen.

ANGELS WE HAVE HEARD ON HIGH

French Carol,
Translated by James Chadwick

Angels we have heard on high, Sweetly singing o'er the plains,
And the mountains in reply. Echoing their joyous strains

Chorus:
Gloria, in excelsis Deo,
Gloria in excelsis Deo.

Shepherds why this jubilee? Why your joyous strains prolong?
What glad-some tidings be Which inspire your heavenly song?

Chorus

Come to Bethlehem and see Him whose birth the angels sing:
Come, adore on bended knee Christ, the Lord, the new-born King.

Chorus

DECEMBER 22

LUKE 1:26-38

In the sixth month the angel Gabriel was sent by God to a town in Galilee called Nazareth, to a virgin engaged to a man whose name was Joseph, of the house of David. The virgin's name was Mary. And he came to her and said, "Greetings, favored one! The Lord is with you." But she was much perplexed by his words and pondered what sort of greeting this might be. The angel said to her, "Do not be afraid, Mary, for you have found favor with God. And now, you will conceive in your womb and bear a son, and you will name him Jesus. He will be great, and he will be called the Son of the Most High, and the Lord God will give to him the throne of his ancestor David. He will reign over the house of Jacob forever, and of his kingdom there will be no end." Mary said to the angel, "How can this be, since I am a virgin?" The angel said to her, "The Holy Spirit will come upon you, and the power of the Most High will overshadow you; therefore the child to be born will be holy; he will be called the Son of God. And now, your relative Elizabeth in her old age has also conceived a son; and this is the sixth month for her who was said to be barren. For nothing will be impossible with God." Then Mary said, "Here am I, the servant of the Lord; let it be with me according to your word." Then the angel departed from her.

Loving God, what beautiful words from the angel to Mary. Mary was filled with wonderment and awe when she heard them. That is what You do, You comfort your people and surely the comfort given to Mary in that moment overpowered her fear. And not only that, but Elizabeth was also gifted with a son! Two miracles and two women who would bear a Divine and human! Some things one must take in with faith, and that is exactly what Mary and Elizabeth did. After all, Elizabeth was well past childbearing age, how else could she become pregnant? Elizabeth's reassurance was instantaneous and rewarded. When women first feel the stirrings in their womb of new life, well it is a miraculous feeling. Thank you Lord, for the gift of carrying a child within and for Mary and Elizabeth who both carried miracles inside. I feel so blessed to feel deeply what that fulfillment meant to all the world. Be with us this day, this moment as we prepare to celebrate again, the birth of Christ Jesus, our Savior. Thanks be to God. Amen.

IT CAME UPON THE MIDNIGHT CLEAR
Edmund Sears

It came upon the midnight clear, that glorious song of old.
From angels bending near the earth to touch their harps of gold:
"Peace on the earth, good will to men,
from heaven's all gracious King!"
The world in solemn stillness lay to hear the angels sing,

Still through the cloven skies they come
with peaceful wings unfurled,
And still their heavenly music floats o'er all the weary world;
Above it's sad and lowly plains, they bend on hovering wings.
And ever, o'er its Babel sounds, the blessed angels sing.

Yet with the woes of sin and strife, the world hath suffered long;
Beneath the angel-strain have rolled two thousand years of wrong;
And men, at war with men, hear not the
love-song which they bring;
O hush the noise, ye men of strife, and hear the angels sing.

For lo! The days are hastening one, by prophet-bards foretold,
When with the ever-circling years shall come the Age of Gold,
When peace shall over all the earth its ancient splendors fling,
And the whole world sends back the song
which now the angels sing.

DECEMBER 23

LUKE 1:35

The angel said to her, "The Holy Spirit will overshadow you; therefore the child to be born will be holy; He will be called the Son of God.

Do you remember that Santa Clause comes from the Anglican tradition of Sinter Klaas, which just happens to be a reference to Saint Nicholas, a Christian bishop from way back in the fourth century?

Lord of all, I pray that all who read the Bible and hear of The Story, or listen to a rendition by a soloist or a full choir, in one's own mind, each one will have their faith renewed and be filled with awe, wonder and Your love. As we celebrate the coming of Christ, may we also remember the selflessness of St. Nick. May his example also remind each of us of our Savior who gave us the greatest gift of all and may his example be a reminder to generously support the message of salvation, especially to those who have not yet received salvation by God's grace alone, through faith alone—and on account of Christ alone. Give us the courage to boldly share Your story.

Merry Christmas! May peace, love and joy be with each one as we share the Christmas message, forgive our sins and be with us always. Amen.

DO YOU HEAR WHAT I HEAR?

Gloria Shane Baker and Noel Regney

Said the night wind to the little lamb:
"Do you see what I see?
Way up in the sky, little lamb
Do you see what I see?
A star, a star, dancing in the night
With a tail as big as a kite
With a tail as big as a kite"

Said the little lamb to the shepherd boy:
"Do you hear what I hear?
Ringing through the sky, shepherd boy
Do you hear what I hear?
A song, a song, high above the trees
With a voice as big as the sea
With a voice as big as the sea"

Said the shepherd boy to the mighty king:
"Do you know what I know?
In your palace warm, mighty king
Do you know what I know?
A Child, a Child shivers in the cold
Let us bring Him silver and gold
Let us bring Him silver and gold"

Said the king to the people everywhere:
"Listen to what I say!
Pray for peace, people everywhere!
Listen to what I say!
The Child, the Child, sleeping in the night
He will bring us goodness and light
He will bring us goodness and light"

LUKE 1:46-56

And Mary said, "My soul magnifies the Lord, and my spirit rejoices in God, my savior, for he has looked with favor on the loveliness of his servant. Surely, from now on all generations will call me blessed; for the Mighty One has done great things for me, and holy is his name. His mercy is for those who fear him from generation to generation. He has shown strength with his arm; he has scattered the proud in the thoughts of their hearts. He has brought down the powerful from their thrones, and lifted up the lowly; he has filled the hungry with good things, and sent the rich away empty. He has helped his servant Israel, in remembrance of his mercy, according to the promise he made to our ancestors, to Abraham and to his descendants forever." And Mary remained with her about three months and then returned to her home.

Lord, this is the day! This is the day that you have made, I shall rejoice and be glad in it. I pray for the faith and love of Mary on this Christmas Eve. May my spirit rejoice in the magic of your wondrous gift to us. I pray for the innocence of each child who is learning of the wonderful, unselfish gift you created to help the people of the world learn to love you and each other. Each Christmas Eve teaches new lessons of your mighty love and power. How we yearn for the innocence of the young children who are so excited for the morning to come. They know something special will happen during the night and long for "things." May your light shine on each one of us, illuminating the love you have for us and bring peace in our hearts for the greatest gift man and woman have ever received. Jesus, the baby in the manger, your gift to the world. An innocent entrance into a world of chaos. In a few short decades he taught us lessons we shall never forget, assisted by disciples, Your word was made flesh and dwells with us each and every day. Thank you Lord

God for the miracle of Christ Jesus, for loving each one, and for the power of faith. Lord, I pray for all the parents of the world, may they raise their children to know you and to love you. Forgive those who are evil, soften their hearts and voices in humble submission to your will. Comfort those who find this Christmas Eve painful, show them your love and mercy and calm their troubled thoughts. May all glory and praise be to you and to your blessed son. In your name, I pray. Amen.

DECEMBER 25

LUKE 2:1-7

In those days a decree went out from Emperor Augustus that all the world should be registered. This was the first registration and was taken while Quirinius was Governor of Syria. All went to their own towns to be registered, Joseph also went from the town of Nazareth in Galilee to Judea, to the city of David called Bethlehem, because he was descended from the house and family of David. He went to be registered with Mary, to whom he was engaged and who was expecting a child. While they were there, the time came for her to deliver the child. And she gave birth to her firstborn son and wrapped him in bands of cloth, and laid him in a manger because there was no place for them in the inn.

Thank you Lord, for the gift of your son, Christ Jesus! You taught us to be unselfish by delivering the Savior. Help us to be more generous without abundance and our attitude towards those in need. Lord, I pray for the homeless, the sick and those who are mentally lost. Help them, heal them, and comfort loved ones who worry about them. Lord, You gave us a most precious gift for a reason, not the season. May we learn to follow and serve. The circumstances of birth do not necessitate failure in the future. Jesus made a life and led many people to Christianity from his humble beginnings. He came that we might have life and have it abundantly. He came to take away the sins of the world and in doing so taught us how we are to live. Help us to live up to those expectations and especially to help those who need assistance. Be with each of your children and save us, I pray in the blessed name of Christ Jesus. Amen.

GENTLE MARY LAID HER CHILD

Joseph Simpson Cook

Gentle Mary Laid her child Lowly in a manger;
There he lay the undefiled, To the world a stranger
Such a babe in such a place, Can he be the Savior?
Ask the saved of all the race. Who have found His favor.

Angels sang about His birth, Wise men sought and found him;
Heaven's star shone brightly forth, Glory all around Him.
Shepherds saw the wondrous light, Heard the angels singing;
All the plains were lit that night, All the hills were ringing.

Gentle Mary laid her child Lowly in a manger;
He is still the undefiled, But no more a stranger.
Son of God, of humble birth, Beautiful the story;
Praise His name in all the earth, Hail the King of glory!

DECEMBER 26
LUKE 2:8-14

In that region there were shepherds living in the fields, keeping watch over their flock by night. Then an angel of the Lord shone around them, and they were terrified. But the angel said to them, "Do not be afraid; for see—I am bringing you good news of great joy for all the people: to you is born this day in the city of David a Savior, who is the Messiah, the Lord. This will be a sign for you: you will find a child wrapped in bands of cloth and lying in a manger." And suddenly there was with the angel a multitude of the heavenly hosts, praising God and saying, "Glory to God in the highest heaven, and on earth peace among those whom he favors."

———————————

Holy God, the wondrous way you directed the shepherds in the fields, was a miracle itself. When one thinks of angels, we generally do not think of them in terms of mapping a way to your beloved and we do not think of them as something for one to fear. I have heard from professionals and others where a loved one whose life is waning "sees" or "hears" a spouse, a family member or a loved one who has passed. We know you are orchestrating a comforting gesture to calm that person as their very life is ending. Those "God Moments" are most comforting and also reassuring. They become calm and almost happy to see familiar faces of loved ones who have gone before them. At times we all need to feel reassurance that you alone are our strength and our redeemer. We confess that we have strayed at times and humbly ask for your saving grace by forgiving our sins and helping us to lead lives pleasing to you. Be with us and save us, Lord, in the name of the One who came to take away the sins of the world, Christ Jesus. Amen

DECEMBER 27
LUKE 2:15-20

When the angels had left them and gone into heaven, the shepherds said to one another, "Let us go now to Bethlehem and see this thing that has taken place, which the Lord has made known to us." So they went with haste and found Mary and Joseph, and the child, lying in the manger. When they saw this, they made known what had been told them. But Mary treasured all these words and pondered them in her heart. The shepherds returned, glorifying and praising God for all they had heard and seen, as it had been told them.

Heavenly Host, help us to follow the angels who have illuminated the way to You. Make our way to you one filled with love and dedication to do your will. Show us the way Lord, you are our shining star. May we make haste to the houses of worship, singing praises and giving thanks. Lord help those who bring fresh eyes to your gospel, making it come alive with life's instructions and filling our hearts with your faith and love. May we hold our faith firm as we move through the stages of our lives and may we teach in our own unique ways, Your ways. Be with those who have lost their way, help them to know your love as you gently guide their ways. Lord, in the days following our celebrations of the birth of your son, help us keep His message alive. Help us show our love for you and Jesus by leading in our own unique ways, helping others learn of your wonderful gift to the world, and to each of us. Help us to "make known" to our brothers and sisters Your love for each of us and the treasure of the infant child, your beloved son whom you sent to save us. Be with us this day and each one of our days, forgive our sins and save us. I pray in the name of Jesus. Amen.

DECEMBER 28

LUKE 2:21-24

After eight days had passed, it was time to circumcise the child; and he was called Jesus, the name given by the angel before he was conceived in the womb.

When the time came for their purification according to the law of Moses, they brought him up to Jerusalem to present him to the Lord (as it is written in the law of the Lord, "Every first born male shall be designated as holy to the Lord"), and they offered a sacrifice according to what is stated in the law of the Lord, "a pair of turtledoves or two young pigeons."

———————————

L oving God, thank you for helping me to understand why giving your son to the world was and is so important. Your ways and your son have enlightened me and have shown the world how to live. Loving you, is just not enough. We have to shine that love on our brothers and sisters, those we know, and those we have yet to meet. Thank you for the bravery of Mary and Joseph. By faith they each raised your son and helped him to become the leader You meant for him to be. As a child of the lineage of Abraham, Jesus, following the law under which he was made and under which he fulfilled the promise. Help us loving God, teach your ways to our children and to those who are searching for the truth in their lives. The truth sometimes is difficult to hear, however, Your truth equals goodness and mercy, all the days of our lives. What a blessing and what a promise you made to each one of us. Be with us this day, save us from our sins, I pray in Jesus' name. Amen.

DECEMBER 29

LUKE 2:25-27

Now there was a man in Jerusalem whose name was Simeon; this man was righteous and devout, looking forward to their consolation of Israel, and the Holy Spirit rested on him. It had been revealed to him by the Holy Spirit that he would not see death before he had seen the Lord's Messiah. Guided by their Spirit, Simeon came into the temple, and when the parents brought in the child Jesus, to do for him what was customary under the law.

Teach us, loving God. Help us to discern the mystery of the early days of your son, Jesus. Make us, like Simeon, a servant seeking to know you and to love you. We think of the "weight of the world" term and realize what Simeon felt must have been beyond comparison. May we seek your love, guidance and forgiveness as we move through our lives however long that might be. Help us Lord God, to be in community with you and to be an example of how our lives can be pleasing to you. May we, like Simeon, not see death before we see You. May we know and serve you throughout walk in life. Lord show us your will and may we ever honor it. Be with those who do not yet know you, help us to shine your light throughout the world in such a way as to honor You. Give grace and peace to those who are searching, yearning to know you. Be with those who live their lives in service to you. Be with each of us this day, forgive our sins, I pray in the name of Jesus. Amen.

DECEMBER 30
LUKE 2:28-35

Simeon took him in his arms and praised God saying,

"Master, now you are dismissing your servant in peace, according to your word: for my eyes have seen your salvation, which you have prepared in the presence of all peoples, a light for revelation to the Gentiles and for glory to your people of Israel. And the child's father and mother were amazed at what was being said about him. Then Simeon blessed them and said to his mother Mary, "This child is destined for the falling and the rising of many in Israel and to be a sign that will be opposed so that the inner thoughts of many will be revealed—and the sword will pierce your own soul, too."

Thank you Lord, for the vision of Simeon! He recognized, he knew the child he held, Jesus was the very one sent to fulfill the prophecy. What joy he felt, knowing he held your beloved son! His words and thoughts were a very profound confession of his faith in you,Lord. We know how comforting it is to know you,to love you, and to follow you. The burden of worry lessens when one knows there is a promise of life in another form. Death, "where is thy sting?" has little meaning to the Christian. The secret is loving and knowing Jesus Christ as our Lord and Savior. Heavenly Father, grant that we may always know you, through the life and teachings of Jesus. May we be good sons or daughters to you, living lives pleasing to you and which augment the societies in which we live. Make us an instrument of your peace and love and mercy. Be with those still searching and help us find them and reassure them that your love and mercy is never ending. Be with us each day as we walk towards a time when we shall live in Your house, Lord God, for ever. Amen.

DECEMBER 31

REVELATION 22:14-21

Blessed are they who wash their robes, so that they will hav e the right to the tree of life and may enter the city by the gates. Outside are the dogs and the sorcerers and fornicators and murderers and idolaters, and everyone who loves the practices of falsehood. "It is I, Jesus, who sent my angel to you with this testimony for the churches. I am the root and the descendant of David the bright morning star." The Spirit and the bride say, "Come." And let everyone who hears say, "Come." And let everyone who is thirsty come. Let anyone who wishes take the water of life as a gift. I warn everyone who hears the words of the prophecy of this book: if anyone adds to them, God will add to that person the plagues described in this book; if anyone takes away from the words of the book of this prophecy, God will take away that person's share in the tree of life and in the holy city, which are described in this book. The one who testifies to these things says, "Surely I am coming soon." Amen, Come, Lord Jesus! The grace of the Lord Jesus be with all the saints. Amen.

Holy God, the time following the death of Jesus was miraculous, frightening and overwhelming. He came among his disciples following the resurrection to fulfill and to reassure a stunned people. People knew what Jesus said, but of course could not understand how it could possibly happen. Lord, we have all been there at some point in our lives. Thank you for sending your son to help us, to reassure and teach and to love us. We know You through Jesus and through historical references in the Holy Bible. The truth is there for us, Lord, help us to teach our children about your love and grace and especially about your promise. We have learned much from you and from Jesus' teachings. Help us to live our lives to your glory and to make our world a better place as we recall the charge you have given us. Jesus' word to the people is one of welcome to those who believe in him. To the non-believer, what is promised is condemnation and exclusion. Jesus is the foundation of all that is good, the light, the bright morning star, it is a light of hope and prophecy. Indeed, Christ's parting words to his church are ones of love and kindness, they are reassuring words to the people that he shall once again return. The closing benediction ends with decidedly proof of Christ Jesus. The Spirit of God teaches all to bless his people in the name of Christ, and then to ask Christ for a blessing. We should aspire for nothing, Lord but the grace of Christ to be with us in our coming in and our going out. We thirst for Christ's grace, his peace and his love. May it abide in each one, now and forever. I pray the new year will bring health to the sick, happiness to the sad, and love of you and Jesus to those who do not yet know you. Be with us all, Lord and save us, I pray. Amen.

EXTRA PRAYER

JULY 3

ACTS 5:29, 32

But Peter and the apostles answered, "we must obey God rather than any human authority."

And we are witnesses to these things, and so is the Holy Spirit whom God has given to those who obey him."

D ear Savior, you have taught us that one shall not anticipate redemption and your saving grace without giving oneself to you. Jesus Christ came into the world to to save us from our sins, not the actual act of sinning. It is Christ's spirit at work within and it is the spirit that awakens our conscience. What moves the innermost being within each heart, the feeling of guilt for a wrong deed, is precisely what causes a change of heart. It is the conscience softening our hearts and minds that enables us to lean into your love and your expectations. Today I pray for a softening of each heart and a re-awakening of consciences. Lord, give each one a renewed sense of what your will is. Help us to make wise and just decisions for others. Be with those who are working for you in so many ways. Give them courage to do the right thing and stamina to stay with the task at hand. Give courage to those whose decisions are technically "right," but that are contrary to the edict of a governing body. May the Holy Spirit live within each of us, I pray. Lord, grant us wisdom and courage for the facing of each day. I pray especially for those working to find a way to help those in need and those who are struggling mentally or physically. May the Holy Spirit dwell in their hearts, and release them from their struggles. Be with those who are hungry, may the food closets in our world be open wide to silence the rumbling stomachs. Comfort your children who are frightened and who are feeling abandoned. Be with us, heavenly savior and save us, I pray in your blessed name. Amen.